The Global Commonwealth of Citizens

The Global Commonwealth of Citizens

Toward Cosmopolitan Democracy

Daniele Archibugi

PRINCETON UNIVERSITY PRESS
PRINCETON AND OXFORD

Copyright © 2008 by Princeton University Press

Published by Princeton University Press
41 William Street, Princeton, New Jersey 08540
In the United Kingdom: Princeton University Press,
6 Oxford Street, Woodstock, Oxfordshire OX20 1TW

Library of Congress Cataloging-in-Publication Data

Archibugi, Daniele
   The global commonwealth of citizens : toward cosmopolitan democracy / Daniele
Archibugi.
      p. cm.
   Includes bibliographical references and index.
   ISBN: 978-0-691-13490-1 (hardcover : alk. paper)   1. International organiza-
tion. 2. Democracy. 3. Globalization. 4. United Nations. 5. Humanitarian
intervention.   I. Title.
   JZ1318.A75   2008
   341.2—dc22   2008013416

British Library Cataloging-in-Publication Data is available

This book has been composed in 10/12 Sabon

Printed on acid-free paper. ∞

press.princeton.edu

Printed in the United States of America

10 9 8 7 6 5 4 3 2 1

To Clara, Orlando, Gabriele, Alamin, and Aurora

Contents

Tables and Figures

Tables

Figures

Acronyms and Abbreviations

AIDS	Acquired Immune Deficiency Syndrome
ASEAN	Association of Southeast Asian Nations
EAC	East African Community
EU	European Union
G7	Group of seven leading industrial states: Canada, France, Germany, Italy, Japan, United Kingdom, United States
G8	Group of eight: G7 plus Russia
GA	United Nations General Assembly
ICC	International Criminal Court
ICJ	International Court of Justice
IDEA	International Institute for Democracy and Electoral Assistance
IGO	Intergovernmental organization
IMF	International Monetary Fund
IO	International organization
IRA	Irish Republican Army
MEP	Member of the European Parliament
Mercosur	Mercado Común del Sur
MP	Member of Parliament
NAFTA	North American Free Trade Agreement
NATO	North Atlantic Treaty Organization
NGO	Nongovernmental organization
OECD	Organization for Economic Cooperation and Development
OSCE	Organization for Security and Cooperation in Europe

SC	United Nations Security Council
UN	United Nations
UNHCR	United Nations High Commissioner for Refugees
UNRISD	United Nations Research Institute for Social Development
SIPRI	Stockholm International Peace Research Institute
WB	World Bank
WEF	World Economic Forum
WP	World Parliament
WPA	World Parliamentary Assembly
WSF	World Social Forum
WTO	World Trade Organization

Preface and Acknowledgments

Contemporary political life is dominated by a paradox. On the one hand democracy has been so successful that it has become the only form of legitimate government. Moreover, countries with the more consolidated democratic systems are those that today are economically prosperous and politically dominant. In this part of the world, which we may define as the West, political power has been partly tamed and citizens have the right to appoint, control, and dismiss those who govern them. However, as soon as we venture outside this circle of privileged countries onto the world political stage, we find that a lust for power marks the relations among countries in which the stronger dominate the weaker.

If the hegemonic countries were authoritarian and despotic, this would not be surprising. But since these hegemonic countries today are highly developed and sophisticated countries in charge of the agenda of world politics, it is indeed surprising and even a reason for indignation. And at the same time an opportunity to understand, to act. It would appear that in the liberal countries, or at least in their governments, no priority is given to sharing the strategic decisions regarding issues of relevance with the other peoples of the world. Indeed, proud that they come from free countries, leaders of liberal countries think they are authorized to treat the other peoples as pariahs.

The leaders of the western world are constantly lecturing others on how alien countries should be governed and exhorting others to modify their own methods of governance so that they more closely resemble theirs. But at the same time they do very little to apply these same principles in the management of global affairs. A state has therefore been reached in which much of the world population, including those who would benefit most from the implementation of democracy in their own countries, accuse the leaders of the western democracies of being hypocritical and egotistical, almost to the same degree as their own home-grown despots. The wars fought by the liberal countries have merely strengthened the opinion that rulers, whether democratic or despotic, are all more or less the same. While the actors, singers, and writers of the West are applauded as heroes wherever they go, their leaders are greeted with vigorous protests. This is an alarming situation, as the West has not only produced good films, songs, and novels but has also and above all perfected a system of government—namely, democracy—that deserves universal approval and to be extended geographically and qualitatively enhanced.

The incapacity of consolidated democracies to exercise their own powers of persuasion has had disastrous effects: some of the most pressing world problems—safeguarding the environment, financial stability, security—are managed by select clubs that act outside all control. Others—defense of human rights, natural catastrophes, epidemics—are not managed at all. At the same time, the process of democratization, which raised so many hopes after the fall of the Berlin wall, seems to have suddenly halted. For their part, the western democracies have to contend with globalization processes that are radically modifying the relationship between those who make the decisions and those who are affected by them. In increasingly extensive areas, the democratic countries are finding they have to face up to external phenomena and decisions made outside their own borders. While increasing efforts are made to boost existing checks and balances on the internal sphere, the internal sphere is gradually decreasing in importance vis-à-vis the external sphere, where the participation and control mechanisms continue to be rudimentary.

This book contains a proposal for radically reversing this situation: to extend democracy not only inside each state but also as a form of management of global affairs. This proposal is not universally accepted; many consider that democracy was born and has grown up inside state borders and is ill-adapted to crossing them. I maintain the opposite thesis: democracy can and must become the method of global governance. Just as democracy has brought considerable benefits to the peoples who have tried it out, so today democracy can benefit for the whole of humankind. However, this assumption means that democracy must be reappraised and reinvented to suit the new historical conditions, and on a different scale. Which rules among those that are applied inside the states can be applied to the global sphere and in international organizations? Which principles must on the other hand be further discussed and reformed? Depending on the scale and the institutions to which it is applied, democracy changes form, although certain basic principles may be identified that remain unaltered whether applied to a small community, a national state, or the entire world.

The present book presents the proposal for a cosmopolitan democracy, which a group of researchers at the end of the Cold War developed, as the management of different levels of governance. This proposal takes into account contemporary historical conditions, in which political communities with different historical and cultural backgrounds interact willy nilly with other neighboring and remote political communities. The form of representation of citizens in the global sphere based on the delegation of governance to a territorial state has become insufficient and in many cases an aberration. For this reason citizens of the world need to be given the possibility of directly participating in global choices through new institutions that are parallel to and autonomous with respect to those that already exist inside the states. Many find the suggestion of a world parliament annoying, as they consider it unrealistic and vague. Yet today it would seem a necessary path to tread in order to ensure that vested interests do not trample the principles of democracy daily and to attain an effective global commonwealth of citizens. A world parliament would give institutional clout and a say in political and social affairs to those global movements that have appeared on the world political scene full of enthusiasm and often with a solid baggage of skills.

The present book does not suggest building up a greater concentration of force. The many problems facing contemporary society cannot be tackled through new coercive powers. It is indeed a matter of strengthening the rules and of imposing penalties for the failure to respect them in order to serve as a stimulus to improve the behavior of political actors. The contemporary world is already based on shared choices, often among specific subjects and in delimited areas. Air transport and telephone communications, trade and finance, culture and information now increasingly involve individuals beyond their specific membership of a given secular state. It is in everyone's interest to participate in these international regimes inasmuch as the failure to participate is itself highly penalizing. Globalization thus offers the possibility of obtaining international integration without using violence to a much greater degree than in the past. But for this to occur requires both identity of intentions and impartiality, at least among those who claim to be champions of democracy.

The first part of this book gives consideration to the foundations of a democratic theory that sets the ambitious task of being applied outside fixed geographic boundaries. Many researchers have studied the conditions required for the democratization of authoritarian countries. It is too often taken for granted that there is a single causal link leading from the democratization of states that are still authoritarian to peace and international cooperation. This causal link is implicitly postulated in the hypothesis that democratic states do not wage war on each other. To argue on the basis of a single causal link ranging from internal democratization to international cooperation is extremely convenient for the consolidated democracies: rather than ponder their own arbitrary and self-interested choices, they lay the blame for international conflicts on others. One other equally important fact has also been ignored, namely, the establishment of international conditions favorable to internal democratization. This is an opposite causal link, and one that postulates the decisive contribution that may be given by the democratization of the world political system to the establishment of democracy within states. The existence of this link lays an obligation on all countries, starting from the hegemonic ones, which are for their good fortune democratic, to harmonize their policies with the actors involved in them.

The topics discussed have a valence that is not only theoretical; quite the contrary. The theory expounded is necessary to address several of the knottiest issues of contemporary politics. It is to these topics that the second part of the book is dedicated, which treats current problems such as United Nations reform, how to go about deciding on humanitarian interventions, suitable instruments for convincing other peoples to adopt democracy, the possibility of resolving conflicts over self-determination and of minimizing violence, the rules for coexistence in political communities inhabited by different peoples. In all these areas of application, I have endeavored to show how the obstacles standing in the way of the attainment of desirable objectives depend on the fact that too much power is concentrated in the hands of too few governments. For this reason cosmopolitan democracy appeals for the creation of new institutional channels that will allow popular participation and the political control over global choices to be increased. Only by creating given individual rights and duties, albeit to a limited degree, will it be possible to attain a democratic global commonwealth of citizens.

This book dedicated to the idea of a cosmopolitan democracy was a long time in the writing. My initial ideas on the topic date back to the gloomy years of the Cold War and the apparently insurmountable rivalry between East and West. The emergence of a new unipolar world order dominated by the western powers modified the original project but without altering its basic thrust. In intellectual symbiosis with David Held and Mary Kaldor, a kind of elective brother and sister, the research project outlined herein, based on the idea that the democratization of the international system is the best guarantee of peace and the respect of human rights, it began to take shape and gradually involved an increasing number of researchers. Richard Falk was a model of inspiration with his capacity to combine disenchanted analysis and bold proposals.

My younger brother, Mathias Koenig-Archibugi, was a true critical conscience and a boundless source of suggestions, criticism, and references. Together with Franco Voltaggio we scoured through the authors of the sixteenth- and seventeenth-century peace projects and discovered them still to be a precious source of ideas. I was honored to receive numerous detailed comments from Norberto Bobbio right up to the time of his death. It is now a quarter of a century since I began my intellectual debate with Mario Pianta, with whom I have shared militant activity in the movements for peace and global justice. Raffaele Marchetti obliged me to engage in some energetic mental gymnastics. To Mariano Croce I owe both encouragement and the checking of bibliographic references. On a number of occasions I benefited from conversations with many Italian colleagues; in chronological order, I am duty bound to mention at least Luigi Cortesi, Luigi Ferrajoli, Luigi Bonanate, Giulio Marcon, Federico Varese, Francesco Gui, Fabrizio Battistelli, Nadia Urbinati, Danilo Zolo, Patrizia Nanz, Mario Telò, Sergio Fabbrini, Filippo Andreatta, Rufo Guerreschi, Sebastiano Maffettone, Alessandro Ferrara, Virginio Marzocchi, Stefano Petrucciani, Luigi Caranti, and Teresa Pullan. No less useful was the dialogue with my foreign colleagues: I learned a lot from David Beetham. My dialogue with Iris Marion Young was interrupted far too early by her premature death, a harsh blow for all those who hope that theory may still enlighten politics. I am equally grateful to Ulrich Beck, Jürgen Habermas, Michael Walzer, Tom Pogge, Tony McGrew, Andrew Linklater, John Dryzek, Carol Gould, Tom Farer, John Keane, Chantal Mouffe, David Chandler, Nancy Kokaz, Andrew Strauss, Hilal Elver, Bruce Morrison, Roland Paris, Ken Booth, Terry and Kate Macdonald, Nieves Zuñiga, Anja Karnein, Inge Kaul, Michael Zürn, Susan George, Rainer Bauböck, Seyla Benhabib, and Étienne Balibar for their comments, criticism, conversations, and emails that, one way or another, helped me revise or reformulate my stance.

I am profoundly grateful to the Italian National Research Council for the wide-ranging freedom it allowed me and for a grant (RSTL-2007). The periods spent at the Centre for the Study of Global Governance of the London School of Economics and Political Science (2003–2004) and at the Center for European Studies of Harvard University (2004–2005), made possible by the two professorships of the Leverhume Trust and the Lauro de Bosis legacy, proved to be particularly fruitful. In London I reaped the benefit of discussion, as well as with David Held and Mary Kaldor, also with a large group of researchers including Chris Brown, Clare Chambers, Mick Cox, Marlies Glasius, Paul Kelly, Janet Coleman,

Eva Nag, and Garrett Brown. At Harvard I enjoyed discussion with Lino Pertile, Peter Hall, Glyn Morgan, Patrice Higonnet, Stanley Hoffmann, Charles Maier, Tricia Craig, Jane Mansbridge, Nancy Rosenblum, Andrew Moravcsik, Richard Tuck, Hélène Landemore, and Daniel Ziblatt. My arrival at Birkbeck College, University of London, in addition to the thrill of teaching at Bloomsbury in John Maynard Keynes's library and Virginia Woolf's bedroom, obliged me constantly to try to match theory with political and economic reality.

Without Ian McGilvray's willing and creative help I would never have succeeded in expressing in English ideas conceived in my mother tongue, Italian. I am extremely grateful to Richard Baggaley of Princeton University Press for his constant encouragement and suggestions for piloting this book through the world of publishing. My brother Alessandro has kindly assisted me for the production of the figures.

Some have accused cosmopolitans of stirring the class consciousness of frequent flyers. Although rigorously in tourist class, I traveled widely to discuss the ideas set out herein and would like to mention the following conferences: "Transnational Democracy," London, Ontario (March 17–19, 2002), International Studies Association, at Portland (February 28, 2003) and at Montreal (March 4, 2004), Società Italiana di Scienza Politica, Trento (September 15–16, 2003), American Political Science Association, Washington, D.C. (September 1–4, 2005), "De-hemonization: The US and Transnational Democracy," George Mason University, Washington, D.C. (April 5, 2006), "Envisioning a More Democratic Global System," Widener University (April 7–8, 2006), "Global Governance without Democratic Foundations?" Development and Peace Foundation and Renner Institute, Potsdam (March 30–31, 2007), "Legality and Legitimacy in International Order," University of California at Santa Barbara (April 27–28, 2007), "The Reform of the United Nations," Centro Studi sul Federalismo, Turin (June 7–8, 2007). I also held numerous seminars, including some at the departments of Political Science of Yale University (April 19, 2001), Columbia University (April 26, 2001), the University of Chicago (March 14, 2002), University of Toronto (May 2, 2002), University of Helsinki (September 7, 2002 and September 21, 2006), University of Westminster (October 7, 2003), University of Southampton (February 19, 2004), Harvard University (November 10, 2004), Birkbeck College, University of London (March 16, 2006), and the European University Institute (March 22, 2007), as well as at the Centre for the Study of Global Governance, Delhi (January 8, 2003), the Jean Monnet Center, New York University School of Law (March 26, 2003), the Fundacion M. Botin, Madrid (April 3, 2003), the Institute of Commonwealth Studies, University of London (February 7, 2004), the Dottorato sull'universalizzazione dei sistemi giuridici, University of Florence (May 23, 2007), and the Scuola per la buona politica, Fondazione Basso, Rome (June 21, 2007).

Discussion with students is the acid test. I therefore wish to thank the students of the courses on International Organization that I have held for a number of years at the University of Rome "La Sapienza," the Ph.D. course in Political Theory at the University of Rome "LUISS," and those of the Master course on Globalization at Birkbeck College, University of London.

Paola Ferretti was kind enough to read and correct the manuscript, but above all to participate in a more modest but equally demanding parenting project, the principal figures involved appear in the dedication to the present book.

Parts of this book have been drawn from previous work and, in particular, appeared in *Constellations* vol. 10, no. 4 (2003): 488–505; *European Journal of International Relations* vol. 10, no. 3 (2004): 437–73; *Alternatives* vol. 29, no. 1 (2004): 1–21, and *Political Studies* vol. 53, no. 3 (2005): 537–55.

I also wish to thank the International Institute for Democracy and Electoral Assistance for permission to use in table 2.1 material from David Beetham, Sarah Bracking, Iain Kearton, Nalini Vittal, and Stuart Weir, eds., *International IDEA Handbook of Democratic Assessment*, and Center for International Development and Conflict Management, to use in figure 2.1 and table 9.1 material from Monty G. Marshall and Ted Robert Gurr, eds., *Peace and Conflict 2005*, and J. Joseph Hewitt, Jonathan Wilkenfeld, and Ted Robert Gurr, eds., *Peace and Conflict 2008*.

In the case of citations originally in languages other than English, I have sometimes altered the existing translations without acknowledging it.

Web sites cited have been accessed on May 8th 2008.

The Global Commonwealth of Citizens

Chapter 1
Introduction: A Queen for the World?

1.1 A Queen for the World?

An American peace thinker, William Ladd, in 1840 published one of the last peace projects which flourished during the European Enlightenment. In his project, he called for the creation of an international congress comprising one ambassador for each state. He envisaged this international congress as a world legislative power that would lay down rules that were shared and respected by all. Ladd realized that such a congress would be insufficient without a judiciary power charged with interpreting the rules and settling disputes, so he also proposed to set up an international court of justice. In a project so explicitly based on the separation of powers that existed in his native America, Ladd could not avoid raising the question of executive power. According to him, executive power was neither conceivable nor probably even desirable and it was therefore necessary to rely on the intangible power of world public opinion, which he optimistically dubbed "the Queen of the World."[1]

The idea that public opinion could be the queen of the world is today even more attractive than it was in the nineteenth century. As championed by numerous visionaries, many international organizations have been set up that are nowadays much more sophisticated than the

1. William Ladd, *An Essay on a Congress of Nations for the Adjustment of International Disputes without Resort to Arms* (New York: Oxford University Press, [1840] 1916), p. L.

thinkers of the past ever dreamed they would be. The United Nations General Assembly and the International Court of Justice, for example, have a much vaster and more ramified jurisdiction than Ladd was proposing. IOs are charged with dealing with a wide range of problems—security, development, communications, trade, environment, childhood, health, and so on. Yet now, as then, no world executive power exists. As a result, at the world level, a huge gap exists between the solemn statements of principle and bleak daily reality.

The violation of human rights, conditions of extreme poverty, periodic recourse to war, and environmental degradation are but a few of the many problems facing humankind today. These ancient problems have taken on a different dimension today, as they are increasingly difficult to confine to, and sometimes even to situate in, a circumscribed geographic area. The capacity for a territorial government to ensure security and promote prosperity is therefore substantially limited. Can a single world power contribute to finding a solution for this? There are many reasons to doubt that it can. Concentration of coercive power is always dangerous, and not even the most sophisticated checks and balances can rule out the danger that this power may be transformed into some new form of planetary despotism. This was the concern of Ladd, and of Immanuel Kant before him.

Restoring the power into the hands of public opinion does not arouse the same concern. Indeed, public opinion does not possess any armies, police forces, secret services, prisons, mental hospitals, or other repressive institutions. Public opinion can only disapprove and express indignation. The public can also express its own opinion through collective action and, in the democratic countries, vote a government that has proved ineffective out of office. But at the world level, public opinion has no voting rights. It has been split into an infinite number of rivulets. Over vast regions of the world, its power to express itself has been limited by dictatorships. Even in the internet age, only a small proportion of the population is duly informed about or even interested in world politics. Its power is, at best, symbolic, and its disapproval is often ineffective and uncertain. To appeal to public opinion and even raise it to the status of queen of the world is therefore a hyperbole. Yet giving public opinion a greater role to play seems to be the only hope we have of tackling the many alarming problems that exist in the modern world.

The present book explores the chances of increasing the legitimacy of world politics by introducing the germs of democracy and subjecting world politics to the citizens' scrutiny. Under what conditions could public opinion become the queen of the world? To what extent can the general public control the actions undertaken by the various subjects, whether national governments, international organizations, or multinational corporations? What institutional instruments are available to confer an effective political role on the inhabitants of the planet? These are the issues to which cosmopolitan democracy—an intellectual project formulated by a group of scholars at the end of the Cold War[2]—must endeavor to find a response. Cosmopolitan democracy is indeed one of the many offspring generated by the great expectations that blossomed after the fall of the Berlin wall. After the collapse of the Soviet empire and the decisive affirmation of the western democracies, it was hoped that there would be some positive repercussions on the global system. It was thus deemed possible to reform the international organizations, to plan the geographic expansion of democracy, and finally to make human rights more certain and to allow world citizens to express themselves through ad hoc institutions. One goal has been achieved: it is no longer sacrilegious to consider that democracy can be applied even outside the state. However, many, too many, of these hopes have so far been dashed. Why? And above all, what hopes remain today that democracy can make its appearance also in world politics?

1.2 The West without Decline

We live in a highly fragmented world that is, however, dominated by a small group of countries that, using a loose but readily understandable term, is defined as the West. The West is an entity composed of countries that have a market economy and consolidated democratic institutions. With the sole exception of Japan, the West involves Europe and its ancient settlements. Too often it is forgotten that this part of the world comprises at most one sixth of the world population. Within the West a single country, the United States, has today emerged as dominant. Never before has such a vast and profound hegemony been witnessed. Suffice it to observe the distribution of resources—production, consumption, knowledge, military capacity—to see how a relatively small part of the world became powerful. This power is not only material; its ideology is equally dominating. Cinema and science, literature and technology, music and mass communications are all in the hands of the West. The principles of political organization that prevail today were also produced by the West: the western visions of freedom and democracy have become

2. Daniele Archibugi and David Held, eds., *Cosmopolitan Democracy: An Agenda for a New World Order* (Cambridge: Polity Press, 1995); David Held, *Democracy and the Global Order* (Cambridge: Polity Press, 1995); Daniele Archibugi, David Held, and Martin Koehler, eds., *Re-imagining Political Community: Studies in Cosmopolitan Democracy* (Cambridge: Polity Press, 1998).

increasingly universal values, and there is no reason to regret this.[3] The West has no cause to be ashamed of having proposed and developed forms of government that have gradually also spread to other parts of the world. The peoples of the five continents have taken to the streets to demand them, often against their own rulers, because they have fully understood that freedom and democracy not only guarantee greater personal dignity but also allow more material benefits to be distributed.

The West, for its part, has endeavored to make converts. Yet these efforts have proved incoherent and ambiguous. Freedom and democracy have been turned into ideological screens to defend vested interests and attack enemies. The vicissitudes of colonialism and then of imperialism show that only too often has the West claimed these values for itself and denied them to others. Can the power that the West wields today be used to involve and include rather than to dominate and subjugate? Is it possible to enlarge the number of subjects among whom to distribute the benefits? Cosmopolitan democracy has the objective of representing an intellectual contribution to the attainment of these objectives.

Cosmopolitan democracy opposes the idea of constructing a fortress in the western area and excluding all those who do not passively accept the new hegemonies. A strategy of this kind cannot but stir up new enemies and lead to futile crusades. Such a vision of the cosmopolitan project is also based on the factual observation that it is impossible to draw a dividing line between "us" and "them," between "friends" and "enemies." The planet is made up of "overlapping communities of fate,"[4] to use the apt phrase coined by David Held, and it is a difficult, and often impossible, task to mark the confines between one and the other. What is the most suitable political community[5] to democratically decide on navigation on the Danube? Does not the spread of contagious diseases affect all the inhabitants of the Earth? And what must be said about issues concerning not only all the present inhabitants of the Earth but also those of the future, such as nuclear waste management or the ozone hole?

There is no obvious, easy answer to these questions. Nevertheless, the modern state—one of the West's favorite offspring—based on the assumption

3. Amartya Sen, among others, usefully reminds us that westerners are too often not knowledgeable enough on similar principles developed by other civilizations. See Amartya Sen, "Democracy Isn't 'Western,'" *Wall Street Journal*, March 24, 2006.

4. David Held, *Global Covenant* (Cambridge: Polity Press, 2005), pp. x and 168.

5. I use *political community* to translate the Latin expression *res publica*.

of sure frontiers and rigid criteria of membership continues to be the main political subject in international relations. In just a few centuries, the territorial state has spread over the entire land surface of the planet. With the sole exception of Antarctica, there is no longer a strip of land that does not belong to or is not claimed by a territorial state. In order to participate in world political life, each individual is obliged to become a member of a state, and each community must contrive to speak with a single voice, that of a monocratic government. World politics is therefore practiced by a small group of actors that have set up a directorate, giving rise to what may be defined as an intergovernmental oligarchy. It cannot be denied that the state plays an essential role in nourishing democracy: without actually deciding, often arbitrarily, who is in and who is out, it would not have been possible to develop self-government. The intensification of the processes of economic, social, political, and cultural globalization, however, has rendered traditional boundaries increasingly vague and uncertain, undermining the capacity for certain political communities to make decisions autonomously. The key principle of democracy, according to which decisions must be taken only after discussion among all those affected by the decisions, is increasingly being questioned.

Today it must be acknowledged that the situation has changed. The rigidity of the frontiers of the political communities, an element that historically enabled self-government to be born and prosper, now stands in the way of democracy's evolving and even surviving. As soon as each political community receives and transmits the echo of its actions from and to the exterior, the state-based democratic procedure is eroded. In order to survive, democracy must undergo a radical transformation comparable to that experienced in the transition from direct to representative democracy. Democracy must be able to create new forms of management of public matters that are also open toward the exterior and to include in the decision-making process those who are affected by certain decisions.

Many attempts have already been made to increase participation and inclusion. International organizations, for example, have increased in number and functions, and almost every country in the world is now a member of the UN. In the so-called Old Continent, a mighty effort is being made to create common institutions, and the European Union has been extended southward, northward, and eastward. Half a century ago, the EU was concerned solely with coal and steel, while today it is competent in all aspects of public policy. Other regional organizations are developing on the other continents. World political life is beginning to assign jurisdiction and legitimacy to subjects other than state representatives, such as nongovernmental organizations, multinational corporations, cultural associations, and transnational pressure groups. This process of institutional integration is still only partial and unsatisfactory, however, compared with the intensity and rapidity of the changes occurring in the global process.

Who is willing to undertake the necessary institutional reforms? The West has preached the lofty principle of the sovereignty of the people, at the same time applying this principle with suspicious parsimony. The West has often declared its intention to promote democracy in other people's back yard but is by no means willing to share the management of global affairs with others. This is what I call democratic schizophrenia: to engage in a certain behavior on the inside and indulge in the opposite behavior on the outside. It is a contradiction that is difficult to justify, although here the West can appeal to a powerful and sophisticated ideological apparatus, the function of which is to demonize any political system that opposes its own. The ideological apparatus is used to disseminate a Manichean view in which anyone opposing the will of the West is presented as a barbarian and a savage. It is certainly not difficult to demonize what happens in the world: you have only to open a newspaper to read about the atrocities committed for political reasons in places far and near. The ideological apparatus does not merely demonize, however; it must also sanctify, and so it proceeds to obscure the atrocities committed by the democratic countries. War crimes are transformed into collateral damage, aggression is converted into prevention, torture is modified to become coercive interrogation. The point is reached in which the democratic states are deemed to be peaceful by nature, and when they fight it is only because other states are not as democratic.

In other words, a consolatory view of democracy arose that demonized its enemies and glorified itself. However, this view is analytically tautological and politically reactionary. It is tautological in that it not only defines democracy as good but also defines what democracies do as good. This prevents any assessment of the relationship between two variables, postulating as an axiom what instead remains to be demonstrated. And it is politically reactionary, as this complacency prevents an analysis of which problems are still open and the transformations needed to fulfill the commitments inscribed in the constituent pact of the democracies. Consoling oneself about what democracy stands for is an obstacle to the democracies' progress.

How far back does this democratic schizophrenia between interior and exterior date? Perhaps it is an intrinsic flaw, already announced in the funeral oration delivered by Pericles, a great democrat, to commemorate those killed in the first year of the Peloponnesian war, a speech that is justly considered the first expression of democratic thought.[6] Pericles lavishes deserving praise on the political order of his city. He refers to Athens as a "living school for Greece,"[7] a model for all civilizations. Thucydides, the chronicler of the war, scrupulously notes the devastation and plundering carried out by the Athenians, but Pericles never asks whether that war was necessary, whether the democratic Athens had been compelled to fight it, or whether it was a war of aggression. Yet Pericles harangues his fellow citizens: "Do not look at the sacrifices of the war in horror."[8] Only by excelling in war can Athens be a "living school." Reading and rereading this famous speech, one gets the impression that the praise of the Athenian democracy is necessary to justify the blood spilt but also that the blood shed on the exterior is necessary to build that democratic society. The Athenian events have unfortunately hung like a shadow over the development of democracy through the centuries.

The democratic regimes are certainly not the only belligerent or unworthy members of the international community. The autocratic regimes are equally and sometimes even more violent on both the interior and the exterior. Students of international relations from both the realists' side and the opposing idealists' side have filled entire library shelves with publications assessing the extent to which the internal regime of a state affects its foreign policies. The method generally used, however, is to compare the foreign policy of the democratic countries with that of the autocratic countries, and it is not surprising to find that the foreign policy of democracies is often, other things being equal, more virtuous than that of the autocracies. Nevertheless, the basis of the comparison is incorrect: the foreign policy of the democracies should be compared with their internal policy. Only when the two are based on the same principles will it be possible to declare democratic schizophrenia to have been cured and the curse that has accompanied this form of government from the time of Pericles to have been lifted.

It is perhaps possible to justify the crimes committed by democracies outside their own borders by the fact that they have so far lived in a composite international system in which the majority of the political communities were managed using authoritarian methods. For years and

6. Domenico Musti, *Demokratia. Origini di una idea* (Roma-Bari: Laterza, 1995), p. 326, has convincingly shown that Pericles' speech can be considered a genuine manifesto of the democratic principles and practice of ancient Athens. For an opposite view, see Luciano Canfora, *Democracy in Europe* (Oxford: Blackwell, 2006), chapter 1.

7. Cf. Thucydides, *The Peloponnesian War*, trans. Benjamin Jowett (Oxford: Clarendon Press, [404 B.C.] 1900), book II, § 41, p. 130.

8. Thucydides, *Peloponnesian War*, book II, § 43, p. 133.

years, democracies have had to defend themselves with the sword as well as with rhetoric. However, this is no longer the situation in the twenty-first century, when the distribution of power is such that the bloc of the democratic states reigns supreme. For these reasons I am often critical concerning what is done and even more of what could be and is not done by the democracies. This criticism is in no way meant to repudiate democracy as a method of managing power, nor is it meant to deny the fact that all the peoples in the world could benefit from democracy. The aim of the criticism is to prevent countries that have succeeded in constructing these regimes—often by means of blood, sweat, and tears—from sinking into complacency, from discharging their aggressiveness toward their exterior and hindering further progress on the interior. Being critical, in other words, by no means signifies a desire to return to a different system but merely a demand that democracies should rise to the expectations that the majority of the world's population has of them. Never before have the western countries been so powerful; never before have their enemies been so weak. The western countries no longer have to fight for survival as they did in the first and second half of the twentieth century. No longer do any external obstacles stand in the way of pursuing a world of democracy.

1.3 The Insidious Perils Facing Democracy and Cosmopolitanism

The key terms of the project illustrated herein—democracy and cosmopolitanism—encapsulate two of the loftiest ideals of political thought. Yet as is often the case with good intentions, both these concepts conceal insidious perils. The democratic idea—based on the principle that power belongs to the multitude—was established by drawing dividing lines between the persons to include and those to exclude. Power may be shared by the whole people but only on condition that we know who is being excluded. Paradoxically, the all-time enemy of democracy, despotism, has not had to face the problem of whom to include: obedience is expected from all individuals.

Throughout their journey, the democracies have gradually increased the number of citizens endowed with political rights: those rights have been extended from exclusively the free males of the polis to all adults. But even though the barriers have been whittled down, perhaps the most decisive one has remained standing: those who are in and those who are out. Extraneous peoples and individuals wishing to be included have been the most frequent victims of exclusion. The need to homogenize those who are different by means of assimilation, expulsion, or even elimination has brought out the dark side of democracy, transforming it into ethnocracy.[9] This dark side has dominated the process of nation building, but it would be wrong to consider this dark side solely as a problem of the past. In a world in which populations are subjected to great migrations, in which natural resources are scarce, and in which the processes of globalization, whether we like it or not, throw together different individuals, this dark side is always liable to re-emerge. The clashes of civilizations are nothing but the latest version of the deviation that can affect democracies at any moment. Cosmopolitanism as a school of tolerance would mitigate this genetic flaw in democracy and should prevent democracy from withdrawing into itself and allow democracy to continue to be a perpetually open and inclusive political system.

The vicissitudes of cosmopolitanism are equally turbulent.[10] In the course of the centuries, cosmopolitanism has cast off its ideal dimension and become a reality. The number of persons—merchants, explorers, writers, intellectuals, and the ever-increasing hordes of tourists—who have been able to travel and get to know the world has grown in parallel with prosperity and the development of mass society. Those who have become familiar with diversity have developed two different attitudes to it. The first is the curiosity (which, as Giovanbattista Vico tells us, is the daughter of ignorance and the mother of science) aroused by the customs of different societies. The second, parallel attitude is the idea that the various civilizations would ultimately converge toward common customs. Cosmopolitanism thus signifies not only knowing but also assessing, comparing, judging, selecting, and ultimately, wherever possible, actually applying the practices and customs deemed to be more valid. Only too often, however, the cosmopolitans have spread the conviction that, by pure chance, the best practices and customs are those of their own civilization.

The cosmopolitanism born as a school of tolerance can thus rapidly turn into its opposite. With the force of its convictions, cosmopolitanism does not fail to desire the assimilation of those who are different, sometimes through persuasion, other times by using violence. The question

9. The impressive and often disturbing research by Michael Mann, *The Dark Side of Democracy: Explaining Ethnic Cleansing* (Cambridge: Cambridge University Press, 2005) and, before him, the theses of Elias Canetti, *Crowds and Power* (New York: Viking, 1963) have not yet been properly digested by democratic theory.

10. For two recent narratives of cosmopolitanism, see Kwame Anthony Appiah, *Cosmopolitanism: Ethics in a World of Strangers* (New York: Norton, 2007) and Robert Fine, *Cosmopolitanism* (London: Routledge, 2007).

is whether this can still be considered cosmopolitanism. It is doubtful. The etymology of the word contains a reference to the citizen, a notion that implies equality and participation. The genes of the cosmopolitan should therefore contain the will to consult those who are different before making any decision. When cosmopolitanism becomes intolerant it is because it has swallowed a dangerous poison, that is intolerance, that has transformed it into fundamentalism. Unlike cosmopolitanism, fundamentalism no longer feels any doubt, wants to impose its view on all and sundry, and does not shrink from using violent and coercive methods. An antidote may be found by marrying cosmopolitanism with democracy: it is not enough for an idea to be a good one in order to be imposed; it is also necessary for that idea to be shared through the required procedures by means of persuasion, not force. This is the ultimate goal of the cosmopolitan democracy project restated in this book.

1.4 Layout of the Book

The first part of the book is dedicated to the theory of cosmopolitan democracy, although a constant effort is made to illustrate theoretical problems by linking them to concrete cases. The second chapter presents the conception of democracy implicit in the cosmopolitan project: democracy is to be viewed as an evolutionary process in which the various communities follow an autonomous itinerary of their own. Also at a time in which democracy has fortunately become a widely accepted concept, differences have continued, and will continue, to exist between the way democracy is interpreted in different parts of the world and at different levels of political affairs management. Rather than force democracy into too narrow a cage, it is preferable to assess these differences and try to see how much can be learned in a laboratory that is destined to grow ever larger and more varied.

Chapter 3 addresses the relationship between democracy and the global system. This is a much more complex relationship than might appear at first sight. It is by no means certain that democratic states are worthy inmates of the global system; democratic states are often as quarrelsome and bullying as any other kind of state. And all states tend to become more bullying when their strength increases. I shall therefore try to shed some light on the links that exist between the international system and internal regimes. What attributes must the international system have in order to perform a maieutic function vis-à-vis internal democracy? Consequently, how can democratic countries contribute to rendering the global system fairer?

Chapter 4 illustrates the institutional architecture of cosmopolitan democracy. The treatment is given on two linked planes. The first refers to the various levels of political management, from the local to the global. The second is performed by comparing cosmopolitan democracy to the two classical types of state unions, the confederation and the federation. The question is asked as to whether a third type may be envisaged that is more cohesive and demanding than a confederation but less rigid than a federation.

In the last twenty years, the problems and prospects associated with transnational democracy have received much attention, up to the point of becoming the subject of several university courses. Cosmopolitan democracy itself has been analyzed, scrutinized, and criticized, and not always in the most benevolent manner. Chapter 5 takes this critical debate into account. I have tried to engage in a fruitful dialogue with the critics, because their observations helped a great deal to table new problems and to clarify some crucial aspects. Regretfully, less attention has been devoted to authors who embraced and developed the project of cosmopolitan democracy; for lack of space priority had to be given to rebuffing the critics rather than to praising one's traveling companions. Nevertheless, I am pleased to see a growing number of young researchers working on these topics and brilliantly treating several key issues of the project in depth.

In part two, cosmopolitan logic is applied to several concrete cases. What does cosmopolitan democracy tell us in connection with daily political action? If cosmopolitan democracy is not to be a book of dreams, it is necessary to determine which steps can be undertaken daily in order to push forward in the direction of cosmopolitan democracy. Chapter 6 is therefore dedicated to the UN, the largest and most ambitious international organization ever conceived. Unfortunately, the UN and the other international organizations were born against a backdrop of great hopes that are daily dashed by political reality. However, much can be done, in the first place to ensure that the UN and its smaller sister organizations carry out the tasks that the states have already assigned them and in the second place to reform those organizations so that they are able to accommodate more decisively the norms and values of democracy. I have already spoken of democratic schizophrenia, and nowhere else is democratic schizophrenia found so extensively as inside the UN headquarters: on the one hand, the western governments protest against the lack of democracy inside the organization, and on the other, they do all they can to prevent any radical reform in that direction.

Chapter 7 tackles the problem of the legitimacy of the recourse to war for humanitarian purposes. Under what conditions is it legitimate to use military force in favor of foreign populations? The problem has been

11

debated on an increasingly wide front in recent years. Military operations for humanitarian purposes have been conducted in Somalia, Bosnia, Kosovo, Sierra Leone, and many other places. But in an equally large number of cases, no such operations have been carried out. Rwanda and Sudan have become paradigmatic cases of genocides that the international community failed to halt. We are thus always teetering between interventions that turn out to be medicines that are worse than the disease and failure to act. In chapter 7 I attempt to trace out a few cosmopolitan principles on which to base intervention so as to prevent humanitarian tragedies taking place in a situation of total indifference, but at the same time are used by some states as a pretext to engage in violence and to impose the will of the powerful on the weak. The main lesson to be learned from recent experience is that it is necessary to progress beyond a logic of emergency in order to set up institutions that are morally, politically, and also militarily equipped to intervene wherever necessary.

Chapter 8 brings us to the historical present: at a time in which two wars are being waged, one in Afghanistan and one in Iraq, the question is whether it is justified to export democracy at bayonet point, which used to be the method employed, or by bombing, as is done today. The prerequisites of democracy include also a preventive pact of nonaggression and the principle of nonviolence. It is therefore easy to understand why the peoples to whom this precious good is offered in the form of military invasion may be somewhat skeptical about the good intentions of their alleged benefactors. The chapter does not dwell exclusively on the negative teachings: in accordance with the theoretical framework of this book, it also explores the most effective methods for exporting democracy. The action of the international organizations, founded on dialogue and cooperation, has proved to be more effective than coercion. This is one of those fortunate cases in which there is no contradiction between the ends and the means: democracy is much easier to export by democratic means than by imposition.

Chapter 9 addresses a typical problem of international relations, the self-determination of peoples. The number of conflicts arising out of clashes among political communities, each claiming its own right to self-determination, is surprisingly large and shows little sign of decreasing. To define what a "people" is that has the right to self-determination is by no means an easy task. The chapter attempts to distinguish among the various interpretations. To what extent can the cosmopolitan idea championed herein be of use in delimiting the various political communities and in minimizing the recourse to violence? I maintain that self-evaluation of self-determination is a contradiction in terms. In the case of dispute, the parties involved should agree to arbitration by a third party. Also in the case of self-determination, I place reliance on a typical figure in democratic thinking—the third-party mediator and arbitrator.

Chapter 10 centers on the possibility of achieving democracy in multi-lingual communities. The ambitions of the cosmopolitan democracy project are worldwide; some object that democracy cannot be cosmopolitan and that cosmopolitanism cannot be democratic. They claim that a democratic community needs a language of communication that is accessible to all; otherwise it turns into an oligarchy. This is no minor objection, and I have taken it into consideration with all due attention. An analysis of linguistic policy actually reveals something of substantial importance for appreciating democratic inclination and how such an inclination can be tested on different scales. A school with students from different ethnic groups, a small country, and an international organization all have to cope with the problem of mutual understanding on a daily basis.

The list of issues tackled is by no means complete. Cosmopolitan democracy has much to say in regard to the enforcement of human rights, managing migratory flows, how to combat terrorism, refugees, the process of regional integration, and cross-border criminal justice. A number of references are made in the various chapters to specific studies on these problems. The aim of the present book is simply to make a contribution to a debate that has been ongoing for many years in the hope that the debate will continue in the years to come and can enjoy greater success not only at the intellectual level but also in the boundless seas of real life.

There is some doubt whether the eleventh and final chapter would be more suitably entitled "Conclusions" or "Sunday Political Rally." Many will probably opt for the latter hypothesis, but this would not trouble me. Also this book is one of those dangerous books written in the hope that our children and grandchildren will have a better world to live in. Such a better world cannot certainly be guaranteed, but at least our children and grandchildren could not reproach us for having ignored the challenge.

PART ONE

THE THEORY OF COSMOPOLITAN DEMOCRACY

Chapter 2
The Conception of Democracy

2.1 Chronicle of an Announced Triumph

It is related in my family that great-grandmother Ada, a very wise woman although not actually an early riser, only once in her life ever got up before the dawn. It was June 2, 1946, and she was among the first to line up in front of the polling station. After two decades of fascism and a fierce war that ended in civil war, Italy had returned to the polls. As a woman, Ada was being admitted to the polling booth for the first time and had no hesitation in contributing to finally ending the Savoyard ruling dynasty, which had stood by so complacently as disaster struck the country. Grandma Ada was in good, indeed excellent, company: the turnout at the election was over 89 percent. A page was being turned, and that small slip of paper placed in the ballot box was the expression of many desires: peace, prosperity, and the dignity of being able to participate in the country's decision-making process.

Ever since the late 1980s, this Italian story has happily repeated in many countries: millions of persons line up in an orderly fashion, sometimes for hours and even for whole days at a time, to participate in the ritual that characterizes democracy: free elections. In Chile and Russia, as well as in Nicaragua, Hungary, the Czech Republic, and Poland, as far as the Philippines and South Africa, peoples have succeeded in exercising the right to choose their own rulers. Many workarounds were needed to guarantee free and fair elections: in countries where registry documents were still unreliable, the voters' index fingers were marked with indelible ink to prevent people from voting twice. In countries with a high illiteracy rate, the candidates' photographs were printed on the ballot paper. Makeshift polling stations were set up everywhere, often using sheets and blankets to guarantee the secrecy of the vote. The desire for liberty and prosperity and to play an active role in political life at the end of the twentieth century gave rise to an unexpectedly powerful mass movement in favor of democracy. Never before in human history had such a genuinely transnational movement been seen; never before had such radical change been achieved with such limited bloodshed. In Poland, South Africa, the Philippines, and Chile, the people swept away existing governments using a much smaller amount of violence than in the past; the unity of the people's intent and the new international situation were sufficient to overthrow the existing totalitarian regimes. In the closing decade of the twentieth century, the goal of democracy was achieved using the predicated method: nonviolence. At the dawn of the third millennium, democracy emerged as a political model that is more than victorious—it is indeed the only political model available.

But what is the real nature of this victory? Can we finally pluck the rose without its thorns? We must ask ourselves, for instance, what is the significance of having free elections in countries under military occupation, such as Afghanistan, Iraq, or Palestine, or whether to vote has any meaning in many African regions when the electoral results in no way differ from the results of an ethnic or religious census. In other countries again, such as in Iran, systematic violations of human rights coexist with the popular vote. What, then, do we really mean by democracy?

The term *democracy* is widely bandied about, and not only in political contexts. In its most current meaning, democracy refers to the government of political communities that—although only for the past few centuries—now coincide with state boundaries. In more remote times, democracy was defined as a form of self-government of small communities that coincided with the city-state or a small republic. In current usage, the term *democracy* is also used to refer to the management of associations: it is applied to the governance of a company, a school, a political party, or a neighborhood committee. This enables us to denote the presence (or absence) of the majority principle, of the respect of rules, of the transparency of decision making, of the accountability of the executive, of the responsibility for decisions taken in the interest of all members rather than only of those closest to the executive. Almost always the reference is to organizations acting within a territorial state, although the same attributes are also applied to international associations: the International Studies Association, the Fédération Internationale de Football Association, and Amnesty International are all institutions to which more or less democratic governance may be attributed. Often *democracy* is used to refer solely to the majority principle; in order to refer to an entire system of rules and procedures that takes in also the respect of human rights and those of minorities, I instead apply the concept of a *democratic system*.

All over the world, power in the twenty-first century seeks legitimacy by calling itself democratic. No important ideological currents now exist that proclaim to be contrary to democracy in state politics. All those who wish to be recognized inside and outside their country declare themselves to be "democratically elected" and speak in the name of their people, even when authoritarian and even brutal political systems lurk behind their rhetoric. When a concept is agreed upon by all, especially when that concept refers to the sphere of power, it runs the risk of losing all meaning. Today democracy is in danger of being destroyed by its very success and of being swallowed up in one of those famous nights in which all cats are gray.

This is not the first time that democracy must be defended from false friends. As early as the 1950s and 1960s, the regimes in the eastern European countries claimed to be "people's democracies" and used the term *people* to qualify and differentiate themselves from the "liberal" democracies. At the same time, the regimes in eastern Europe claimed that their power was as legitimate as, if not more legitimate than, that in the western systems. The task of many researchers of the time was indeed to challenge this indiscriminate use of the term and to restrict it to those regimes in which governance was actually expressed and controlled by the people.[1] A purely terminological issue—which country deserves to be defined as democratic—was thus turned into a political clash between the liberal-democratic bloc and that of real socialism.

Today, nearly twenty years after this fresh wave of democratization, we must measure ourselves with many countries that have extremely imperfect political systems and that declare themselves to be formally democratic even though in reality they are not.[2] On what grounds can a country like Iran, in which 60 percent of the population votes, be considered as undemocratic? In the academic community, disagreement has been much reduced over the past few years. The assessment criteria used

1. The classical work by Giovanni Sartori, *Democratic Theory* (Westport, CT: Greenwood Press, [1962] 1973), for instance, was an attempt to oppose those who, in the eastern bloc countries, were endeavoring improperly to appropriate the label of "democracy."

2. Among those that signaled this problems, see Fareed Zakaria, *The Future of Freedom: Illiberal Democracy at Home and Abroad* (New York: Norton, 2003).

may change, even though the results obtained converge substantially. When we leave academe, however, the assessment of the democratic level reached by a state or a government directly enters the sphere of politics: a sensitive nerve is touched that leads directly to the legitimacy of power. Experts and institutions who would be called upon to define criteria to determine which governments and which states may be deemed "democratic" thus accumulate substantial power. Just as the label of "heretic" applied to a secular prince could deprive him of legitimacy vis-à-vis his subjects, so today defining a government as "nondemocratic" can lead to mobilization, revolt, and international isolation.

However important it may be to lay down distinguishing criteria, we must also necessarily avoid being dogmatic, which merely leads to the belief that only one single form of organization of the political community can be compatible with the values of democracy. Conversely, it is possible and necessary to identify different models of democracy, each one with its own legitimacy, that respond to historical and cultural differences.[3] History has revealed different systems to us and, as far as the present era is concerned, one of the main tasks of political scientists is to weigh the pros and cons of each system vis-à-vis the characteristics of each separate state. Both the researcher and the politician championing the cause of democracy should therefore shun seeking the absolute "best practice" in order to try out many "good practices." The ways of democracy are not infinite, but there are certainly more than one way.

2.2 Five Mainstays of the Nature of Democracy

The proposal put forward in the present book is based on five mainstays of the nature of democracy.

1. *The journey toward democracy is not yet over.* In all countries, including those in which the principles of democracy are more firmly entrenched and developed, the process is still under way.[4] In the democratic countries, strong pressures are at work to extend democ-

---

3. I thus move away from the conception of democracy as expressed by Giovanni Sartori, *Democrazia: cosa è* (Milano: Rizzoli, 1994), to embrace the approach whereby the existence of a plurality of models is given priority. See C. B. Macpherson, *The Life and Times of Liberal Democracy* (Oxford: Oxford University Press, 1977); David Held, *Models of Democracy* (Cambridge: Polity Press, 1987); Frank Cunningham, *Theories of Democracy* (London: Routledge, 2002).
4. John Dunn, ed., *Democracy: The Unfinished Journey, 508 BC to AD 1993* (Oxford: Oxford University Press, 1992).

racy into other spheres, with reference to procedures and content. Concerning content, the current debate is focusing on the need to extend economic and social rights, while new categories of rights are demanded regarding the environment, future generations, and even animals. Concerning procedures, the essential principle according to which each vote has the same weight is now being challenged, and sophisticated models have been developed to group together individual preferences in such a way as to weight the decision-making clout of individuals on the basis of their effective involvement in a choice. The principle of equality is thus reinforced by the idea that not every aspect of political life involves all citizens to the same extent and that to apply equality means accepting the difference.[5] A new and promising line of research—that of discursive democracy—actually claims that considering democracy solely as a way of aggregating preference votes is reductive: the path followed in making a decision is as important as the decision itself, and it is conceivable that consensual modes of decision making may be found.

This is not just a theoretical debate. In both democratic and autocratic countries there are daily conflicts, albeit of a different nature, in order to extend or achieve democracy. It is not possible today to predict which developments will favor democratic communities. The uncertainty surrounding the future democratic system does not, however, prevent us from observing how democracy has evolved over a period of more than twenty-five centuries. It is possible to identify a number of *milestones of democracy*: the majority principle, universal suffrage, minority rights, constitutional guarantees, and so on. Individual political communities have managed to achieve these milestones in different historical situations and not necessarily in the same order. Within Marxist thinking, Lev Trotsky evolved the theory of the "permanent revolution" in order to maintain that the economic and social development of a country does not necessarily follow in the footsteps of the predecessors.[6] The thesis illustrated herein is of the same ilk, as it rejects the idea that the order in which the various stages of the democratic journey occur is the same for each political community.

The thesis that democracy is an unfinished journey leads us to wonder in which direction a democratic community must look in order to appreciate how its own political system can be improved.

5. Iris M. Young, *Justice and the Politics of Difference* (Princeton: Princeton University Press, 1990).
6. Lev Trotsky, *The Permanent Revolution, and Results and Prospects* (New York: Merit Publishers, [1929] 1969).

The answer is twofold: by means of *introspection* and *extroversion*. First and foremost is introspection, as only by an internal assessment of the problems acknowledged by a given political community is it possible to appreciate how to improve one's trajectory. But extroversion, that is, the observation of the democratic procedures applied in other countries to assess which norms tried and tested in some communities can be transmitted to others, is equally necessary.

2. *The journey toward democracy is endless.* Democracy is much more than a set of rules and procedures. Democracy must be understood as an interactive process involving the needs of civil society and political institutions. In order to appreciate its nature, one must consider which *democratic pathway* is being followed, which is represented by a progressive evolution aimed at satisfying the individuals' demands for participation. When this process will end, let alone the direction it will take, cannot be known. In this sense, democracy is an open system. To write out a recipe for the democracy of the future is not possible today. Whatever form the political systems of the future will take, however, their legitimacy must be grounded on consensus.

Theoretical debate often precedes the social innovations introduced, which sometimes take even centuries to implement. Even today, imaginative thinkers and political minorities have demanded more of democratic systems, and their demands are often conflicting. It cannot be excluded that subordinate employment will be deemed incompatible with democracy, as it creates a de facto disparity between the employer's position and that of the employee, which contradicts the principle of equality among citizens.[7] In the distant future, perhaps we will find highly evolved political communities that require all their citizens to be vegetarians,[8] and perhaps we will find political communities that allow animals to be eaten may actually be deemed illiberal. Nor can it be ruled out that vegetarian communities will consider it so abhorrent to eat animals as to desire to break off all relations with political communities that allow their people to eat animals and that perhaps vegetarian com-

---

7. This is the thesis of Robert A. Dahl, *A Preface to Economic Democracy* (Cambridge: Polity Press, 1985), chapter 4; C. B. Macpherson, *The Rise and Fall of Economic Justice and Other Essays* (New York: Oxford University Press, 1985), chapter 3; Philippe Van Parijs, *Real Freedom for All: What (If Anything) Can Justify Capitalism?* (Oxford: Oxford University Press, 1995).
8. As urged, for example, by Peter Singer, *Animal Liberation* (New York: Avon Books, 1975) and his increasingly numerous followers.

munities will even impose sanctions on the barbarous peoples who feed on sausages and steaks. We can bet that the democratic political communities of the future will consider our political systems with the same condescension that we display today toward the Athenian democracy, in which neither women nor slaves nor aliens enjoyed the right to vote. Our constitutional systems will no doubt be criticized and considered unbearably backward, perhaps because they allow the buying and selling of labor, the butchering of animals, or the destruction of nonrenewable resources.

In this sense, the democratic pathway has not yet attained its goal, nor can it, as it is on an interminable journey shrouded in uncertainty. In a word, democratic faith clashes with the millenarist idea that political organization has a purpose and that certain individuals or institutions can actually predict or worse, dictate its future form. Democracy's great vitality lies precisely in its ability to set itself new goals and critically to evaluate what has been achieved. A democracy that does not progress by virtue of the work performed by its institutions is already defunct. Democracy is essentially progressive, while different political systems, such as autocracy, oligarchy, or anarchy relegate the task of innovating outside the political dialogue. The task of modifying the political system is entrusted, respectively, to a charismatic leader or to an elite or is indeed expelled from politics and it is assigned exclusively to individual's own resources.

This vitality of democracy is expressed by constantly setting up in the political arena new objectives that only very slowly transform into additional, universally shared milestones. In the long and controversial journey of democracy, and observing its vicissitudes from the vantage point offered by the early twenty-first century, one may note that none of the main milestones of democracy have so far been removed. Suffrage has gradually been extended, the checks and balances have become more sophisticated, the rule of law has been consolidated, minorities have enjoyed greater protection, and the forms of representation have been further developed. This perhaps authorizes us to believe that the democratic process has developed in an incremental fashion, acquiring and consolidating the lessons of the past. At the same time, democracy must address new problems such as control of the mass media, the protection of confidentiality in the age of information technology and of the interconnections that distinguish a global society. In the very instant in which democracy stopped evolving, it would become a static set of rules and procedures doomed to lose its validity.

3. *Democracy is meaningful in its own historical context.* Since the democratic process is historical in nature, the very concept of democracy should be viewed in a *comparative* rather than *absolute* sense. Ancient Athens was democratic in comparison with other city-states of the fourth century B.C., but democracy in Athens would not satisfy any of the criteria commonly applied today. The denial of voting rights to the majority of the population would today produce a system very similar to that of South African apartheid. Nineteenth-century Great Britain and the United States were quite democratic countries even though most of the population, including women, was excluded from suffrage. This critical point must be taken into account when the democratic level of countries with different historical traditions and levels of development are compared at a given point in time: even if all states were to apply this system, each state would be characterized by its own specific features and by being at a different stage from other states. As democratic practice has become more generalized it has inevitably been accompanied by an increase in observed variety. The idea of democracy extended in all directions must therefore be based on the acceptance of a multiplicity of models and stages.

Let us take the case of Switzerland, one of the first countries to have democratic cantons and a consolidated tradition of participation. In this country, voting rights for women (that is, for the majority of the population) were granted only in 1971, much later, for example, than in India. Yet it would not be correct to conclude that Switzerland was not a democratic system prior to 1971, or that India in 1952 was more democratic than Switzerland. This paradoxical case shows that each community follows its own itinerary and that, in 1952, both Switzerland and India, despite the substantial differences in income levels, education, and civic tradition, had something to learn from each other.

This does not rule out that however many different paths there may be to democracy, milestones exist that each community must adhere to. It would not be acceptable for a country that first adopted a democratic system in the twenty-first century to exclude the female or male population from its active or passive electorate. Nevertheless, in evaluating a democratic system, it is necessary to take into account both the level attained vis-à-vis the given historical conditions and the system's capacity to travel along the democratic pathway.

4. *Democracy is based on competition and not on conflict.* The democratic process is an integral part of social dynamics and, as

such, arises out of the daily social and political struggles. Democracy, no less than its development, is an achievement and, like all achievements, is the outcome of a struggle. What distinguishes democracy from other political regimes is the nature of the struggle: the competing parties do not pursue the annihilation of their adversary; they merely endeavor to ensure their own ideas prevail within the framework of a shared system of rules.[9] Democracy is nevertheless characterized by constant struggles in which, however, the use of violence is kept to a minimum: the parties implement a competitive logic rather than an antagonistic or even polemical logic. Even though use is often made of terms borrowed from warfare (words such as *battle*, *defeat*, and *enemy* are used daily), democratic practice more closely resembles a sporting ritual than warfare.

The competitive logic followed in democracy is also associated with the fact that the political formations are not permanent. Individual citizens may vote from time to time for different solutions and parties. Political factions are continuously formed and modified on the basis of substantial issues that are under discussion and have not been crystallized. Majorities and minorities are therefore dynamic and not static constructions. Moreover, when a majority is elected to government, as Pericles observed, the majority is required to govern in the interest of all, not just in the interest of those that are part of the majority.[10]

5. *In order to work, democracy requires an endogenous fabric.* In order to be substantial and effective, a democratic system cannot do without an extensive endogenous support. Only in the presence of bottom-up pressure can democratic institutions function materially. Even when the democratic institutions have been imposed by external forces, such as in the case of Germany, Japan, and even Italy, after World War II those democratic institutions became established only thanks to the reconstruction of the social fabric, including political parties, unions, and social movements, inside these countries that allowed the acceptance and daily application of the democratic rules.

Some claim that a political community, in order to achieve certain democratic conditions, needs to attain a certain level of eco-

9. Norberto Bobbio, *The Future of Democracy*, trans. Roger Griffin (Minneapolis: University of Minnesota Press, 1987); Chantal Mouffe, *The Democratic Paradox* (London: Verso, 2000).
10. Cf. Thucydides, *Peloponnesian War*, book II, § 37, p. 128.

nomic development, education, and social infrastructure.[11] They actually claim that, without these conditions, democracy cannot be achieved or is doomed to be unstable.[12] I do not agree with this thesis; to acknowledge the importance of an endogenous fabric does not necessarily mean believing that it is possible to identify a priori the historical conditions necessary for democracy to exist. Prosperity and a high educational level facilitate the introduction and consolidation of democratic systems, but it is deterministic to associate socioeconomic conditions with a given political system and vice versa. The socioeconomic conditions of ancient Athens or the republican cities of the Italian renaissance also existed in many other places without similar power-sharing systems being produced. At the same time, we have seen democracy stifled in countries that formally satisfied all the ideal conditions (suffice it to take Italy and Germany in the period between the two world wars).

But above all, to decide ex-cathedra when a political community is mature or suitable for democracy instead of trusting in the people's will to construct a political system that is better suited to satisfy their needs serves no useful purpose. We have seen democratic systems, albeit only rudimentary ones, rise and prosper in conditions that may be considered historically as unacceptable. Choosing democracy as one's political credo also means allowing members of the various political communities to autonomously decide when and how to introduce a democratic system in line with their own needs and conditions.[13]

2.3 A Definition of Democracy

Precisely because democracy is now accepted by all and sundry, and precisely because this acceptance brings together sincere champions and cynical profiteers, it is necessary to define the cardinal principles. The theory of democracy I propose here is based on three distinct criteria that may be summed up as *nonviolence*, popular *control*, and political *equality*. The first criterion is drawn principally from the thinking of

11. See the classical essay by Seymour Martin Lipset, *Political Man: The Social Basis of Politics* (Garden City, NY: Doubleday, 1960) and the consequent debate.
12. Robert A. Dahl, *Democracy and Its Critics* (New Haven, CT: Yale University Press, 1989), p. 264.
13. See Amartya Sen, "Democracy as a Universal Value," *Journal of Democracy* vol. 10, no. 3 (1999): 3–17.

Norberto Bobbio, while the other two criteria were developed and refined by David Beetham.[14] Let us examine these three criteria in detail.

NONVIOLENCE

Karl Popper defined democracy as that political system in which the citizens can change their government without causing a bloodbath.[15] Although this definition is not sufficient to characterize a democratic government exhaustively, it captures one essential aspect, namely, the preexisting will of the political parties to take turns at governing without the need for violence. Political parties must be interpreted in the broad sense and may be made up of social, ethnic, and religious groups that live side by side in the same political community. Even more than a requirement, nonviolence is therefore a prerequisite. Bobbio claimed that the very essence of democracy must be sought in the willingness to accept shared rules and to adhere to an implicit preemptive nonaggression pact.[16] Reflecting precisely on the Italian experience, Bobbio saw in the Constituent Assembly of 1946, as well as in the Constitution it gave rise to, the commitment to accept diversity and to establish common rules of living together. What happened in Italy at the end of World War II is actually an exemplary case of the authentic will of a wide range of political forces to reach a prior agreement on the rules of living together.

The principle of nonviolence as a foundation of democracy is reflected in the willingness of the various political components to accept a priori the rules of the game and consequently the rule of law. Nonviolence must not be interpreted in the absolute sense but as a commitment to use force only as a last resort and even then to exercise it within the bounds of legality. Nonviolence by itself does not fully characterize a democratic system; one can easily imagine communities that are not violent but authoritarian, for example, because those communities are based on a theocracy largely accepted by the population or because certain ethnic, political, or religious groups passively allow themselves to be dominated

14. Bobbio, *Future of Democracy*, in particular chapter 1; David Beetham, *Democracy and Human Rights* (Cambridge: Polity Press, 1999), chapter 1; see also David Beetham, Sarah Bracking, Iain Kearton, Nalini Vittal, and Stuart Weir, *International IDEA Handbook of Democratic Assessment* (Dordrecht: Kluwer, 2002).
15. Karl R. Popper, *The Open Society and Its Enemies,* 5th rev. ed. (Princeton: Princeton University Press, 1971), p. 124.
16. Bobbio, *Future of Democracy,* p. 42.

by the ruling elites. For this reason, nonviolence a is necessary but not sufficient condition. In order for nonviolence to translate into democracy, the principles of control and equality are also necessary.

POPULAR CONTROL

A democracy is characterized by the fact that government action is constantly under public scrutiny. The actions undertaken are subjected to the people's control during decision making and throughout the administrative action. In other words, both decisions and decision makers are under control. This means that political action must be authorized and accountable and, in order to allow popular control, it must be shaped by transparent rules. This presses the administration to respond to people's needs.

POLITICAL EQUALITY

The principle of equality demands that all the members of the community have the same rights, in the first place the right to participate in political life. All members must be able to contribute, directly or indirectly, to the process of making appointments to public office and to be appointed themselves. For this condition to be possible, the political system must be able to guarantee adequate representation, and at the same time the political community must view the promotion of equality and solidarity as a priority task.

This is not the only possible definition of democracy. The right to vote, periodic elections, the existence of several political parties competing among themselves, free availability of information—these are all aspects required to define a democracy.[17] Many other aspects could be added, for instance, respect for institutional rules, alternation in public officials, pluralism, and protection of human rights. A definition based on the three principles of nonviolence, equality, and control would seem, however, to be the most general, to grasp the spirit of what we commonly term *democracy*, and to be useful in identifying different models. Indeed, as shown in table 2.1, through the use of suitable mediation values, requirements, and institutional means, this definition allows all the other aspects deemed to be essential to be

17. See Dahl, *Democracy and Its Critics* and Robert A. Dahl, *On Democracy* (New Haven, CT: Yale University Press, 1998).

Table 2.1

Democratic Principles and Mediation Values

Basic principles:

Nonviolence in the way public choices are made

Popular control over public decision making and makers

Political equality among citizens in the participation and exercise of control

Values	Requirements	Institutional Means for Achieving Them
Pacification	Peaceful settling of disputes	Autonomy of the judiciary
	Codification of norms restricting the use of force	Enforcement of court decisions
		Use of arbitration
Security	Security of political forces	Loyalty of the institutions to the constitutional pact
	Absence of threats against those in office or running for office	Disarming of armed factions
	Guarantees for minorities, oppositions, and dissidents	Parliamentary control over army and police
Participation	Right to participate	System of civil and political rights
	Availability of resources and instruments for participation	Economic and social rights
	Fostering of participation	Elections, parties, associations
		Civic education
Authorization	Validation of the constitution	Referendum
	Choice of candidates and programs	Free, fair, and recurrent elections
	Control of elected persons over nonelected executive personnel	Subordination of the powers of the state to the elected representatives
Representation	Legislative representation of the principal currents of public opinion	Electoral system and parties
	Public institutions that are representative of the social composition of the electorate	Antidiscrimination legislation

(Continued)

Table 2.1 (*Continued*)

Values	Requirements	Institutional Means for Achieving Them
		Affirmative action policies
	Integrity of public servants and judiciary	Independent evaluation process
		Legally implemented standards
		Legislative control of power
Transparency	Government action open to scrutiny by the legislative power and the general public	Legislative protection of the freedom of information
		Independent means of communication
Responsiveness	Accessibility to government to voters and different groups of public opinion in the formulation and distribution of policies and services	Regular and open procedures for public consultation
		Effective legislation evolution
		Local government close to the people

Source: Elaboration from David Beetham, Sarah Bracking, Iain Kearton, Nalini Vittal, and Stuart Weir, *International IDEA Handbook of Democratic Assessment* (Dordrecht: Kluwer, 2002), p. 14.

included.[18] Moreover, as will be discussed in chapters 4 and 5, the above definition also makes it possible to identify which norms and values can be extended from the national sphere to the international sphere.

18. Beetham, *Democracy and Human Rights*, pp. 6–13; Beetham et al., *International IDEA Handbook*.

2.4 The Expansion of Democracy

At the end of the eighteenth century, only a few states—the Swiss Cantons, England, France, and the United States of America—had begun to sow the seeds of democracy. In 1989, the countries where free elections were held numbered 69. By 2005, according to some sources, that number had become 122.[19] A simple count of the countries holding free elections is, of course, not enough to describe the wide range of different political experiences. As is only to be expected, the process of democratization is uneven and piecemeal. A substantial democracy has not (so far?) always accompanied the procedural aspects, and many new regimes have simply introduced free elections in order to obtain admission to the advanced nations club, more in the aim of doing business and receiving aid than through belief in the principles those regimes claimed to respect.[20] It actually became necessary to invent new terms—such as *dictablanda* and *democradura*—to describe the mixture of formal democracy and substantial authoritarianism that still prevailed in countries in transition.[21] This historical process was accompanied by a flourishing literature aimed at assessing the problems and limits of the new democracies.[22] The academic debate became so intense that scholars founded new reviews such as the *Journal of Democracy* and *Democratization*.

Despite the imperfections in many of the newly democratic countries, democracy was making giant strides. Figure 2.1 sets out a classification of countries according to their political regime between 1946 and 2006, drawn up on the basis of information garnered from the Polity

19. Two most comprehensive classifications of democratic regimes at the world level are Freedom House, *Freedom in the World 2007: The Annual Survey of Political Rights and Civil Liberties* (Lanham, MD: Rowman & Littlefield, 2006) and Polity IV; see J. Joseph Hewitt, Jonathan Wilkenfeld, and Ted Robert Gurr, eds., *Peace and Conflict 2008* (Boulder, CO: Center for International Development & Conflict Management, 2007).
20. Zakaria, *Future of Freedom.*
21. See Guillermo O'Donnell, Philippe C. Schmitter, and Laurence Whitehead, *Transitions from Authoritarian Rule* (Baltimore: John Hopkins University Press, 1986), p. 17.
22. Juan J. Linz and Alfred Stepan, *Problems of Democratic Consolidation: Southern Europe, South America, and the Post-Communist Europe* (Baltimore: Johns Hopkins University Press, 1996); Adam Przeworski, ed., *Sustainable Democracy* (Cambridge: Cambridge University Press, 1995); David Potter, David Goldblatt, Margaret Kiloh, and Paul Lewis, eds., *Democratization* (Cambridge: Polity Press, 1997).

31

Number of countries

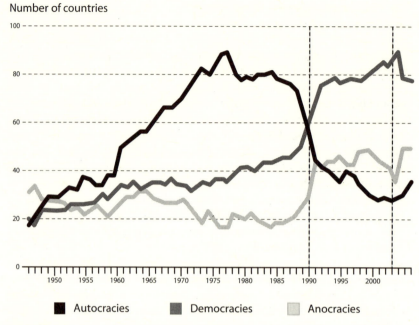

FIGURE 2.1 Types of World Regimes, 1946–2006
Source: Monty G. Marshall and Ted Robert Gurr, eds., *Peace and Conflict 2005: A Global Survey of Armed Conflicts, Self-Determination Movements, and Democracy* (College Park, MD: Center for International Development & Conflict Management, 2005), p. 16; J. Joseph Hewitt, Jonathan Wilkenfeld, and Ted Robert Gurr, eds., *Peace and Conflict 2008* (College Park, MD: Center for International Development & Conflict Management, 2007), p. 27. States with a population of fewer than one million have been excluded.

IV database.[23] This classification separates countries into three groups: democracies, anocracies (i.e., intermediate), and autocracies. The most striking fact is the increase in the number of states in the postwar period, which occurred because of decolonization. The national state, this creation of sixteenth-century Europe, rapidly spread to the four corners of the Earth. The next most striking fact is the slow but gradual increase in the number of democratic states and the relative decrease in the number of autocracies.

23. Monty G. Marshall and Ted Robert Gurr, eds., *Peace and Conflict 2005: A Global Survey of Armed Conflicts, Self-Determination Movements, and Democracy* (College Park, MD: Center for International Development & Conflict Management, 2005), p. 16; and Hewitt et al., eds., *Peace and Conflict 2008*, p. 27.

Political commentators have been discussing when the latest wave of democratization began. The most commonly accepted date, proposed by Huntington, is April 25, 1974, with the collapse of the fascist regime in Portugal.[24] This dating, however, is historically unconvincing; the establishment of democracy or its return in European countries such as Portugal, Greece, and Spain was still a geographically limited phenomenon. Only with the fall of the Berlin wall did democracy spread to states with political systems that had hitherto been antithetical, such as the eastern European countries, and even to areas of the world that had substantially lower annual incomes. The democratization of the European countries in the 1970s simply denoted a tardy and necessary allignment of the internal regimes to the dominant ideology of the bloc of international alliances to which those regimes belonged at the end of World War II, whereas after 1989 democracy began to be extended well beyond its traditional boundaries.

In fact, the number of democracies grew significantly after 1989. This growth is not just the consequence of the formation of new states; new democracies have replaced autocracies. Although several of the new democracies are still unstable and weak, as many as thirty new states joined the democratic club between 1990 and 2003, while the number of autocracies has consistently dropped. Figure 2.1. however, shows a significant decrease since 2003: more than ten countries have stopped being democratic, causing a sharp U-turn in this long-term trend. It is too early to assess if this trend is a contingent or a structural phenomenon, and the next chapters (in particular chapter 8), will explore if this trend can be related to the foreign policies adopted by western democracies after 9/11.

The more the number of democratic governments increases, the more important it becomes to ask oneself about what future democracy may expect. Today we hear about new predictions, which are all far from agreement. A quarter of a century ago, Michael Doyle forecast that all states would embrace this political credo and that in just over one century practically every country in the world would become democratic.[25] This already optimistic forecast has been updated by Diamond, who claimed that in the course of a single generation we

24. Samuel P. Huntington, *The Third Wave: Democratization in the Late Twentieth Century* (Norman: University of Oklahoma Press, 1991), chapter 2.
25. Michael W. Doyle, "Kant, Liberal Legacies, and Foreign Affairs," *Philosophy and Public Affairs* vol. 12, nos. 3 and 4 (1983): 205–35 and 323–54.

are likely to see all the countries in the world governed demo-cratically.[26]

Conversely, others claim that democracy is a specifically western cul-tural value and that there is very little hope of extending it to any great extent outside the boundaries of its native cradle, as though democracy were a value reserved to a select circle.[27] In a more comprehensive way, some believe that the conditions that allowed democratization—such as a minimum level of income, education, and infrastructures—do not ex-ist in many parts of the world and that the absence of those conditions stands in the way of any change of regime.[28] If a democratic system is "imposed" from outside, as happened in many African countries at the end of colonial domination, the structural conditions of the state itself are too weak to ensure their survival, leading to the often violent re-placement of elected governments by authoritarian regimes.

The regulatory implications of this hypothesis are nevertheless to be viewed with caution, as those implications could lead us to believe that we must shelve the struggle to achieve democracy until economic condi-tions improve. Authoritarian regimes have often used this argument and have asked their citizens to concentrate on other objectives—economic growth, defense, national unity—before thinking of their own political and civil rights (through which the citizens might challenge the legiti-macy of their ruling government).

The concept of democracy outlined above elicits very different ques-tions and answers. The struggle for democracy, which has mobilized such huge masses both in the West and elsewhere, is perhaps showing for the first time that democracy has been a universal system of values not just in treatises on political philosophy but because there has been an explicit request for democracy by the only subjects that can legiti-mize power—the world's inhabitants. If we reject the idea that certain conditions must necessarily give rise to democracy, and that in the ab-sence of these conditions democracy is impossible, then we move away from the deterministic notion that it is possible to decide who is mature and who is not, and we accept that the attainment of democracy must start from the bottom rather than from the top.

In fact, there have been more mistaken forecasts than accurate ones. While the Berlin wall was coming down, many influential democratic

26. Larry Diamond, *Can the Whole World Become Democratic? Democracy, Development, and International Polities* (Irvine CA: Center for the Study of Democracy, 2003).
27. Huntington, *Third Wave*, p. 294.
28. Lipset, *Political Man*; Robert J. Barro, "Determinants of Democracy," *Journal of Political Economy* vol. 107, no. 2 (1990): S158–83.

theorists were already expressing doubts as to whether democracy could be spread any further, a forecast that, as shown in figure 2.1, fortunately proved to be false.[29] Recent empirical analysis has indicated that low income is not necessarily an obstacle to democracy.[30] Any further broadening and deepening of democracy will therefore be the outcome of a project and of a political conflict. That is how political systems have evolved for centuries and centuries and as it will apparently be also in the future.

2.5 Assessment of Democratic States

One of the ways to protect, consolidate, and extend democracy is through the constant assessment of the way in which democracy operates. This assessment can be carried out in different ways. Elections are one method for assessing the work of the agents to whom a mandate has been given (members of the government, parliament, or administration). Likewise, the constitutional courts have the function of assessing whether and in what way to accept modifications to the constituent rules of a political system. The control authorities are then called upon to supervise the administration's activity in defined areas. Public opinion—through accountability and transparency—is in a position to control the executive. These assessment systems are an integral part of a democracy, which is actually characterized by being able to rely on antidotes and self-corrective measures. These methods could be defined as *internal assessment*. However, a democratic society can also benefit from assessment methods that are not part of the constitutional system and that may therefore be defined as *external assessment*.

One might object that a truly democratic system should contain within it the procedures for and the possibility of self-correction and thus not even need any external assessment. Indeed, democratic systems allow the current administration to be changed when that administration proves unsatisfactory and even allow the constitutional rules to be revised whenever this is deemed necessary. However, the internal assessment channels are not always enough. The members of the government, parliament, and constitutional courts are, for example, part of the establishment and could prove reluctant to identify any distortions in the system or to accept any radical modifications demanded by the general public. Voters might have only limited information on highly complex

29. Dahl, *Democracy and Its Critics*, p. 314.
30. UN Development Program, *Human Development Report 2002: Deepening Democracy in a Fragmented World* (New York: UN, 2002), p. 57.

issues and when called upon to express their opinion, in elections or referendum, might express themselves too synthetically: neither the vote for a candidate or a political party nor the vote in a referendum communicates sufficient information regarding the public's perception of the political system. For the above reasons, even an external assessment may be of assistance and is part of that necessary introspection and extroversion mentioned earlier as characterizing democratic systems. It should be added that, while internal assessment has a direct political fallout, in the sense that a government in which voters fail to confirm their confidence at election time must step down, external assessment has much more indirectly political consequences. External assessment is essentially more of a fact-finding tool than a political one.

External assessments may be of different kinds.[31] Sometimes external assessments are official and performed by IOs to comply with treaties and agreements. One of the most consolidated external assessments is that of the human rights regime carried out by the United Nations and its agencies. Backed up by the Universal Declaration subscribed to by all the member states and the numerous subsequent pacts, the UN is endowed with a complex assessment procedure. Other regional organizations, for example, the Council of Europe, also use this form of assessment.

The external assessment of democracy is still in its early stages and has not been accepted to the same extent as that of human rights. The values of democracy have still not been generally accepted on the international scene to the same extent as human rights: a Universal Declaration of Human Rights exists but (so far?) there is no analogous Universal Declaration of Democratic Principles.[32] Also from the point of view of methods and procedures, assessing democracy is more difficult than assessing the regime of human rights, as it involves norms that are essentially prescriptive rather than interdictive.

Two different approaches to external assessments carried out by civil society have been followed so far. The first approach consists in an assessment made by independent experts who, using given parameters, assess the level of democracy prevailing in the various countries (a kind of external/external assessment). This is the method used ever since the 1950s by Freedom House for political and civil rights and more recently

31. For a review, see UN Development Program, *Human Development Report 2002*, pp. 53–54; Beetham et al., *International IDEA Handbook*, p. 12.
32. See, however, the *Universal Declaration on Democracy* of the Inter-Parliamentary Union adopted in Cairo on September 16, 1997; see www.ipu .org/cnl-e/161-dem.htm.

in the Polity IV database.[33] Numerous other attempts were developed later.[34]

The second form of external assessment requires the involvement of a group of citizens from the state concerned who are asked to weigh existing problems in their own political system. (This form of external assessment could be called external/internal assessment.) The International Institute for Democracy and Electoral Assistance carried out a pilot project involving the comparison of eight countries.[35] In this method, the citizens, that is, those who on the basis of the etymological meaning of the word *democracy* ought to control power, are allowed to determine how democratic the country they live in is and to point out the modifications that they believe would increase the democratic level of the community. The two approaches, and their respective application methods, are not contradictory but complementary. Their essential elements are set out in table 2.2.

The institutions and the assessment tools used in those assessment excercises highlight different aspects of political life. For example, the elections indirectly express the assessment made by the public of the outgoing administration, the constitutional courts assess the compliance of the legislative action with the constitutive pact, and opinion polls express the degree of temporary approval of a policy or simply of a politician. The phenomena assessed are heterogeneous, although what distinguishres democracy from the other forms is precisely the existence and the variety of these tools, so much so that the vitality of a system may be judged in terms of the quantity and effectiveness of the existing assessment tools.

External assessment forms an integral part of the above-mentioned conception of democracy that indeed refers to a constantly evolving system based on extroversion. However, external assessment is also an essential part of cosmopolitan democracy since both embrace the notion that it is not sufficient for the institutions of a political system to declare themselves democratic for them to be such, nor can these institutions be validated by suffrage only. The effective modes of government and the

---

33. Freedom House, *Freedom in the World*; Hewitt et al., *Peace and Conflict*. These information sources are periodically updated and made available on the internet. For Freedom House see www.freedomhouse.org; and for Polity IV, www.cidcm.umd.edu.

34. For a review, see Alex Inkeles, ed., *On Measuring Democracy* (New Brunswick, NJ: Transaction Publishers); David Beetham, ed., *Defining and Measuring Democracy* (London: Sage, 1994); UN Development Program, *Human Development Report 2002*, chapter 3.

35. Beetham et al., *International IDEA Handbook*.

Table 2.2

Assessment of Democracy

Type of Assessment	Tools and Methods
Internal: procedures and checks envisaged in the constitutional framework	Periodic elections, referendum
	Control of legislation by the constitutional courts
	Control of judiciary, political, and economic work of the administration carried out by independent bodies, such as the judiciary, guarantee, authorities, auditing institutions
External/internal: procedures and checks not envisaged in the constitutional system but performed inside the political community	Opinion polls run by the government, political parties, and nongovernmental organizations. Auditing exercises performed by impartial subjects and involving political community citizens
External/external: assessment procedures carried out by subjects outside the political community	Assessment carried out by international organizations on the basis of treaties (Council of Europe, Human Rights Commission, UN, etc.)
	Assessment carried out by external institutions (Freedom House, IDEA, Polity IV, World Bank) for fact-finding purposes

constitutional norms themselves, even when they result from a democratic procedure, can and must be assessed from the outside, which is beneficial for the very nature of the political dialectic. They open up the way to defining a democratic system as a system that is responsive to dialogue and external criticism rather than a closed and self-referential system.

The two external assessment methods pursue different aims. The external/external one aims to compare different countries or to check a country's evolution over time and therefore gives a comparative perspective. This comparison has one advantage and one disadvantage. The advantage is that more is learned about the potential of a political community when that community has to measure itself with other experiences. The disadvantage lies in the risk involved in evaluating an experience that occurs outside its historical context. The external/internal method, on the other hand, is used to identify the points deemed "weak" by the citizens of each country with a view to detecting the critical aspects and suggesting the improvements to make to the institutions and the political forces. The latter method demands greater resources because it requires the involvement of a sufficiently large group of citizens to ensure that a statistically representative sample is obtained. Unlike public opinion polls, this method also demands that the interviewees devote a large amount of their own time to acquiring the necessary information and to providing a comprehensive response.

The information gleaned from these investigations then acts as a guideline for public policies. Third-party governments and IOs, for example, can then decide to channel their economic aid, trade, and cooperation agreements toward democratic countries or countries that intend to consolidate their democracy. The same sources are also consulted whenever international or regional organizations have to decide whether to accept new members. The most significant case is that of the European Union, in which the eastward enlargement has always been linked to a thorough assessment of the level of democracy and of the respect of human rights shown by the candidate countries and for which also sources of information produced by independent groups are often consulted. Corporations and other institutions of civil society can refer to this information before deciding where to invest, where to hold their meetings, and so on. Even individuals can decide where to spend their holidays or even which bananas to purchase, after examining the political system prevailing in foreign countries.

The methods of external/internal and external/external assessment raise conceptual problems. In the first case, problems emerge when the information is interpreted in a comparative light. The citizens of a state with longstanding liberal traditions might be particularly demanding and critically assess their own political regime. Moreover, an exacting public opinion and a participative population guarantee the high level of democracy attained by these countries. Conversely, the citizens of a state in which democracy has only recently been established as a replacement of an authoritarian regime might express satisfaction over what has been achieved. On an absolute scale, the first country might have a substantially higher level of democracy than the second, and in spite of this the citizens of the second country might feel much more satisfied than those in the first country.

Nor is it necessary to wait until the public opinion has clearly identified the most important problems facing a democratic society. If this were the case, the public would have already addressed the problem through the existing institutional channels. Instead, the results of the assessment might be found surprising. Auditing carried out in Switzerland in the 1960s, for example, might not have shown up as a fundamental problem the fact that women did not have the right to vote. Likewise, any auditing performed in the United States in the 1950s would have failed to detect the existence of strong discrimination against the black population. It is therefore not surprising that in some countries, including Italy, public opinion considers the concentration of the ownership of the means of information in the hands of its head of government only marginally important.

The problems raised in external/external assessment are even more radical. In the first instance, who assesses the assessors? What democratic procedure has been set up to decide who assesses the democratic procedures? External/external assessment is open to the customary criticism: who sets the criteria for deciding what "democracy" is? Neither the Freedom House experts nor those of Polity IV, to mention but two commonly used sources, have been given a popular mandate. We thus find ourselves in a conflict in which a group of technocrats (in the literal sense of the term) claim the right to judge when a country is democratic. In this specific case, Freedom House is certainly deserving of praise for the pioneering role it has played, and even today the data Freedom House provides are the easiest to access. However, the criteria followed by the Freedom House experts are not completely transparent, their assessments are highly subjective, and there is the suspicion of a tendency to give judgments that are aligned with U.S. foreign policy. The funding for Freedom House's activities comes not only from government sources but also from associations that are a direct offshoot of the political parties and large corporations. In Freedom House's reports, frequent comments are found on U.S. foreign policy as though world freedom were a problem regarding the United States alone and not the whole world.

In available classifications of political systems, a numerical ranking is assigned to the various countries: Freedom House from 1 to 7, Polity IV from +10 to −10. The very fact that regimes are ranked according to a scale confirms the thesis proposed herein (see § 2.2) that democracy is a matter of relative intensity. On the other hand, these analyses set a maximum limit that is fixed in time. For example, a good fifty-eight countries have obtained the highest Freedom House score. Some of them have had the same maximum score for a quarter of a century. This might seem to indicate (1) that these countries have in no way improved their political systems, which would be a very poor outcome, or (2) that they have completed the full course and there is no further margin of improvement, a hypothesis that contradicts the conception of democracy illustrated above. If we accept the principle that democracy can always be improved, the ranking should be on an open scale.[36]

36. Recent research in progress carried out in Europe is trying to provide indicators able to account more accurately for differences in democratic practice in the OECD countries. See Marc Bühlmann and Lisa Müller, *Quality of*

2.6 What Is to Be Gained by Democracy?

In addition to its ideal component, are there any practical reasons for citizens to prefer living in a democratic system rather than in some other system of government? The existence of a purely material advantage would not be decisive; there would be excellent reasons for preferring democracy even in the absence of material advantages. Democracy has an intrinsic value that does not entail only practical advantages.[37] It does not seem, however, that we are in a situation in which it is necessary to sacrifice one's interests to live in a more dignified political system, in other words, for the intrinsic value to overshadow the practical value. However varied the empirical assessment may be, it seems that individuals enjoy more advantages than drawbacks in living in a democratic country. What are these advantages and how important are they? On the basis of available historical and empirical analyses, I shall examine (i) exposure to political violence, (ii) exposure to international conflicts, (iii) respect of human rights, (iv) standard of living, economic development, and wage level, and (v) life expectancy and risk of being victims of famine.

EXPOSURE TO POLITICAL VIOLENCE

I previously cited Karl Popper's definition according to which democracy can allow a change of government without bloodshed. More precisely, as Bobbio asserts, democracy is a political system in which change is nonviolent. These theoretical tenets have a clear empirical correspondence: in the consolidated democracies, the number of individuals subjected to violence for political reasons is far smaller than in nondemocratic systems (if we limit ourselves to *internal* political violence). Let us begin by examining the most serious violence a government can inflict: mass extermination for racial, religious, social, or political reasons.[38] Out of the twenty major democides that occurred in the world between 1900 and 1987, only one was carried out by a democratic regime—imperial Britain in its colonies.[39] Likewise, the list of countries attempting democide starting from 1955 includes only two cases out of forty-one in the

---

Democracy: Democracy Barometer for Established Democracies (Zürich: NCCR, 2006).

37. As persuasively argued by Sen, "Democracy as a Universal Value," p. 10.

38. What Rudolph J. Rummel, *Death by Government* (New Brunswick: Transaction Publishers, 1994) termed "democide."

39. Rummel, *Death by Government*, p. 4.

West: Bosnia in the period 1992–1995 and Yugoslavia in 1998–1999.[40] The result is partially tautological: it would be difficult to define as democratic a government that carries out the mass killing of its own *demos* because it would be violating the principle of nonviolence. A certain congruency is expected between input and output in the democratic process and historical experience tends to confirm this expectation. This does not mean that a government that carries out democides cannot be an elected one. The case of Adolf Hitler is an example of this. However, by the time the democide occurred, Nazi Germany had long ceased to satisfy the criteria of a democracy.

Statistical analyses are problematic and open to criticism.[41] For instance, statistical analyses do not take indirect responsibilities, such as those deriving from funding, fomenting, or supplying arms to others, into account. The data cited exclude the victims occurring in the course of wars, while it is historically difficult to distinguish between victims in time of peace and those of war, as governments often unleash political violence, even against their own citizens, in times of war. A democratic government can also start wars that cause a large number of victims in other areas, such as those inflicted by the United States during the Korean and Vietnam wars and more recently in Afghanistan and Iraq. The observed absence of violence in the interior is certainly not a reason for satisfaction if the violence carried out in the exterior is very high. Likewise, countries with a long liberal tradition such as Great Britain, France, and the Netherlands were embroiled in long and bloody colonial adventures.[42] Even if these factors are taken into account, the fact remains that a state that perpetrates or allows a democide involving its own citizens cannot be deemed democratic.

Important research by Michael Mann has situated the relationship between democracies and genocide in a new context. Mann claimed that political communities with a high level of participation ensure the

---

40. Marshall and Gurr, *Peace and Conflict 2005*, p. 58.

41. The data collected by Rummel are not considered reliable by everyone and tend to overestimate the crimes committed by despotic regimes and underestimate those committed by democratic ones; for a critique see, for example, Tomislav Dulic, "Tito's Slaughterhouse: A Critical Analysis of Rummel's Work on Democide," *Journal of Peace Research* vol. 41, no. 1 (2004): 85–102. Some of these analyses belong to that form of democratic self-congratulation that feeds also on the manipulation of statistical data. However, more objective data do not significantly alter the present discussion.

42. See Domenico Losurdo, *Controstoria del liberalismo* (Roma-Bari: Laterza, 2005).

safety of their own members but can prove dangerously lethal to those who do not belong to them. This is the often neglected "dark side of democracy."[43] Typical examples of this dark side are the massacre of the indigenous populations by European colonists in North America and Australasia. These massacres were often carried out by small communities with a high level of internal participation and solidarity (often at local rather than state level) but that did not hesitate to defend themselves and physically eliminate native populations who those communities felt represented dangers or obstacles to them. In many cases simply because those native populations were different.

Ethnic cleansing was practiced in the majority of eastern European countries when those countries established themselves as national states and founded their own legitimacy on the people, which was, however, defined in ethnic terms. In recent times we saw in the Balkans how the democracies being set up felt an almost physiological need to emphasize their difference from other groups, even when the ethnic dividing lines (for instance, between Croats, Serbs, Slovenians, Bosnians, Albanians, Montenegrins, and Macedonians and so on) were anything but obvious. As soon as the homogenization of the community had been obtained by such coercive means as forced assimilation, expulsion, or even genocide, those democracies became oblivious to the blood they had spilt. There is nothing like self-satisfaction for helping to remove the horrors of the past and to perfect peaceful cohabitation.

This confirms that even though democracies minimize the amount of political violence inside their boundaries, democracies can be extremely harmful to those they do not recognize as members, whether they belong to ethnic minorities or other nations. External enemies are useful for developing a common identity on the interior by means of an outward pouring of violence repressed on the inside. As Hegel had already observed, "successful wars have prevented civil broils and strengthened the internal power of the state."[44] The risk of this is all the more frequent at the stage in which a given democratic community is being established.

EXPOSURE TO INTERNATIONAL CONFLICTS

The good performance of democracies in controlling internal political violence has no equivalent in international conflicts: democracies are as

43. Mann, *Dark Side of Democracy*, pp. 61–68.
44. Georg Wilhelm Friedrich Hegel, *Philosophy of Law*, trans. S. W. Dyde (Kitchener: Batoche Books, [1821] 2001), § 324, p. 259.

belligerent as non-democracies.[45] However, the wars that democracies wage are simply somewhat less bloody than those fought by non-democracies. Empirical analysis shows that a small margin exists in favor of democracies, although that margin is narrow compared to what would be expected from political systems established on the internal principle of nonviolence. Why are democracies so warlike? Why does the principle of nonviolence, which is indeed a constituent of the internal political system, not have favorable repercussions also on international relations? This represents a central point of the problem addressed in the present book, namely, the extension of democracy at the global level, to which I shall return in the next chapter.

Although democracies are warlike, there are advantages in being citizens of them. One advantage is that democracies tend to win their wars: the control exercised by the general public over the government and the existence of a degree of transparency mean that the executive is unlikely to embark upon a war the country is doomed to lose.[46] One of the reasons why democracies win wars is that democracies manage to form coalitions of several states, many of which are also democratic. Democracies win also by virtue of the solidarity that exists among democratic regimes. Moreover, democracies must keep their casualties to a minimum. Soldiers are also citizens, and the government must account to the public opinion for any losses sustained, while in an autocracy the government has an easier task to dodge the will of the people and can use its power of repression to force the people to fight.

The existence of a democracy is not necessarily good news for its neighbors, however. Indeed, when a democracy is engaged in a conflict, not only does the democracy tend to be victorious, but it also inflicts on its enemies much greater losses than it itself sustains. This is the trend that emerged in World War II and is directly linked to U.S. superiority in technology, notably in aerospace technology. In the latter postwar period, we saw how this supremacy caused victims in Korea, Vietnam, the Persian Gulf, and the Balkans. Nowadays this supremacy is denoted in strategic studies as an asymmetric conflict, which leads to wars in which the vast majority of casualties are on only one side. This was seen in Kosovo, Afghanistan, and Iraq prior to the deployment of troops on ground. This supremacy of the democratic states may lead them to think less about using force against others. However, this is linked less to their

45. Karen A. Rasler and William R. Thompson, "The Monadic Democratic Puzzle and an 'End of History' Partial Solution?" *International Politics* vol. 40, no. 1 (2003): 5–27.
46. Dan Reiter and Allan C. Stam, *Democracies at War* (Princeton: Princeton University Press, 2002).

democratic nature than to the resources available to them: there is no evidence that authoritarian governments would make a more sparing use of the same political, economic, and military resources.

Nor would it be good news for the neighbors if a state is transformed from authoritarian to democratic. As pointed out by Mansfield and Snyder, in their constituent phase, democracies are surprisingly belligerent.[47] The destruction of the earlier autarkic order makes not only the use of internal political violence more likely (as may legitimately be expected in the case of regime change) but also warlike behavior directed against their neighbors.

RESPECT OF HUMAN RIGHTS

One of the principal justifications of democracy is its respect of human rights, and so it is meet and fitting to expect a link between the input (a democratic system) and the output (the safeguarding of human rights). It is not surprising that there is an almost complete correspondence between countries with a democratically elected government and countries in which violations of human rights are less frequent. Yet it is important not to overlook the difference that exists between democracy on the one hand and human rights on the other. Indeed, a political system with a government elected by an ethnic majority that does not respect its minorities could conceivably exist. In many eastern European countries and in the former Soviet republics, ethnic discriminations have indeed increased with democracy. Likewise, there are situations in which human rights are scrupulously respected even though the general public plays no part in the election of the government; Hong Kong under British dominion is a case in point. Today, a small state such as Singapore extends broad civil rights to its citizens except that of electing the government.

Keeping human rights and democracy separate also makes it possible to assess the differences among the various systems. Some forms of government show a greater sensitivity toward the protection of certain types of rights than others. Among democratic regimes a distinction may be made between the liberal family and the egalitarian one. While the liberal family tends to safeguard civil rights, including the right to property, even to the detriment of equality, the egalitarian family tends

47. Edward Mansfield and Jack Snyder, "Democratization and the Danger of War," *International Security* vol. 20, no. 1 (1995): 5–38 and, more comprehensively, Edward Mansfield and Jack Snyder, *Electing to Fight: Why Emerging Democracies Go to War* (Cambridge, MA: MIT Press, 2005).

to restrict the right to property (for instance, by means of taxation) for the purpose of guaranteeing economic and social rights such as health, education, or unemployment benefits. Let us try to distinguish among the three types of human rights identified by T. H. Marshall—civil, political, and socioeconomic rights—and see the extent to which each of those types is safeguarded in a democratic regime.[48]

Civil rights (religious freedom, freedom of expression, freedom to own private property, etc.) established themselves historically by bringing the executive under control, which gradually led to increased public participation in the choice of government. Some civil rights, such as the right to property, flourish in a democratic system but are not an exclusive part of that system: numerous authoritarian systems of the twentieth century, for example, guaranteed the right to property, or indeed defended that right against the claims of workers' movements. Other civil rights, such as freedom of worship and expression, may instead be linked directly to a democratic regime. In a competitive political system, the minorities can use the vote as an instrument for demanding that the government safeguard their rights.

However, exceptions do exist. Several ethnic minorities are not safeguarded even in democratic systems. Gypsies in Europe, colored minorities in the United States, and aboriginal populations in North America and Australasia have not been adequately protected, in part because the minorities themselves were often slow to use the vote as an instrument to protect their own community. Today the problem recurs in the new democracies of eastern Europe. In these new democracies, the correctives traditionally applied in a democratic system may prove too weak and ineffective, to the extent that it becomes necessary to implement public policies aimed at boosting them, an argument put forward in a growing body of literature.[49]

Political rights can instead be linked directly to democracy. A democratic government cannot exist without an active and passive right to vote. The suppression of political rights means rendering democracy impossible and vice versa; there can be no democracy without political rights.

The relationship between democracy and *economic and social rights* (such as education, health, housing, and income) is more complex. Many

---

48. Thomas H. Marshall, *Citizenship and Social Class* (London: Pluto Press, [1949] 1992).

49. Young, *Justice and the Politics of Difference*; Will Kymlicka, *Multicultural Citizenship: A Liberal Theory of Minority Rights* (Oxford: Oxford University Press, 1995); Seyla Benhabib, *The Claims of Culture: Equality and Diversity in the Global Era* (Princeton: Princeton University Press, 2002).

of these rights are inadequately safeguarded in many democratic systems, while some authoritarian systems have endeavored to guarantee them. Albeit rather inefficiently, the countries of real socialism guaranteed income and the right to work, as well as the availability to everybody of public services. From the regulatory standpoint, Beetham argues that a democratic system also requires the safeguarding of economic and social rights, because citizens deprived of such protection are unable to participate fully in political life.[50] An extension of economic and social rights could, however, lead to a restriction of the right to property should, for example, extensive use be made of taxation of income and wealth to fund social welfare programs. Conversely, it has been denied that there is a trade-off between economic rights and social and political rights (as claimed by the Stalinist regimes in the 1950s); nothing prevents both batteries of rights from being safeguarded simultaneously.

LIVING STANDARD AND ECONOMIC DEVELOPMENT

Today the wealthier countries are those that are more democratic. The states with the highest per capita income are all democratic, except for a few anomalous cases in which wealth, often concentrated in the hands of the few, comes from oil. Democracies enjoy the same dominant position on the basis of other indicators of prosperity. If we examine, for instance, the top thirty countries ranked in terms of human development, all have democratic institutions, with the sole exceptions of two small countries, Hong Kong and Singapore.[51] However, observing an association does not mean that also a causal link may be identified. Is it the existence of a democratic system that produces a high standard of living or vice versa, a high standard of living that produces a democratic system? I previously challenged the deterministic view that democracy needs must be associated with specific conditions of prosperity. Nevertheless, empirical literature has so far suggested that a high standard of living makes democracy a more stable arrangement that is less exposed to regime changes.[52] It should, however, be pointed out that this was not always the case: in the period between the two world wars, some of the

50. Beetham, *Democracy and Human Rights*, chapter 5.
51. The human development index is a composite indicator made up of life expectancy at birth, rate of literacy, and per capita income. See the Annual Report by the UN Development Program, *Human Development and Climate Change 2007* (New York: UN, 2007), tab. A1.2.
52. Larry Diamond, "Economic Development and Democracy Reconsidered," *American Behavioral Scientist* vol. 34, nos. 4–5 (1992): 450–99; Barro,

richest countries in the world abandoned their own democratic systems in favor of totalitarian regimes. After World War II, several eastern European countries had higher standards of living than some democratic countries in Africa, Asia, and Latin America. Yet from the vantage point of the twenty-first century, it would seem that prosperity is anchored with increasing stability in democracy.

Prosperity is an acquired status. For developing countries, the fundamental issue is not what elements are associated with prosperity but what elements generate prosperity. The question therefore is: does democracy favor economic development, allowing those who are not yet rich to become so? Here, historical evidence is less conclusive. Soviet Russia under the heel of Stalin and Germany under that of Hitler enjoyed a much higher rate of economic development than democratic countries such as France and Great Britain.[53] This problem persists today: countries such as South Korea, Taiwan, Singapore, and Hong Kong have had a strong rate of economic development under authoritarian regimes. Since the Tiananmen massacre in 1989, China has enjoyed a soaring rate of economic growth. This can largely be accounted for by the fact that these countries were "in pursuit" of the richer nations. Indeed, precisely the need to "overtake" the richer (and often democratic) countries meant that the oppositions and internal dissent could be repressed on the pretext that repressing them was necessary to defend the national interest.

But it is not possible even to trace a causal link between authoritarianism and economic development. Many authoritarian countries have had quite unsatisfactory rates of development, in spite of favorable conditions. Available empirical analyses seem to indicate there is no clear relationship.[54] In particular, while the growth rate is more regular in democracies, in authoritarian regimes the growth rate varies widely, with some spectacular successes (South Korea, Taiwan, People's Republic of China) and many cases of lack of development. Empirical analysis suggests that when authoritarian regimes turn into democratic regimes, a positive effect is exerted on economic development.[55] However, this effect ceases when the level of democracy increases.

"Determinants of Democracy": UN Development Program, *Human Development Report 2002*, p. 58.

53. Angus Maddison, *The World Economy in the 20th Century* (Paris: OECD, 1989), pp. 15 and 120.

54. Diamond, "Economic Development and Democracy Reconsidered"; John F. Helliwell, "Empirical Linkages Between Democracy and Economic Growth," *British Journal of Political Science* vol. 24, no. 2 (1994): 225–48.

55. Robert J. Barro, *Determinants of Economic Growth: A Cross-Country Empirical Study* (Cambridge, MA: MIT Press, 1997).

Yet individual freedom and the possibility of public opinion exerting control over the government have become increasingly important also for economic development. Contemporary social systems are characterized by rapid change that demands the testing, transmission, selection, and dissemination of cultural, economic, and technological innovations.[56] An autocratic system, which limits individual freedom, does not allow this change to occur and indirectly hinders prosperity. It is as though while development associated with heavy industry can apparently coexist even with authoritarian regimes, development linked to the information society calls for political systems based on participation and freedom of communication. Under existing historical and technological conditions, economic development is increasingly becoming linked to democracy.

Finally, it is no surprise to learn that wages are higher in democratic regimes, even taking other factors into account, such as income levels and labor productivity. Rodrik estimated that if Mexico had the same level of democracy as the United States, wages would be between 10 percent and 40 percent higher.[57] Similar estimates have been made for a group of over ninety countries. It is clear that lack of democracy is a drawback for employed workers: autocratic regimes often repress trade unions and prevent the formation of political parties that have to compete for popular support. As soon as an employed worker becomes a citizen, also that worker's bargaining power increases. The stronger position of workers in the labor market could lead other social categories, such as entrepreneurs and investors, to have less power and lower incomes.

LIFE EXPECTANCY AND FAMINE

There is no proof that democracy guarantees longevity. If we consider life expectancy, the evidence is quite uncertain: life expectancy is linked to a high income level and, to the extent that democracy is associated with prosperity, democracy then also offers the hope of a longer life. But this is not a decisive argument, as this is the effect of income rather than of democracy. It must be ascertained whether, for an equivalent income, life expectancy is higher in democratic regimes than in other regimes. A significant comparison may be made between two large countries, China and India, which have had very different political systems since the last

56. Nathan Rosenberg and Luther E. Birdzell, *How the West Grew Rich: The Economic Transformation of the Industrial World* (New York: Basic Books, 1986), chapter 8.
57. Dani Rodrik, "Democracies Pay Higher Wages," *Quarterly Journal of Economics* vol. 114, no. 3 (1999): 707–38.

war. Yet in the period 1950–1955, the two countries had similar life expectancies: 40.8 years in China and 38.7 years in India. In 1975–1980, China soared to 65.3, while India stopped short at 52.9. Only in the period 1995–2000 did a certain degree of convergence occur, even though life expectancy in China, now 69.7 years, is considerably higher than in India, which stands at 62.1.[58] Equally great successes have been achieved in Cuba, the Latin American country with the highest life expectancy despite a very low income level and the denial of civil and political rights.

The research of Amartya Sen and colleagues has instead shown that famines are less frequent in democratic countries, even for equal income levels.[59] This finding is explained by the fact that a democratic system ensures better distribution of information, thus allowing individuals to react promptly to an adverse situation. Moreover, democratic governments must cater to the citizens' interests by acting in a timely fashion to save the population. An autocratic state, on the other hand, can ignore these demands and prevent information flows, also by virtue of its control over the media.

OVERVIEW

The historical and empirical data described above are partial; a survey of the advantages and disadvantages accruing to individuals in the various political regimes could be much more detailed. Although the overall picture is very fragmentary, it shows that democracy does not stand in the way of achieving substantial objectives. Quite the contrary. It is obvious that a rational individual should prefer to live in a democracy even when he or she has no interest in participating in political life. Democratic countries offer a long list of advantages: they limit internal violence, allow greater wealth, win wars, provide more comfortable life, have drinking water and cinemas with plush armchairs. Many of these indicators are correlated and merely point to the fact that one part of the world, the West, has a much higher standard of living than the others. Although the relationships of cause and effect are much more complex than can be examined here, at least one conclusion can be inferred: there is no evidence that democracy is an obstacle to well-being and prosperity; indeed, there is considerable evidence to indicate that democracy facilitates them.

58. Graziella Caselli, Jacques Vallin, and Guillaume Wunsch, *Demography: Analysis and Synthesis* (Amsterdam: Academic Press, 2006), p. 71.
59. Amartya Sen, *Development as Freedom* (Oxford: Oxford University Press, 1999), chapter 7.

The communist pipe dream, which nevertheless had such a strong effect on the course of what Eric Hobsbawm has termed "the short century,"[60] can today offer very few material advantages to rival those in democratic systems, and these advantages are limited to the enhancement of life expectancy achieved in developing countries such as China and Cuba. The benefits distributed by the communist countries, neglecting their well-known side-effects, may be associated with societies in the early stages of industrialization and in which the value of communication assets—knowledge, information, initiative—are still relatively unimportant. Yet the fact that democratic systems lavish benefits on their communities does not mean that they distribute those benefits evenly to all their inhabitants. When democracy is associated with capitalism, it distributes benefits, although in a fashion that is anything but uniform. Internal social, ethnic, political, or economic discriminations lead to several groups enjoying much greater advantages than others and has meant that several groups gain nothing. However, the main issue as far as the present analysis is concerned is different: a democracy that distributes benefits to its own population does not necessarily also distribute them to its neighbors. Indeed, a democracy often discharges toward the exterior its own political violence and appropriates the resources of others.

2.7 Not Resting on One's Laurels

Democracy has been on the march for more than twenty-five centuries. Its progress has been difficult and controversial, although its advance has actually been overwhelming in the more recent historical period. Such a sensational victory would not have been possible without the pressure of the people's demanding to take over the reins of their own destiny. But we must not overlook how instrumental the consensus that exists today has been, and to consider that consensus irreversible would be a howling error.

This chapter has brought out two critical aspects. The first aspect refers to the need to have a variety of democratic models. In the short space of a few years, dozens of countries with different historical traditions, income levels, and social capital have turned to democracy. New electoral systems and constitutions have been tried out; myriad political parties and associations have arisen in civil society. All this makes up a vast testing ground that has involved a process of selection and will continue to do so. The paths followed by democracy are numerous, and

60. Eric J. Hobsbawm, *The Age of Extremes: The Short Twentieth Century* (London: Michael Joseph, 1994).

even if many of those paths turn out to be blind alleys, much is to be learned from what is currently being tried out. While fixing a few rigid principles, it is necessary to safeguard the theoretical and political legitimacy of models of democracy that differ from those that exist in western society. It is necessary to guard against a form of creeping democratic fundamentalism that tends to dignify only forms that have been tried and tested in the western countries and that are publicized by highly remunerated preachers.

The second aspect is related to the benefits that democratic regimes, both old and new, will be able to deliver to their citizens. For years, the West has been making a solemn promise to the peoples of the South and East: accept democracy as your ideology rather than communism, fascism, third-worldism, or Islamism, and in exchange you will be given freedom, dignity, and material prosperity. Despite the oversights, the empirical and historical analysis set out in the previous section shows that, overall, democratic systems have paid greater dividends to their own citizens than competing systems. And it is also to obtain these promised benefits that the peoples of the South and the East have turned to democracy. Available empirical analyses refer, however, only to the past, to before the group of democratic states was enlarged to include a large number of developing countries. It would be incorrect to believe that the same benefits can be granted automatically to new democracies in ten to twenty years' time.

If we examine the group of poorest countries in the world, those with the lowest indexes of human development, we find a dozen or so countries in which democratic elections are held. In these countries the majority of the population is engaged in a daily struggle for survival. They have adopted democracy as an act of faith in what western countries have promised them. If these countries are to continue to be democratic, and if their political systems are to acquire greater stability, it will depend largely on the international political choices made. But should these benefits cease, there is a danger that the democratic wave will be replaced by a backlash in the opposite direction and of uncertain nature, the consequences of which are hard to predict. The fact that since 2003, for the first time since the end of World War II, the number of democratic countries is decreasing is already a very warning sign.

The West has made another implicit promise to the developing countries: become democratic and we will accept you into our exclusive club of nations, giving you the same dignity we have accorded the other members. So far, this promise has not been kept. This promise depends on the extension of democracy to the global sphere, a topic that will be addressed in the next few chapters.

Chapter 3
Democracy and the Global System

3.1 From the Fiction of the Sovereign State to the Global System

In the preceding chapter I set out the mainstays of democratic theory pertinent to the analysis carried out in this book using a fiction that has accompanied democratic theory ever since its origin: imagining autonomous political communities that are isolated from each other. This expedient is both common and useful. It made it possible to elaborate the democratic doctrine, test that doctrine in small communities, and then gradually extend it to large national states. Without the conviction that self-government can be attained in a given community believed to be reasonably free of external influences, it would not have been possible to set up any democratic laboratory.

However, the time has come to do away with the fiction and to accept reality for what it is: no political community is free from outside influences. Trade, wars, environmental issues, financial flows, tourism, epidemics, mass media, migrations, and a thousand other aspects of human life mean that each political community is linked to the others, both near and far. Immersed as they are in a global context, political communities are intrinsically shaped by external influences.

This is a problem faced by all states, not just democratic ones. In a world made up of countries with a wide range of political systems, each state experiences the influence of and exerts an influence on its neighbors, whether those neighbors have similar or different political regimes.

Nor is it necessarily true that the influence of states that are similar is less bothersome than the influence of states that are different. The conception of democracy outlined in chapter 2 has shown, however, that even if all the countries in the world were finally to adopt a democratic system this would not mean the end of diversity. We may therefore expect that the differences will persist, even though this expectation does not entitle us to rank countries hierarchically as advanced or backward, democratic or autocratic, good or bad. However probable as well as preferable it is for self-government to be extended to more and more communities and gradually become more sophisticated, the interstate system is and will continue to be composed of different elements. Each community, whether democratic or not, is obliged to live together with other communities in a heterogeneous and often quarrelsome condominium.

Those wielding power, whether democratic or autocratic, never have absolute control. The power exercised inside a political community has always had to come to terms with two kinds of counterweight. The first kind is represented by the constraints imposed on a government by other governments, the second kind by the existence of a plethora of actors, groups, and institutions—in a word, by a public sphere that approves or disapproves, permits or prevents, obeys or resists. In a world of interdependence, these groups not only perform an internal function but also can participate in different ways in external political life.[1]

For the purposes of the explanation, it may prove useful to represent the global system as being composed of democratic and nondemocratic states. In each country, three entities are at work: the general public, the state, and the government. Figure 3.1 provides a graphic representation comprising only four states, two democratic (A and B) and two autocratic (C and D). In the democratic states, the government represents the general public as the result of a process of legitimization, and this is shown in Figure 3.1 by the direction of the arrow. In the autocratic states, the process of legitimization is absent, and so the government has an impositional power. What are the effects on democracy due to the dialectic between the system inside the states and the interstate system?

3.2 Globalization and Democratic Autonomy

With the sole exception of the monastic republic of Mt. Athos, no political community has ever been effectively independent of the external

1. As emphasized long ago by Robert O. Keohane and Joseph S. Nye, eds., *Transnational Relations and World Politics* (Cambridge, MA: Harvard University Press, 1971).

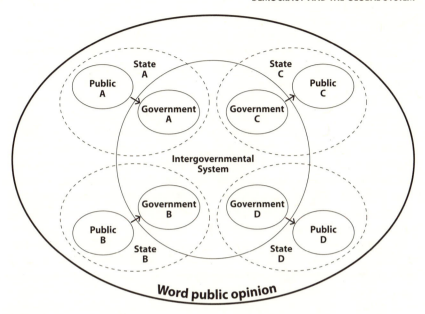

FIGURE 3.1 Schematization of the Interstate System

environment, neither the Greek city-states nor the Italian renaissance communes nor even the modern nation-states. While the conventional internal/external dichotomy postulates the existence of a clear-cut de-limitation between areas, the two dimensions are growing increasingly interrelated, as can be seen in the literature on international regimes and on global governance.[2]

The increasing globalization of recent years has strongly augmented the qualitative and quantitative importance of external influences, mod-ifying the way power is exercised in all the states. The areas in which a state political community can make its own decisions autonomously are therefore increasingly limited. The governments of authoritarian states have experienced growing difficulty in preventing their own subjects from autonomously entertaining relations with the exterior. The fact that the population of an authoritarian state has access to information originating from other countries via the radio, television, internet, trade

2. See James N. Rosenau, *Along the Domestic-Foreign Frontier: Exploring Governance in a Turbulent World* (Cambridge: Cambridge University Press, 1997); and Mathias Koenig-Archibugi, "Mapping Global Governance," pp. 46–69 in *Governing Globalization*, ed. David Held and Anthony McGrew (Cambridge: Polity Press, 2002).

relations, and tourism has weakened the authoritarian regimes and proved to be a decisive factor in favoring democratization. In the past, external pressures played a decisive role in upsetting the authoritarian regimes of eastern Europe, a phenomenon that is now observed in China and in many other countries.

While globalization may be perceived as a threat by authoritarian regimes, as it undermines their control over their own people, globalization also causes problems for democratic states.[3] The fact that a community has to cope with an external environment distorts the institutive democratic pact. All three constitutive criteria for democracy—nonviolence, control, and equality (see § 2.3)—are being challenged. The principle of nonviolence is weakened when interstate disputes are resolved outside a constitutional pact through diplomacy, intimidation, or even war. Control of those holding public posts may be exercised inside a community, but not when the decision makers are located outside it. The very criterion of equality is overshadowed if only a few of the persons involved in the decision-making process take part in the political process. Let us examine these effects more closely.

NONVIOLENCE

In external relations, the preventive nonaggression pact explicitly or implicitly agreed upon internally ceases to exist. The outcome of a possible external threat may simply depend on the power and the resources available to the adversaries. While on the interior the community has emerged from a state of nature, on the exterior the community plunges back into it. For a democratic state, the problem emerges (or *should* emerge) both when the state is meek and when it imposes itself. If a democratic state is subjected to the decision-making process after a military defeat or finds itself in the condition in which other communities

3. The literature on the impact of globalization on democracies, pioneered by Held, *Democracy and the Global Order*, has grown exponentially in recent years. See, among others, Ian Clark, *Globalization and International Relations Theory* (Oxford: Oxford University Press, 1999); Philip G. Cerny, "Globalization and the Erosion of Democracy," *European Journal of Political Research* vol. 36, no. 5 (1999): 1–26; Michael Goodhart, "Democracy, Globalisation and the Problem of the State," *Polity* vol. 33, no. 4 (2001): 527–46; Esref Aksu and Joseph A. Camilleri, eds., *Democratizing Global Governance* (Houndmills: Palgrave, 2002); Robert O. Keohane, "Global Governance and Democratic Accountability," pp. 130–59 in *Taming Globalization: Frontiers of Governance*, ed. David Held and Mathias Koenig-Archibugi (Cambridge: Polity Press, 2003).

decide on its behalf, it is no longer in a position to meet its commitments vis-à-vis its own citizens. Let us take the paradoxical case of Denmark during the German invasion in World War II (1940–1943).[4] Despite the fact that the country had retained its own institutions, external domination had distorted political life to such an extent as to render it unrecognizable. But the situation is no better when the democratic state imposes its will on others. This may allow contingent benefits to be obtained, but these benefits are paid for at the cost of forgoing the constituent principles of one's own political system. Let us take for example the French occupation of Algeria in the late 1950s. While elections and parliamentary debates continued to take place in France, the occupation was eroding some of the constituent principles of the republic.[5]

The cases of Denmark under Nazi occupation and of France during the Algerian adventure are extreme, as those cases refer to situations involving the explicit dominion of one political community over another. But similar problems arise also in much more ordinary situations, such as joining a military alliance or the imposition of economic exploitation. Karl Marx warned that a people that oppresses other peoples cannot be free, a statement more of a principle than a fact. If freedom is considered an individual condition, it is easy to imagine that certain groups enjoy their own freedom by depriving others of theirs. To be free, a community may for instance imprison those who commit crimes. But if we replace the word *freedom* with the word *democracy*, the principle stated takes on a more certain meaning, as democracy has more to do with a collective system of rules. To claim that a people that oppresses other peoples cannot be democratic means giving full value to the concept of democracy as participation.

POPULAR CONTROL

Control by the people ceases to exist in the instant in which the decisions are made outside the political community of reference. Even when the decisions of state A have important consequences outside its frontiers, for example, in state B, they are made exclusively by state A. Likewise, state A must submit to decisions made in any other state even

---

4. See the fascinating account by Richard Petrow, *The Bitter Years: The Invasion and Occupation of Denmark and Norway, April 1940–May 1945* (New York: Morrow, 1974).

5. For a recent account of how the Algerian colonization affected the French Republic, see Todd Shepard, *The Invention of Decolonization: The Algerian War and the Remaking of France* (Ithaca, NY: Cornell University Press, 2006).

when those decisions have an impact on the internal living conditions. The contemporary world is full of "overlapping communities of fate" with common interests on limited aspects but that are equally important for community life that crosses state borders.[6] The management of a lake situated among several countries, the existence of a religious or linguistic community whose members are scattered over remote areas of the world, the dependence of workers from several countries on the strategic choices made by the same multinational corporation, and the ethical code of an international professional society are all issues that elude democratic control in a global system based on the predominance of states.

POLITICAL EQUALITY

How must the political community be constructed at the time it is called upon to deliberate and make decisions? Who must be included in this community and who not included? This is one of the principal problems regarding democratic theory and practice, to which no satisfactory response has so far been given. The most significant evolution occurring in democratic practice over the past twenty-five centuries has been the gradual expansion of holders of political participation rights. Today the political equality of all adults is widely acknowledged inside democratic states, although the principle is lost in each issue that crosses the border. The institutional communities continue to be established in a rigid fashion, corresponding to the present-day territorial states. They call upon their own members to discuss and decide on the problems on the agenda but ignore those problems that lie outside it. Whenever a decision-making process has external fallout, the principle of political equality according to which everyone involved must participate in the political debate is violated. This originates out of the nature of citizenship, which allows the individual to participate in the political process in state A or state B but not in both states, regardless of what the individual's exact involvement actually is.[7]

Let us take the striking case of the atomic tests carried out by France in 1995–1996 at Mururoa atoll. The French government decided to

6. Held, *Global Covenant*, p. 168.
7. Raffaele Marchetti, "Interaction-Dependent Justice and the Problem of International Exclusion," *Constellations: An International Journal of Critical and Democratic Theory* vol. 12, no. 4 (2005): 487–501.

carry out the tests in accordance with wholly democratic principles.[8] Obviously, however, the entire community of stakeholders was not involved: the Pacific Ocean populations were exposed to nuclear radiation, while the French people (allegedly) obtained the benefits in the form of national security and/or nuclear power. Although there were some protests also in France, French public opinion would certainly have had a different reaction if the same tests had been carried out in the Paris region rather than thousands of miles away.

Intergovernmental organizations are one of the institutional modes in which the states attempt to set up political colleges to deal with existing problems. The IGOs apply several of the principles of democracy that are known in the states, and are widely used to resolve any contradictions encountered. But, as IGOs are composed of representatives of the governments rather than of the direct stakeholders, IGOs are inclined to favor choices that facilitate the interests of governments rather than those of the individual stakeholders. In the case in which these IGOs are composed exclusively of countries with elected governments, the decision-making process regarding these issues does not follow the democratic principle according to which all those involved should have a say in the matter, if for no other reason than because the principle of equality applies to the states but not to individuals (this topic will be taken up again in chapters 4 and 5).

3.3 International Conflicts and Democracy

The interstate system exerts a direct and decisive influence on the way power is exercised inside the states. The possibility of a state becoming a democracy or boosting its current democratic status is directly linked to the existing international climate. The absence of a peaceful international climate blocks dissent, mortifies the opposition, and restricts freedom inside the states. Citizens' rights are curtailed and, in order to satisfy the need for security, civil and political liberties are often impaired. In wartime, people are prepared to place their freedom in the hands of the war leaders who promise victory. The threat of war, even more than war itself, bolsters the existing regime and anyone daring to criticize his or her own state is immediately viewed as antipatriotic and banned from social life. The elites in power thus have a covert interest in

8. Between September 1995 and May 1996, France carried out eight nuclear tests in one of its old overseas possessions, the Mururoa atoll, in the Pacific. This provoked the reaction of IOs, of countries such as New Zealand, and of world public opinion.

promoting international conflicts in order to consolidate their own internal power.

This is certainly no novelty. Already in the sixteenth century, Erasmus observed: "I am loth to suspect here what only too often, alas!, has turned out to hold true: that the rumor of war with the Turks had been trumped up with the aim of mulcting the Christian population, so that being burned and crushed in all possible ways might have been all the more servile towards the tyranny of all kind of princes."[9] In the eighteenth century, Jean-Jacques Rousseau pointed to the internal/external link: "war and conquest without and the encroachment of despotism within give each other mutual support. . . . Aggressive princes wage war at least as much on their subjects as on their enemies, and the conquering nation is left no better off than the conquered."[10] These observations took on fresh significance during the Cold War: in the eastern bloc the external threat was used to prevent democracy, and in the West to restrict its potential.

The case of the Cold War is illuminating precisely because of its unreal and "imaginary" nature.[11] A potential war, a looming threat that for decades is expressed only obliquely, can be much more effective than war itself in restricting internal participation. The instant the war becomes real, the consequences are unpredictable. The need to mobilize the population can lead to upheavals in the social structure. A defeat and even a victory can be accompanied by radical changes in the political system of the belligerent countries, perhaps even leading to the constitutional norms being rewritten and the former leadership being completely removed and replaced. Paradoxically, the looming external threat (the *cold* war) may be more effective than an actual conflict (the *hot* war) in enfeebling internal opposition and in consolidating the support of the public for the incumbent government; when a war ends, there are probably a winner and a loser, and accounts have to be settled inside each country. Many countries have actually embraced democracy after experiencing the horrors of a war imposed by an autocratic system.

However, the latent conflict may be prolonged, even indefinitely, and may represent an effective way of keeping an authoritarian regime in place. In *Nineteen Eighty-Four,* George Orwell had already warned of

9. Erasmus of Rotterdam, *The "Adages" of Erasmus*, ed. and trans. M. Mann Phillips (Cambridge: Cambridge University Press, [1536] 1964), pp. 347–48.
10. Jean-Jacques Rousseau, "Judgement of Saint-Pierre's Project for Perpetual Peace," pp. 53–100 in *Rousseau on International Relations*, ed. Stanley Hoffmann and David P. Fidler (Oxford: Clarendon Press, [1758–1759] 1981), on p. 91.
11. Mary Kaldor, *The Imaginary War* (Oxford: Blackwell, 1990).

such dangers: "War is now a purely internal affair. In the past, the ruling groups of all countries, although they might recognize their common interest and therefore limit the destructiveness of war, did fight against one another, and the victor always plundered the vanquished. In our own day they are not fighting against one another at all. The war is waged by each ruling group against its own subjects, and the object of war is not to make or prevent conquests of territory, but to keep the structure of society intact."[12] The end of the Cold War has not meant the elimination of extremist parties, even in democratic states, and those extremist parties maintain their power by pouring oil on the flames of international conflict.

In figure 3.1 this means that the introduction of democracy in states C and D and its extension in states A and B are hindered by the existence of relationships of conflict in the intergovernmental system. Of course, it is not necessary for all the countries to be involved in the same conflict. The international threat, whether real or assumed, may be limited or even come from non–state subjects, such as terrorist formations. The schema provided also enables us to focus on the difference between the agenda pursued by the government and that corresponding to the interests of the general public. In a democratic regime, the government wields considerable power over foreign policy and defense, which is generally not subjected to public scrutiny to the same extent as other branches of the executive. Out of fear that potential enemies may come into possession of confidential information, foreign policy and defense matters are not subjected to the rules of transparency and control. A vicious circle is set up in which those responsible for foreign policy and defense matters might have a vested interest in blowing on the flames precisely because this would encourage the general public to rally around the executive, and the executive could thereby gain some contingent advantage such as that of being reelected. Strife might thus be stirred up to obtain a "rally round the flag" effect.

The absence of external conditions and of the will to create them thus affects the internal development of democracy. It is certainly significant that the recent project of the International Institute for Democracy and Electoral Assistance, the most elaborate attempt so far to make an informal external assessment with the help of national experts (see § 2.5), assesses democracy within a state also on the basis of the foreign policy it pursues and of the existing conflicts in global society.[13] For the purpose of weighing the overall degree of democracy, IDEA also deemed

12. George Orwell, *Nineteen Eighty-Four* (London: Penguin, [1949] 1989), p. 207.
13. Beetham et al., *International IDEA Handbook*, p. 66.

61

important to assess the external conditions on the basis of the following criteria:

i.   How free is the governance of the country from subordination to external agencies, economic, cultural, or political?
ii. To what extent are government relations with external donors based on principles of partnership and transparency?
iii. To what extent does the government support UN human rights treaties and respect international law?
iv. To what extent does the government respect its international obligations in its treatment of refugees and asylum seekers, and how free from arbitrary discrimination is its immigration policy?
v.   How consistent is the government in its support for human rights and democracy abroad?

The basic assumption is that the development of democracy is inextricably linked to a peaceful world order based on legality.

Here we have outlined a strong causal link to which we shall return later: from world peace to internal democracy. This link must not be interpreted in an absolute sense; the absence of international conflicts may also allow a regime to consolidate authoritarian power on the inside. However, this link becomes explicit in its negative version: the absence of peace, that is, latent or explicit conflict, is an obstacle to democracy.

3.4 Democracy and War: Theory and Reality

THE INVOLVEMENT OF DEMOCRACIES IN WAR

We have maintained that in a democratic system there is a willingness among the parties to accept an a priori nonaggression pact. Indeed, the very existence of this pact is necessary for the implementation of the other constituent principles of control and political equality. To what extent do democracies apply the principle of nonviolence, or more exactly, of violence exercised within the bounds prescribed by legality, in their external relations? Are democracies more inclined to use means other than war to resolve international disputes?

Popular control should restrain the executive from waging wars that jeopardize the life and welfare of its citizens. According to one noble liberal tradition, popular control should act as an antidote to the indiscriminate use of violence. Jeremy Bentham claimed that, in order to limit war, it is necessary to abolish the secrecy shrouding the work of the foreign office.[14] This would allow the people to ascertain whether foreign policy was in line with its own interests rather than with that of restricted elites. James Madison believed that wars could be reduced by subjecting the will of the government to that of the people.[15] Madison was aware that a government expressed by the people would not be sufficient to eliminate all wars; if wars, Madison observed, were supported by popular fervor, there was little chance of avoiding them except by making each generation pay the costs incurred by them. Immanuel Kant believed that if each state had a republican constitution, wars would be reduced because "if the consent of citizens is required to decide whether or not war is to be declared, it is very natural that they will have greater hesitation in embarking on so dangerous an enterprise."[16]

The arguments of Bentham, Madison, and Kant are based on an essentially utilitarian logic: because the people generally have no interest in engaging in a war, and because the population rather than the ruling elites have to pay the consequences, yoking the executive to the people's will allows the general interest to be served. However, available historical and statistical analyses unfortunately prove the hopes of the founding fathers of liberal thought to be partly wrong. As pointed out in the preceding chapter, the incidence of wars waged by democracies is comparable to that waged by autocracies.[17]

It is nevertheless true that democracies are proportionately somewhat less embroiled in wars than autocracies and that the wars democracies wage are slightly less bloody than the wars autocracies wage.[18] Indeed, democracies have an understandable resistance to putting their soldiers in harm's way and even more their own nonbelligerent citizens. At the same time, the democracies, even in the course of a war, tend increasingly to minimize the casualties among the civilian population of the enemy

14. Jeremy Bentham, *A Plan for an Universal and Perpetual Peace* (London: Sweet & Maxwell, [1786–1789] 1927).
15. James Madison, "Universal Peace," pp. 191–94 in *The Mind of the Founder: Sources of Political Thought of James Madison*, ed. Marvin Meyers (Hanover: Brandeis University Press, [1792] 1981).
16. Immanuel Kant, "Towards Perpetual Peace: A Philosophical Project," pp. 93–130 in *Kant: Political Writings*, ed. Hans Reiss (Cambridge: Cambridge University Press, [1795] 1991, 2nd ed.), on p. 100.
17. See, for instance, Rasler and Thompson, "Monadic Democratic Puzzle."
18. See, respectively, Kenneth Benoit, "Democracies Really Are More Pacific (In General): Re-examining Regime Type and War Involvement," *Journal of Conflict Resolution* vol. 40, no. 2 (1996): 636–57; and Rudolph J. Rummel, "Democracies ARE Less Warlike Than Other Regimes," *European Journal of International Relations* vol. 1, no. 4 (1995): 457–79.

countries. Yet it is odd that one of the constituent principles of democracy, nonviolence, has hitherto spread so little and with such difficulty on the exterior.

It is therefore a question of mulling over the utilitarian hypothesis and of seeking to account for the fact that democracy has been so unsuccessful in reducing conflict. One possibility is that the general public is relatively uninformed and "led astray" by demagogues. In the ancient Athenian democracy, those in public office who misled the demos were actually punished. Alternatively, it could be claimed that a war is not necessarily against the interests of a state, for example, because damage is limited and more than compensated by the benefits accruing not only to the elites but also to the population at large. Benefits can be quantified only after the war is over, although a government wanting to wage war could lead people to believe that there are some benefits, and the general public might not be sufficiently well informed to be able to disprove this. In such circumstances, the moderating role of public opinion in encouraging peace might not be exercised for the simple reason that there is an objective alliance of interests between the elites in government and the people, as is demonstrated by the colonial ventures of Great Britain, France, and the Netherlands. In order to reduce wars, it would thus be necessary to find ways and means of extending the constituent pact of democracies also to the exterior.

The strategic picture regarding war has moreover changed radically in the last fifteen years: the war waged by democracies in Iraq (1991), Kosovo (1999), Afghanistan (2002), and again Iraq (2003) caused far fewer casualties among the troops of the democratic countries than among their enemies (combatants and civilian victims). With their technological supremacy, the United States and its allies succeeded in reducing their losses to a minimum. Whether or not these wars have produced any benefits for the population of the democratic countries is debatable; however, one of the reasons why these wars have not led to a negative surge of public opinion like that which occurred during the Vietnam War is probably related to the limited number of casualties suffered by the country.

Here we find one of the most disturbing features of contemporary democracies, particularly of today's dominant democracy, the United States. On the one hand, the United States has advanced so far that it possesses resources and technology capable of winning a war (although not necessarily the peace) with limited casualties, or in any case far fewer losses than those inflicted on its enemies. On the other hand, the United States does not display the will or the capacity to resolve international conflicts by any means other than war and which would be more similar to conflict-resolution procedures applied on the interior. It cannot be denied that liberal thinkers were right to consider that war in many cases is against the public interest and so popular control could be a remedy against war. However, the question is to find ways and means of rendering this control more effective.

A SUBHYPOTHESIS: DEMOCRACIES DO NOT FIGHT EACH OTHER

In the face of the repeated and disturbing participation of the democracies in war, which continued also after the fall of the Berlin wall, it would perhaps have been logical to expect that researchers would devote their efforts to trying to understand why democratic regimes continue to be so belligerent and what means could be used to make them less aggressive. These issues have instead been considered of secondary importance, while the attention of the study of international relations over the past twenty years has focused on a subhypothesis: democracies do not fight each other.[19] In his study of international justice, Rawls actually raised this hypothesis to one of the constituent premises of his theory.[20] Those taking part in the debate not only are champions of democracy but, it goes without saying, live and work in consolidated western democracies.

The decision to wage war is not a unilateral one. It depends on an external context that can either facilitate or make more difficult peaceful diplomatic solutions of disputes. In order for a war to break out there must be at least two sides, and if either side is a bully even the meekest of states is forced to defend itself. Therefore, another line of inquiry has started to investigate whether democracies are intrinsically peaceful except when external conditions are unfavorable. In particular, in an international system composed of democratic and autocratic states and, above all, of autocratic states that up to a decade ago quantitatively dominated the world, democratic states would be unable to extend the principle of nonviolence also to the exterior through lack of reciprocity. It is postulated that this could explain the involvement of democratic states in so many wars. This hypothesis is extremely benevolent to the

19. Doyle, "Kant, Liberal Legacies, and Foreign Affairs" was among the first to launch this hypothesis. The most convincing formulations can be found in Bruce Russett, *Grasping the Democratic Peace* (Princeton: Princeton University Press, 1993) and Bruce Russett and John Oneal, *Triangulating Peace: Democracy, Interdependence, and International Organizations* (New York: Norton, 2001).
20. John Rawls, *The Law of Peoples* (Cambridge, MA: Harvard University Press, 1999), pp. 54 and 58.

democracies, as it suggests that the democracies are forced to fight against their will and attributes the existence of war to the evil company that is found in the international system.

It was actually Demosthenes who claimed that the reasons why democracies wage wars are essentially different when they clash with oligarchies than with other democracies:

> Let it also be considered that you, my fellow-citizens, have waged many wars against states both of democratic and oligarchic government. Of this you are not to be informed: but perhaps you have never once reflected what were the causes of your several wars with each. With democratic states your wars arose from particular complaints, which could not be decided in a national council; or from disputes about districts and boundaries; or from the love of glory or pre-eminence. But of your wars with oligarchies, there were different causes: with these you fought for your constitution, for your liberty. So that I should not scruple to avow my opinion that it would be better for us to be at war with all the states of Greece, provided that they enjoyed a democratic government, than to be in friendship with them all, if commanded by oligarchies; for with free states I should not think it difficult to conclude a peace whenever you were inclined; but with oligarchic governments we could not even form a union to be relied on: for it is not possible that the few can entertain a sincere affection for the many; or the friends of arbitrary power for the men who choose to live in free equality.[21]

The keenest champions of the thesis of peace among democracies are only too well aware of its limits.[22] There is no denial that democracies wage wars, that they themselves may declare them, and that they can form alliances with autocratic regimes or that they can engage in "covert" hostile actions against other democracies.[23] In the terms of figure 3.1 it cannot be ruled out that state A may form an alliance with

21. Demosthenes, *The Oration for the Liberty of the Rhodians* (351 B.C.), trans. T. Leland, at www.4literature.net/Demosthenes/Oration_for_the_Liberty_of_the_Rhodian.

22. Russett, *Grasping the Democratic Peace*, p. 131. I prefer to call it "peace among democracies" rather than "democratic peace" because there is no indication that the content of peace also includes elements of democracy.

23. On the hostile actions by the United States against the elected governments in Iran (1953), Guatemala (1954), Indonesia (1955), Brazil (1960s), Chile (1973), and Nicaragua (1980s), see David P. Forsythe, "Democracy, War, and Covert Action," *Journal of Peace Research* vol. 29, no. 4 (1992): 385–95.

state C to wage war against state D, or that state A may help C while the latter is fighting against B, or that A may engage in indirect hostile action against the government of B in order to overthrow state B's government and replace it with a dictatorial regime. The hypothesis merely asserts that states A and B do not wage war against each other *directly*.

In the absence of laws regulating the behavior of states on the international scene, it is something exceptional, as has often been observed, to find one having a general value. In the ongoing debate between the so-called realists and idealists regarding international relations, it seems to have finally been proved that not all states are equal and that at least in one limited aspect the nature of the internal regime is able to influence foreign policy. This apparently shows that democracies are able to extend the practice of nonviolence toward the exterior, although only with states that are also democratic, in a kind of separate peace that applies only between similar states. "Dog does not eat dog," it might be said, although the saying is not valid for other animal breeds; wars between authoritarian regimes are as frequent as those between authoritarian regimes and democratic ones. The wolf bites not only the dog but also other wolves. If we take this hypothesis to its logical conclusion, we might say that the phenomenon of war can be eliminated when all world states have become democratic. Therefore an opposite causal link to the one illustrated above may be discerned, which goes from internal democracy to international peace: the greater the increase in the number of democratic states, the greater the reduction in the risk of war.

Even if we consider this thesis within the narrow limits imposed, significant exceptions are apparent, exceptions that have been set aside lightly, sometimes even with annoyance, by those who champion the idea of peace among democracies.[24] While the more prudent and perceptive limit themselves to claiming that wars between democracies are unlikely, thus supporting a probabilistic hypothesis, the more enthusiastic assert that no wars between democracies have ever occurred,

---

24. Several Italian researchers have stepped out of the chorus of Anglo-American literature and have made a critical assessment of the hypothesis of democratic peace—see, for example, Luigi Cortesi, *Storia e catastrofe* (Napoli: Liguori, 1984); Luigi Bonanate, *Una giornata del mondo. Le contraddizioni della teoria democratica* (Milano: Bruno Mondadori, 1996); Angelo Panebianco, *Guerrieri democratici. Le democrazie e la politica di potenza* (Bologna: Il Mulino, 1997); Filippo Andreatta, "Democrazia e politica internazionale: pace democratica e democratizzazione del sistema internazionale," *Rivista Italiana di Scienza Politica* vol. 35, no. 2 (2006): 212–33.

going as far as to subscribe to a deterministic thesis.[25] Let us see, for example, how several historical cases are treated. The American Civil War is defined as an internal conflict rather than a conflict between two states, even though the high degree of autonomy achieved by each member of the Union prior to 1864 should lead to the American Civil War's being considered an interstate war. As far as World War I is concerned, France, Great Britain, and Italy are classified as democratic countries, but not Germany. This classification may seem arbitrary, and above all, the difference in democratic status among the various states does seem to be sufficiently large to justify the different classification.

Also excluded from the case histories are the short war between the newly founded Roman Republic and France in 1849;[26] the war between Serbia and Croatia between 1991 and 1995; and the war waged by the North Atlantic Treaty Organization, the members of which are all democratic, against Serbia. The justification for exclusion in these cases was the fact that the democratic regimes of the Roman Republic, Serbia, and Croatia were not sufficiently consolidated. The proponents claim that this hypothesis is valid only after a country has consolidated its democratic regime for at least several years. Indeed, the transition from an authoritarian regime to a democratic one can even have the opposite effect: the likelihood of being involved in conflicts actually increases.[27] Transition implies a change in the ruling elites and at the same time the unity of intent of the people may often be associated with new or renewed nationalistic claims accompanied by the outbreak of violence against neighboring communities.

It is indicative that the thesis of peace among democracies also has been studied in societies that have differed substantially from modern democracies over the past two thousand years.[28] It may obviously be wondered what sense it makes to compare such different conflicts as

25. See Russett and Oneal, *Triangulating Peace* for the probabilistic thesis and Spencer R. Weart, *Never at War: Why Democracies Will Not Fight One Another* (New Haven: Yale University Press, 1998) for the deterministic one.
26. This is certainly a minor case of interstate warfare but equally dear to me since my ancestors Francesco and Alessandro Archibugi died as combatants of the Rome University Battalion defending the democratic Roman Republic from the aggression of the equally democratic French Republic. At the time, the French foreign affairs secretary was the most authoritative democratic theorist of the nineteenth century, Alexis de Tocqueville.
27. Mansfield and Snyder, "Democratization and the Danger of War," Mansfield and Snyder, *Electing to Fight*.
28. Cf. Russett, *Grasping the Democratic Peace*, chapters 3 and 5; Weart, *Never at War*.

those between Greek city-states and medieval Italian republics, or between Andean populations and modern states. But it is precisely the historical material examined that, in my opinion, reveals an intrinsic flaw in the hypothesis of peace among democracies, namely, that this hypothesis takes into consideration political systems on the basis of a dichotomic variable (democratic/autocratic) without considering the existing difference and the historical evolution of those systems.

This is not the only problem. This tendency to extend the modern concept of democracy in very different eras is always marked by exceptions: for example, the clashes between the western settlers in America and Australasia, who often lived in communities with a high degree of self-government, and the native tribes are not deemed sufficient to confute the hypothesis of peace among democracies. Russett, for instance, points out that the European and American settlers did not believe it was possible for the indigenous inhabitants of the colonized territories to have self-governing institutions.[29] This brings us back to the case of ethnic cleansing carried out by the liberal regimes in the process of becoming established, which represents that dark side of democracy pointed out by Mann.[30] It may therefore be inferred that, had the settlers of the Far West realized that the Indians were governed by a council of tribal elders elected by a majority vote, would the settlers have refrained from exterminating the Indians? May we think that, should the United States recognize Iran as a democratic country and vice versa, there will no longer be a risk of war?

Ever since the time of ancient Athens, democracies have been evolving, and huge differences still exist between countries with elected governments such as Sweden and Iran. The hypothesis would therefore have to be reformulated: similar democratic systems, which recognize each other as such, have a low probability of fighting each other. This is a highly reductive hypothesis and also a much more acceptable one. The key thus becomes the process of recognizing the other performed by a democratic regime. Nevertheless, ancient and recent historical experience shows the extent to which democracies, particularly when those democracies are dominant, bestow this recognition with selectiveness, intolerance, and self-interest.

There is thus no lack of ad hoc hypotheses, of questionable evaluations of the historical material, or of attempts to ignore inconvenient exceptions. A skeptic would be less inclined to consider peace among democracies as an absolute truth and would be more likely to consider it the result of a specific international scenario, that of the Cold War

29. Russett, *Grasping the Democratic Peace*, p. 34.
30. Mann, *Dark Side of Democracy*, pp. 502–9.

between 1946 and 1989, which led to the democratic countries' uniting to form a common front against the Soviet threat.[31] The hypothesis is therefore less solid than its supporters declare: even when the hypothesis is considered in its probabilistic rather than determinist version, it does not seem to point to any significant difference between the behavior of democracies and the behavior of non-democracies. Any difference may be linked to how the small number of sporadic cases challenged are considered.[32]

However, it is worth considering the normative implications, also because they are not all adequately illustrated in the literature. Those who have developed the thesis do not deny there is an actual intention to state a kind of self-realizing prophecy: to claim that democracies do not fight each other may serve the purpose of convincing them to find pacific means of resolving their own disputes.[33] Unfortunately the peace among democracies hypothesis was not enough to allow a peaceful solution to be found to the conflict between Serbia and NATO countries in 1999, even though the two sides had elected governments. But the same hypothesis has also had quite the opposite effect: for example, it can lead democracies to wage war against autocracies.

By means of a syllogism that has never been actually explained, the thesis of peace among democracies may suggest that if war persists to the present day it is because certain states are not democratic and therefore in the final analysis the blame for wars lies with the authoritarian states. This belief has led to the idea that it is enough to compel states to become democratic to achieve a peaceful international community. If the causal nexus runs from democracy to peace, even war may be justified as a means for achieving the aim of democracy even though Russett himself had already warned against such a simplistic interpretation, declaring that "the model of 'fight them, beat them, and then make them democratic' is irrevocably flawed as a basis for contemporary action. It would not work anyway, and no one is prepared to make the kind of effort that would be required. A crusade for democracy is not in order."[34]

31. This is the result of the empirical investigation by Joanne Gowa, *Ballots and Bullets: The Elusive Democratic Peace* (Princeton: Princeton University Press, 1999), p. 113: "The most unambiguous and important message of this book is that the democratic peace is a Cold War phenomenon."
32. Cf., for instance, James L. Ray, *Democracy and International Conflict: An Evaluation of the Democratic Peace Proposition* (Columbia: University of South Carolina Press, 1995).
33. See, for instance, Russett, *Grasping the Democratic Peace*, p. 136.
34. Russett, *Grasping the Democratic Peace*, p. 136.

However, the U.S. political decision makers paid no heed to this warning when they were working out the public justification for military intervention in Somalia, Kosovo, Afghanistan, and Iraq. Peace among democracies became a more significant part of the political debate than is normally the case for an academic theory, although not, as had been hoped, to avert wars between democracies but indeed to promote the waging of war by democracies against the autocracies. Two U.S. presidents have made reference to peace among democracies in their speeches. Bill Clinton drew upon the hypothesis to assert that the best strategy for guaranteeing national security is the progress of democracy. George W. Bush was more direct: during the days of the Iraq invasion, he pointed out that, after their defeat in World War II, Japan and Germany were transformed into democratic countries, which had the effect of consolidating the security of the United States, as these countries became political and trading partners of the latter and no longer a threat. Pursuing the same argument, Bush defended the invasion of Iraq, claiming that a democratic Iraq would cease to be a threat to the United States.[35] It should be noted how the external mission of exporting democracy is coupled with the internal objective of increased security.

Yet the hypothesis is not necessarily accompanied by any sensible normative indications. Even the Latin American countries have never waged war against each other, perhaps because they all love dancing, and the few skirmishes that there have been can easily be explained away using ad hoc arguments. It would nevertheless be quite singular if all the countries in the world were asked to dance more often as a way of abolishing war. It would be even more singular if the countries of Latin America, in order to increase their own security, started preemptive wars in order to get other peoples to dance. Democracy can fortunately be justified by means of much stronger arguments. The bitter and critical observations by Russett are therefore not surprising: "Many advocates of the democratic peace may now feel rather like many atomic scientists did in 1945. They created something intended to prevent conquest by Nazi Germany, but only after Germany was defeated was the bomb tested and then used—against Japanese civilians whose government was already near defeat. Our creation too has been perverted!"[36]

35. See, for instance, the State of the Union speech by President Bill Clinton of January 25, 1994 and the speech delivered by George W. Bush on November 6, 2003 to the "National Endowment for Democracy" dedicated to the democratization of the Middle East.
36. Bruce Russet, "Bushwhacking the Democratic Peace," *International Studies Perspectives* vol. 6, no. 4 (2005): 395–408, on p. 396.

3.5 Internal and External

War is the extreme event of international conflict; however, there are an infinite number of behaviors other than war that characterize a state's foreign policy: respect of international law and treaties, capacity to negotiate or to provide economic aid, and so on. Let us try to generalize these observations and extend them to the complex relationship between internal regimes and international system. To what extent do the internal regimes influence the international system and vice versa? Norberto Bobbio asked two penetrating questions in this regard:

> Is an international democratic system possible among solely autocratic states?
> Is an international autocratic system possible among solely democratic states? [37]

Bobbio claimed that "the negative answer is automatic in both cases." Observing figure 3.1, one may assert that, if all states were autocratic, the interstate system could only be autocratic. Conversely, should all states be democratic, also the interstate system would be democratic.

The two questions asked by Bobbio are extremely pithy: they take the hypothesis of peace among democracies to its extreme consequences. The hypothesis no longer stops short at an exceptional event such as war but extends to the entire relationship between the interstate system and the internal regimes of its component parts. A negative answer to both questions signifies opting for congruence between the nature of internal regimes and the international system deriving from this. Not only, but the answers provided to the two questions also imply that the real-life presence of even one autocratic state could prevent the international system from being fully democratic. Unlike the case of the idealist tradition in international relations, these hypotheses no longer refer to the individual behavior of the states but to that of the international system as a whole.

Although these questions proved very useful for framing the problem, my answer is diametrically opposed to the one given by Bobbio.[38] There is not necessarily any congruency between internal systems and the interstate system. In theory and in historical experience, a significant lack

---

37. Norberto Bobbio, "Democracy and the International System," pp. 17–41 in *Cosmopolitan Democracy*, ed. Archibugi and Held, on p. 17.

38. Bobbio has partially modified his position, as shown by our private correspondence. However, I have retained the positions expressed in his essay in view of their exemplary expositive clarity.

of congruency is actually found. There is no conclusive evidence that the increase in the number of democratic states, as has occurred over the past fifteen years, has actually led to an increase in democracy in the international system.

At the theoretical level, let us take the example of the model of international organization envisaged by thinkers such as Emeric Crucé and the Abbot of Saint-Pierre, in which kings were invited to create a permanent suprastate union composed of their ambassadors, with the task of guaranteeing peace among states and, at the same time, of putting down their subjects' revolts.[39] Inside the union, these thinkers proposed to make decisions by majority vote, and all members were supposed to respect them. This model could only infuriate progressive thinkers like Voltaire, Rousseau, Madison, and many others, who saw in the model a way of protecting the arbitrary power wielded by kings and tyrants. In this model, the suprastate organization was very similar to that of a council of heads of family, in which the collective decisions were taken in the most democratic of ways but in which each member could then return home and beat his wife and children at will. This is not just a theoretical case; the Congress of Vienna closely resembled the model envisaged by Crucé and Saint-Pierre, as it represented a forum in which sovereigns debated until they reached an agreement, even though practically none of the states attending applied the principles of democracy on the interior. Indeed, the Holy Alliance generated by the Congress of Vienna also served the purpose of discouraging and, if necessary, repressing democratic demand on the inside. In the terms set out in figure 3.1, a pact of nonaggression and the recognition of formal equality exists among governments. However, these attributes are not transposed into the relationship between governments and those whom they govern, who are treated as subjects and not as citizens. Democratic consultation in this nucleus, as it is not extended to include the subjects, is turned into what I have defined as intergovernmental oligarchism.

Likewise, the fact that all the components of the interstate system are democratic is no guarantee that the system will be also democratic. Let us take the case of the Greek city-states: Athens dominated and the

---

39. For an analysis of the principal seventeenth- and eighteenth-century peace projects, see Sylvester J. Hemleben, *Plans for World Peace through Six Centuries* (Chicago: University of Chicago Press, 1943); Frances H. Hinsley, *Power and the Pursuit of Peace* (Cambridge: Cambridge University Press, 1963); Daniele Archibugi, "Models of International Organization in Perpetual Peace Projects," *Review of International Studies* vol. 18, no. 18 (1992): 295–317; and Cornelius F. Murphy, *Theories of World Governance: A Study in the History of Ideas* (Washington, DC: Catholic University of America Press, 1999).

other less powerful *polis* had to submit. NATO, although composed of democratic states, is dominated by one member who on many occasions has succeeded in imposing its own agenda on all the other members. It is recent history that an alliance of democratic states, the coalition of the willing, waged a war of aggression against an authoritarian state. I postulate, therefore, that the existence of a large number of democratic states ought to help achieve the democratization of the international system but that this democratization is not automatic, just as it is possible to have an international system based on shared rules and agreement even if the individual member states are not democratic.

The reason why there is no congruency between an internal system and the international system is to be sought in the fact that the democratic countries are only too often reluctant to apply the principles and values that inform their internal system also in their foreign policy. Already Thucydides showed how Athenian democracy had imperialistic ambitions and described with dispassionate realism how the citizens of the polis had voted very enthusiastically, "amongst a pile of other fascinating nonsense," in favor of the campaign against Sicily without any clear idea of how far away and large the island was; in a word, Thucydides showed how an elite can manipulate the demos to its own advantage.[40] Today the privileged position of Athens is occupied by the United States, and often, as had already happened when the Athenian democracy was at its acme, the conviction of being a society in which progress and freedom flourish is sufficient justification in the eyes of the citizens for actions of foreign policy that would revolt their conscience if carried out on the interior.[41]

Practically every day we read in the press news items that reveal the total difference between external and internal behavior in the democracies. Democratic states periodically breach the basic rules of international law. Only in certain cases do the democracies develop self-corrective measures that can condemn and make up for the abuses committed. Of course, not only the democracies carry out this kind of abuse. The authoritarian states also periodically violate international law and rules. If the authoritarian countries were to concentrate in their own hands the power available to the democratic countries, the violations of international

40. Thucydides, *Peloponnesian War,* Book VI, § 8, p. 184. See also § 1, p. 178 and § 24, pp. 197–98 in the same book.
41. Alan Gilbert, *Must Global Politics Constrain Democracy?* (Princeton: Princeton University Press, 1999), chapter 4, offers an instructive comparison between ancient Athens and the United States. For a very severe analysis of U.S. foreign policy, see Noam Chomsky, *Hegemony or Survival: America's Quest for Global Dominance* (New York: Metropolitan Books, 2003).

legality would be even more numerous because the actions by the groups in power would not be limited by the checks and balances of constitutional states. Nevertheless, when these abuses are committed by democracies, they violate the democracies' own constituent pact. Some justify these actions on the grounds that it is impossible for democracies to apply similar methods to those who do not respect them, whether they are rogue states or terrorists, or that it is possible to act as gentlemen only with gentlemen, while a gentleman surrounded by rabble has no option but to conform. Bobbio's two questions lead to a third, related question: "Is it possible to be fully democratic in a non-democratic world?"[42]

This question may be broken down into two parts. The first part, which we have already answered negatively, is whether it is legitimate and coherent for a democratic system to use different methods in an external environment. The second part is whether it is possible to behave democratically in foreign policy without jeopardizing the very existence of the political community. One can easily argue that it is illegitimate and incoherent but that a democratic state has often no better option for surviving in a hostile environment. But the latter question needs to be put into historical perspective: considering the resources available *today* to democratic states, no credible threat from autocratic states seems to exist; in the twenty-first century, democracies can easily afford, even unilaterally, to use on the outside the methods they apply on the inside.

Actions that in no way depend on the existence of a hostile external environment are authorized and permitted daily by democratic states. Let us take, for example, the exportation of conventional weapons. It is a known fact that the principal exporters of conventional weapons are Russia, the United States, France, Germany and the United Kingdom, in that order.[43] These are all democratic countries, and only one of them, Russia, is a recently founded regime. These arms are sold to all states, including those states in which human rights are more frequently violated and where arms are used to repress internal oppositions. By their arms sales, the democratic states have materially helped many dictatorships to survive.

Must it be inferred that all states are equal and that the nature of the internal system is irrelevant as far as the determination of a state's foreign policy is concerned? This point of view, which the realist school in its various manifestations vigorously maintains, has been dissected in all its forms in international relations. The problem is what terms of

42. Bobbio, "Democracy and the International System," p. 18.
43. SIPRI, *Yearbook 2007: Armaments, Disarmament and International Security* (Oxford: Oxford University Press, 2007).

comparison to choose. In studies on international relations, the behaviors of democratic and authoritarian states are frequently compared. It is not surprising that in many cases the foreign policy of the democratic states is generally found to be more virtuous than of non democratic states. This gives the lie, at least partially, to the realist thesis that the nature of the internal political regime has no influence on a state's foreign policy. However, this does not mean that all the foreign policy acts of democratic states must be considered virtuous. From the normative standpoint, the error lies in considering that the comparison must be made between the foreign policies of democratic states and those of autocratic states. But it will be much more significant and normatively useful to compare the congruency between the foreign policy and internal policy of democracies.

3.6 The Birth of Global Political Players

It was stated earlier in this chapter that it is an invention to claim that a state—whether democratic or not—lives in a condition of autonomy. But also the schematic representation of the international system provided in figure 3.1 is only a first approximation, as the system assumes that the only actors on the global political scene are the states and their governments. If this assumption were true, the problem of postnational democracy could be solved by boosting and reforming IGOs.

Many actors appear on the other hand in the global system, some very ancient, others modern. All these political actors today have a fresh opportunity to express themselves and are not necessarily represented in an exclusive fashion by the governments of territorial states.[44] Multinational corporations, global movements, and international organizations themselves are all cross-border actors and satisfy criteria of legitimacy, obedience, and fidelity that do not coincide with state dynamics. These new actors are actually challenging the legitimacy of the dominant intergovernmental oligarchism.

In the private sector, multinational corporations have played an increasingly important role in the world economy, to the extent that they often have a turnover that is even greater than that of many small or medium-sized states.[45] Even though modern multinational corporations

44. For an overall mapping of these opportunities, see Rosenau, *Along the Domestic-Foreign Frontier*, part IV.
45. Comparing the gross domestic product of countries with the added value of large corporations, it is found that as many as 37 of the 100 largest institutions are multinational corporations and the other 63 are territorial states. Cf. Sarah

no longer possess their own private armies and fleets, as did the famous East India Company, the economic and political resources multinational corporations can command justifiably intimidate many state institutions. The decisions that multinational corporations make can cause either a crisis or an economic expansion in a country, create thousands of jobs or destroy them. The smaller or weaker the states, the less able those states are to impose their own agenda on the multinational corporations. Nokia is a Finnish company no less than Finland is a part of Nokia. But even larger and more powerful countries have to cope with large multinational companies that daily engage in cross-border transactions, and this raises problems regarding numerous prerogatives typical of sovereign states: Who must pay taxes and where? Which economic subjects are entitled to public incentives?

From the institutional point of view, IOs have seen a substantial increase in their own political clout and decision-making autonomy. Even though IOs are bound by the will of their governments, they have come to perform an autonomous political role, often thanks to a deliberate policy of the states themselves granting powers and functions. The priorities imposed by the various member states do not necessarily coincide with the priorities imposed by the administrations of IOs, and the latter are not necessarily subordinated to the former. The EU is the most advanced case: its institutions have not only access to independent financial resources but also a parliament to express peoples' voices directly and legal channels such as the European Court of Justice, which have the competence to assess whether government actions comply with the shared norms.

Changes are also occurring in how the individual perceives his or her political, social, and cultural community. On the one hand, through the new information and communication technology channels, we are exposed to an increasing number of events taking place in distant localities. There is a "passive" mode of belonging to the global village that affects lifestyles, economic choices, and cultural customs. This mode of belonging is very unevenly distributed among people: company executives and sailors generally make more contacts outside their own community than policemen and farmers. However, there is a growing active transnational participation that is often linked to new forms of organization of interests: membership of professional associations, tourism, and political and social presence, for example, increasingly take on features that cross the borders between states.

Anderson and John Cavanagh, *Field Guide to the Global Economy* (New York: New Press, 2005).

The urge felt by the general public to achieve a political association among the peoples of the planet is not just a response related to economic and social globalization.[46] While globalization increases the need to coordinate interstate policies, as required by the interests of the individual components, the drive toward a global ethics would not be reduced even if it were possible to reestablish the pristine condition of each state's autonomy. Human rights, natural catastrophes, and conditions of extreme poverty are uniting the various peoples of the world as never before as though, for the sake of hypothesis, these phenomena did not have any perceptible consequences on the global scene. Human beings are experiencing a feeling of solidarity that with growing frequency is crossing the borders between states. Even the feeling of global solidarity is itself linked to the availability of information channels, which amplifies the attention paid to phenomena and problems that exist outside the local community, even to the extent of modifying the perception of identity of the world population.

Surveys indicate that about 15 percent of the world's inhabitants perceive the supranational identity as the principal one, compared with 38 percent for the national identity and 47 percent for the local identity.[47] If these data can be trusted, only a minority of the world population believes that its own principal identity lies in the institutions that hold the Weberian monopoly of the legitimate use of force. Again, considering that the global identity is increasing among young people and those with a higher educational level, it is legitimate to ask: what results will the same surveys give us in 20, 50, or 100 years' time?

There are many reasons why individuals feel they belong to political entities other than the state. These reasons may be cultural or economic; they may be dependent on the increased weight of foreign interests or on empathy for those who are different. Nor should it be thought that membership of the global village entrains a desire to participate actively in world political life. The collective identity, whether local, national, or cosmopolitan, is felt much more strongly in sporting, religious, or cultural rituals than in politics.

Transnational movements are certainly not new,[48] but the emergence of a global public sphere is one of the most significant novelties in con-

46. As noted by Michael Saward, "A Critique of Held," pp. 32–46 in *Global Democracy: Key Debates*, ed. Barry Holden (London: Routledge, 2000), on p. 33.
47. Pippa Norris, "Global Governance and Cosmopolitan Citizens," pp. 155–77 in *Governance in a Globalizing World*, ed. Joseph S. Nye Jr. and John D. Donahue (Washington, DC: Brookings Institution Press, 2000).
48. Steve Charnovitz provides an original and accurate account of the long march of transnational movements in "Two Centuries of Participation: NGOs

temporary politics.[49] As in the case of the national public sphere, the global one comprises a wide range of different associations and institutions having different objectives and often opposed to each other. The World Economic Forum and the World Social Forum, churches and lay movements, professional associations and trade unions, the Socialist and Christian Democracy Internationals are the significant and visible representatives of global public sphere, although they are accompanied by a much closer-knit network of enterprises, ethnic and linguistic groups, and even individuals and families. The emergence of this global civil society raises fresh conceptual concerns, and even the name of the academic discipline that studies these phenomena, *international* relations, has become too constraining and needs to be replaced by the more general term *global studies*.[50]

Even though this public sphere is developing in the absence of unifying institutions, it is nevertheless increasingly successful in taking over the functions of conventional powers. The widespread feeling of participation in global problems is expressed in a growing number of nongovernmental organizations and of movements pursuing global objectives.[51] Not only is global identity perceived "passively," but positive action is focused on phenomena that occur outside the borders of one's state of origin.[52]

---

and International Law," *Michigan Journal of International Law* vol. 18, no. 2 (1997): 183–286.

49. This point has been stressed by thinkers as different as Richard Falk, *On Human Governance: Towards a New Global Politics* (Cambridge: Polity Press, 1995) and Jürgen Habermas, *The Postnational Constellation: Political Essays* (Cambridge, MA: MIT Press, 2001).

50. For different views and definitions of global civil society, cf. Mary Kaldor, *Global Civil Society: An Answer to War* (Cambridge: Polity Press, 2003) and John Keane, *Global Civil Society?* (Cambridge: Cambridge University Press, 2003). The Centre for the Study of Global Governance at the London School of Economics publishes annual reports that include both analyses and statistics. See Marlies Glasius, Mary Kaldor, and Helmut Anheier, eds., *Global Civil Society Yearbook 2007/2008* (London: Sage, 2008).

51. Mario Pianta, "Parallel Summits of Global Civil Society," pp. 169–94 in *Global Civil Society 2001*, ed. Helmut K. Anheier, Marlies Glasius, and Mary Kaldor (Oxford: Oxford University Press, 2001); Donatella Della Porta and Sydney Tarrow, eds., *Transnational Protest and Global Activism* (Lanham, MD: Rowman & Littlefield, 2005).

52. The link with cosmopolitan democracy is investigated in Martin Koehler, "From the National to the Cosmopolitan Public Sphere," pp. 231–51 in *Reimagining Political Community*, ed. Archibugi et al.; Molly Cochran, "A Democratic Critique of Cosmopolitan Democracy: Pragmatism from the Bottom Up,"

The global movements have increased in clout and quality. They came to public attention during the World Trade Organization summit held in Seattle in November 1999 and have since become an essential part of world political life. Although associated in the early years with spectacular forms of protest on the occasion of the summits held by organizations or intergovernmental bodies of the NATO, WTO, Group of Eight, or International Monetary Fund, in recent years these movements have increasingly put forward their own autonomous agenda. While their early image was negative, branded with the "No Global" label, today, through the various social forums organized on all the continents, these global movements have become political subjects capable of pursuing a political strategy by means of targeted campaigns. The "No Global" label, which the mass media still use to refer to these movements, is to a large extent misleading: the movements are in fact essentially global in their composition, themes, and objectives; paradoxically these movements are at the same time the darlings of globalization and the ones that challenge its rules. It is therefore more accurate to define them as global movements or movements for a different globalization.[53] One of the more innovative aspects is represented precisely by the way these movements act in the political sphere, both within themselves and toward the general public. In circumscribed areas, global movements have even been able to provide goods and services, taking responsibility, particularly in the developing countries, for functions that the welfare state should be performed.

It is not surprising that, at the same time, there has been an increase in the number of NGOs and their associates, as well as in events and organized campaigns.[54] In an increasing number of cases, the campaigns of these global movements are imposing a different agenda on governments, multinational corporations, and IOs. If the British government has decided to use more environmentally friendly methods to dispose of the Brent Spar oil rig, if an international treaty was agreed on to ban antipersonnel mines and the International Criminal Court was set up, if some multinational corporations have relinquished their interests and

---

European Journal of International Relations vol. 8, no. 4 (2002): 517–48; John S. Dryzek, *Deliberative Global Politics* (Cambridge: Polity Press, 2006).
53. As rightly suggested by Susan George, *Another World Is Possible If . . .* (London: Verso, 2004), p. X and Mario Pianta and Raffaele Marchetti, "Global Justice Movements: The Transnational Dimension," pp. 29–51 in Donatella Della Porta, ed., *The Global Justice Movements: A Cross-National and Transnational Perspective* (New York: Paradigm, 2007).
54. Mario Pianta and Federico Silva, *Globalisers from Below: A Survey of Global Civil Society Organizations* (Rome: Globi Research Report, 2003).

agreed to the dissemination of anti-AIDS drugs in Africa, or even if military action has been taken to protect human rights, this has been due also and above all to an active world public opinion.[55] IOs have increasingly had to come to terms with these global movements. These movements have often occupied a grandstand seat, as is shown by the history of the thematic summits promoted by the UN, starting from the Rio summit on the environment in 1992.[56] Although still far from reigning supreme in the world, public opinion has been adopting transversal and transnational forms and will be increasingly hard to ignore.

Yet public opinion has often failed to attain its objectives, in both the past and the present. For several decades, the pressure of world public opinion was unable to end apartheid in South Africa, to prevent wars or major human rights violations. Perhaps the most striking case of the failure of public opinion was the invasion of Iraq: on February 15, 2003 demonstrations were held in more than eight hundred cities on the five continents, with millions of people involved. The scale of the mobilization was so sensational that the *New York Times* named the new global movements a sort of superpower opposed to the U.S. government.[57] Not even a mobilization of this size succeeded in stymieing the war plans of the U.S. and British governments.

These new movements raise the fundamental issue of the democratic legitimization of global society: what is the most appropriate political constituency? In one of several countersummits held on the occasion of the G8 meeting in Genoa in July 2001, demonstrators wore T-shirts displaying the slogan "You are G8, we are 6 billion." Why should just eight governments discuss the problems concerning the entire planet, among other topics, without being controlled by anyone? While we know for certain that an agreement on interest rates negotiated at a G8

55. See, respectively, Gwyn Prins and Elizabeth Sellwood, "Global Security Problems and the Challenge to Democratic Process," pp. 252–72 in *Reimagining Political Community*, ed. Archibugi et al.; Marlies Glasius, "Expertise in the Cause of Justice: Global Civil Society Influence on the Statute for an International Criminal Court," pp. 137–68; Hakan Seckinelgin, "Time to Stop and Think: HIV/AIDS, Global Civil Society, and People's Politics," pp. 109–36, both in *Global Civil Society Yearbook 2002*, ed. Marlies Glasius, Mary Kaldor, and Helmut Anheier (Oxford: Oxford University Press, 2002); and Mary Kaldor, "A Decade of Humanitarian Intervention: The Role of Global Civil Society," pp. 109–43 in *Global Civil Society 2001*, ed. Anheier, Glasius, and Kaldor.
56. Mario Pianta, *UN World Summits and Civil Society: The State of the Art* (Geneva: UNRISD Programme Paper 18, 2005).
57. Patrick Tyler, "Threats and Responses: News Analysis; A New Power in the Streets," *New York Times*, February 17, 2003.

summit has an impact that may involve the creation or destruction of millions of jobs anywhere in the world, the decisions made at these summits ignore the needs of the majority of the population and are outside all control. The use of the slogan "No Globalization without Representation" raises a fundamental issue of legitimization regarding both governments and IOs.[58]

Yet global movements often cloak themselves with an improper legitimacy. The head of a G8 government could easily retort: "I have been elected. Who elected you?" Students of the decision-making structures of NGOs have pointed out that the effective decision-making processes are in the hands of small groups that are not necessarily controllable by or accountable to public opinion.[59] Even if NGOs were totally transparent, it would not be easy to respond to the questions, Whom do you represent? What is your source of legitimacy? Not even all the NGOs lumped together have a total number of members equivalent to the voters in a medium-sized country such as Italy, France, or the United Kingdom. Even though these governments do not possess an electoral mandate from the Indian, Chinese, or Brazilian people, these governments nevertheless do have an electoral mandate, while the global movements do not. As Wendt pointed out, it is not necessarily true that the demos, which is theoretically the main beneficiary, is prepared to support global policies.[60] The interest of the world population to the issues raised by global movements needs to be demonstrated rather than taken for granted.

It is sometimes argued that increasing the role and functions of stakeholders and developing new forms of deliberative democracy for transnational issues could bridge the global democratic deficit. An increasing role of informed groups, epistemic communities, and other nonterritorial associations can certainly increase popular control over transborder decision making: I have already noted how some bold groups have often managed to change the agenda of intergovernmental politics. But even if these associations grow in terms of numbers, legitimacy and power they will always be less representative than traditional forms of political

58. Clark, *Globalisation and International Relations Theory.*
59. The One World Trust, through its periodic accountability reports, provides an important assessment of the transparency, participation, evaluation, and responses of IGOs, NGOs, and multinational corporations. See Monica Blagescu and Robert Lloyd, *The Global Accountability Report: Holding Power to Account* (London: One World Trust, 2003).
60. Alexander Wendt, "A Comment on Held's Cosmopolitanism," pp. 127–33 in *Democracy's Edges,* ed. Ian Shapiro and Casiano Hacker-Cordón (New York: Cambridge University Press, 1999), on p. 129.

representation. A global commonwealth based on voluntary participation will bridge some aspects of the democratic deficit but will also generate new problems. The problem of inclusion cannot be addressed solely by giving voice to stakeholders or people of good will only; a more solid form of legitimacy based on citizens should be established. Democratic vanguards should today be concerned with the content of current global governance as much as with the institutional innovations needed to increase legitimacy and participation.[61] To return to the definition of democracy used here, the strengthening of a global civil society, spearheaded by the global movements, increases public control without guaranteeing political equality. The various interest groups can today assess the actions of governments, corporations, and IOs and bring them under public scrutiny, but their capacity to intervene is selective and limited. It is not enough to mention the existence of numerous stakeholders, in the first place because the problem is to define their relative weight and in the second place because there is no guarantee that the stakeholders can achieve results more in line with the general interest. The World Energy Council is without doubt a stakeholder in environmental issues no less than the Union Cycliste Internationale, although the World Energy Council has a much greater power to influence public policy. As we shall see in the following chapter, the involvement of stakeholders raises problems for democratic theory: who must be consulted and to what extent? And with what decision-making power?

This is certainly not the first time that specific needs have been perceived by vanguards. Examples of vanguards are the English liberals, the U.S. colonists, the French Jacobins, the worker and socialist movements, the anticolonial liberation fronts, and the feminist movement. Many, if not all, of the demands made by these movements gradually became established as a shared patrimony of contemporary political life. However, global movements often have not disdained to champion given causes, which they are fully entitled to do, but claim to do so in the name of humankind ("you are G8, *we* are six billion"). There is always the danger that the global movements, even when championing just causes, like the odd Prussian Jacobin Anacharsis Cloots, proclaim themselves to be "orators of the human race" even when they have no mandate to do so.[62] In order to retrieve the cosmopolitan sentiments of

61. See Dryzek, *Deliberative Global Politics* and, more recently, Terry Macdonald, *Global Stakeholder Democracy: Power and Representation Beyond Liberal States* (Oxford: Oxford University Press, 2008).
62. Anacharsis Cloots, an enthusiastic and wealthy pro-French Prussian baron turned Jacobin, was a forerunner of the global activists. On July 19, 1790, Cloots led a delegation to the French National Assembly composed of some

Cloots and of many other enthusiastic thinkers, the movements must today be transformed into institutions, and political legitimization must be sought not solely by displaying good intentions but also through the procedures of democracy. This is the aim of the cosmopolitan project, the institutional structure of which will be introduced in the next chapter.

---

thirty representatives of all peoples, as a demonstration of humankind's acceptance of the Declaration of the Rights of Man and of the Citizen. This was the first World Social Forum. When Cloots saw that there was no worthy representative of the African continent, he had the face of several of his servants blackened and had them parade in colorful turbans. After this event, he declared himself "orator of the human race" and later directed a newspaper of the same name. These sentiments must have met with the approval of the French revolutionaries, as they actually elected him to the National Assembly (the only foreigner, together with Tom Paine), and he was one of the eighteen foreigners who were granted honorary French citizenship in 1792, together with Bentham, Hamilton, Madison, Paine, Pestalozzi, Schiller, and Washington. Unfortunately his luck was soon to run out, and Cloots fell victim to political realism: for no reason, like other Hebertists, he was sent to the guillotine by Robespierre on March 22, 1794.

Chapter 4
The Architecture of Cosmopolitan Democracy

4.1 The Global Laboratory

Wars and genocide, migrations, poverty, and epidemics are but a few of the many problems facing the global society. These are not new problems, although today they have an intensity and an immediacy that were unprecedented in the past. These problems have thrust their way to the fore on the world stage, but can they also be managed at the same global level? Global processes are much less amenable to public regulation than those processes taking place inside individual nations, yet only a small minority of people are in favor of international anarchy. Indeed, from left wing to right wing, from North to South, an increasingly impelling appeal is arising for global processes to be regulated. A new term, *global governance*, has begun to be used in the media and by public opinion. This term implicitly acknowledges that a worldwide *res publica* exists that must be managed using instruments that differ from those used so far. Global governance is bandied about in G8 summits and by demonstrators in the movements, by the World Economic Forum, by the World Social Forum, by autarkic governments, and by IOs. But the actual form that global governance should take remains a highly controversial subject.[1] Even more than controversial, it is a terrain of political conflict.

1. A variety of perspectives on global governance can be found in Held and Mc-Grew, eds., *Governing Globalisation* and Mathias Koenig-Archibugi and Michael Zürn, eds., *New Modes of Governance in the Global System* (Houndmills:

Some consider that a new imperial hegemony, today exercised de facto by the United States, is the best way to manage a complex world. The champions of this thesis are, of course, extremely numerous in the United States. Bolstered by the Bush administration, these authors claim that a powerful hegemonic guide is necessary and can lavish advantages on all parts of the world.[2] Others again feel deeply skeptical about the capacity of the public authorities to govern the world's problems and suggest leaving the prime responsibility for this to the market, in particular to the large multinational corporations.[3] They point out that economic interests can achieve substantial results far more effectively than political action. Lastly, some would like to see global governance entrusted to multilateral institutions, with existing accords being boosted and new ones developed.[4] However, not all the multilateralists express the same preferences. Many multilateralists believe that a solution based on the harmonization of policies among sovereign states is the most effective way, as such a solution would restrict involvement to a limited number of actors—the governments of the nations concerned—that have the necessary authority and resources to make decisions and ensure those decisions are enforced.[5]

This chapter sets out a different and much more ambitious project: it outlines the possible constitutional structure of a cosmopolitan democracy. A cosmopolitan democracy is but one of the possible forms of global governance, but it is one that tilts heavily toward a democratic management of the global commons. Choosing cosmopolitan democracy is based on two considerations. The first consists of asserting a conviction: democracy is better able to satisfy the demands of the world's population than any other form of governance. We cannot expect all to share this claim. The normative theory, especially when operating outside the boundaries of what has already passed the test of history, cannot provide evidence in support. Never before has the world had so many inhabitants; never before have there been such significant interconnections among the various parts. And never before has a cosmopolitan democr-

Palgrave, 2006). See also Stanley Hoffmann, "World Governance: Beyond Utopia," *Daedalus* vol. 132, no. 1 (2003): 27–35.

2. Charles Krauthammer, *Democratic Realism: An American Foreign Policy for a Unipolar World* (Washington, DC: American Enterprise Institute, 2004).

3. Kenichi Ohmae, *The Next Global Stage: The Challenges and Opportunities in Our Borderless World* (Upper Saddle River, NJ: Wharton School Publishing, 2005).

4. Anne-Marie Slaughter, *A New World Order* (Princeton: Princeton University Press, 2004).

5. Hedley Bull, *The Anarchical Society: A Study of Order in World Politics* (Houndmills: Macmillan, 1977); Robert Jackson, *The Global Covenant: Human Conduct in a World of States* (Oxford: Oxford University Press, 2003).

racy been tried out. As is often the case in politics, doctrine is over-whelmed by individual interests and choices. To opt for a democratic management of global problems is a partisan choice. I make this choice, but not only as an act of faith. Just as democracy has bestowed more ad-vantages than disadvantages on individual nations, I deem that democ-racy can bring long-term benefits to all the inhabitants of the Earth.

The second consideration pertains instead to the democratic goal. Looking back over the long and successful journey of democracy, we observe that it remains incomplete until such time as the problem of in-clusion is solved.[6] Not only, but in the absence of any extension of the global sphere, the democratic breakthroughs achieved in individual countries are in jeopardy today. The democracy achieved inside a grow-ing number of individual countries is liable to be sapped by globaliza-tion and will be reduced to a mere formality unless it succeeds in linking up also with the higher echelons of actual of power management.[7]

Such a context sheds new light on the self-governance experiments carried out in the course of nearly three thousand years. Those experi-ments may actually be viewed as a laboratory in which a yet-to-be-attained goal is pursued. This is not the first time that, in order to survive, de-mocracy has had to change its skin.[8] When the first American settlers devised a system of participation based on the universal suffrage of all free adult men, and on a much larger scale than that of the ancient Greek cities or the Italian renaissance republics, the settlers did not even use the old word *democracy*, as this would have suggested "direct" de-mocracy, something infeasible in their situation. Tom Paine defined di-rect democracy as "simple," and the authors of the *Federalist* preferred to use the term *republic*, explicitly asserting that "in a democracy the people meet and exercise the government in person; in a republic, they assemble and administer it by the representatives and agents."[9]

Yet the two systems, although different, share common values linking old democracy to the modern form: the legal equality of the citizens, the majority principle, the fact that, once established, the government must

---

6. Jürgen Habermas, *The Inclusion of the Other: Studies in Political Theory* (Cambridge, MA: MIT Press, 1998); Iris M. Young, *Inclusion and Democracy* (Oxford: Oxford University Press, 2000); Raffaele Marchetti, "Global Govern-ance or World Federalism? A Cosmopolitan Dispute on Institutional Models," *Global Society* vol. 20, no. 3 (2006): 287–305.
7. Held, *Democracy and the Global Order.*
8. Dunn, *Democracy: The Unfinished Journey*; Held, *Models of Democracy.*
9. Thomas Paine, *Rights of Man* (Secaucus, NJ: Citadel Press, 1794), p. 173; Alexander Hamilton, James Madison, and John Jay, *The Federalist* (Chicago: Encyclopædia Britannica, [1788] 1955), no. 14.

govern in the interest of all, the requirement that majorities should be transitory and not permanent, the idea that decisions must be taken after a public comparison of the various positions. These principles, which underscore the material advantages bestowed by democracy, may also be transferred with the necessary changes to the global sphere.

4.2 Areas of Intervention

So what is the significance of reinventing democracy in order to enable it to govern the contemporary world? It is a matter of sharing a minimal list of substantial objectives, the responsibility for which is to be entrusted, although not necessarily in an exclusive fashion, to the global institutions. Without sharing certain minimal substantial objectives, a cosmopolitan democracy would boil down to mere procedure. These objectives must for the time being be minimalist: whatever form of transnational democracy is adopted, it is highly unlikely that it will possess the necessary resources and competencies to deal with street lighting or the ban on smoking; most competencies would therefore remain within the purview of the present-day power structures. Five areas of priority action may be listed.

1. *Control over the use of force.* Try to keep political violence to a minimum both within and outside nation-states, until force is used solely as a last resort and regulated by previously established rules and procedures. This implies an extension of the principle of nonviolence.
2. *Acceptance of cultural diversity.* Global system architecture must allow existing differences to be preserved and promoted. The successful attainment of a convergence of governance methods and even lifestyles must not be imposed by one party on the others, but achieved endogenously by free choice.
3. *Strengthening of the self-determination of peoples.* It is necessary to ensure that every people is actually in a position to govern itself. This self-governance involves both the internal dimension, namely, the citizens' effective participation in the choices affecting their own political community, and the external dimension, namely, the absence of domination.
4. *Monitoring internal affairs.* Self-determination also must be subjected to constraints in order to avoid individual political communities being governed in an authoritarian manner to the detriment of their subjects or those communities imposing their own dominion over subcommunities. It therefore becomes necessary to open up a channel of intervention in internal

affairs that, although not appearing as an imposition by one party on the others, is concerned with the protection of human rights and has a place in the existing self-governance modes expressed in the various political communities. This entails collective action being placed if necessary under the political control of external agents.

5. *Participatory management of global problems.* Unlike other forms of global governance, cosmopolitan democracy gives prominence also to the management modes. By embracing the democratic cause, cosmopolitan governance therefore sets out to strengthen the dimension of political equality in global matters. In other words, it aims to extend the principle of political equality as far as the management of the global commons is concerned.

However minimalist, this list might conceivably be viewed as a mere pipe dream, with little relevance to the ruthless practice of world politics.[10] The daily press is full of reports on how these aims are ignored and trampled upon, and realist critics ridicule the underlying aspirations. Nevertheless, political theory has the task of setting objectives and endeavoring to identify the instruments to achieve them, if for no other reason than to identify adverse projects. Cosmopolitan democracy may best be conceived of as involving different levels of governance. These levels are bound not necessarily by hierarchical ties but rather by a set of functional relations. Five paradigmatic dimensions may be taken into consideration: local, state, interstate, regional, and global. These levels correspond to what Michael Mann termed "socio-spatial networks of social interaction."[11] It is a matter of verifying the extent to which the rules of democracy can be applied to each of these dimensions and their respective interactions. At the end of this exercise, the similarities and differences between existing state representative democracy and a possible global democracy will emerge.

THE LOCAL DIMENSION

Today it is hard to imagine a state democracy without a local network of democratic institutions, associations, and movements. This dimension is

10. Chris Brown, *Sovereignty, Rights and Justice* (Cambridge: Polity Press, 2002), p. 226.
11. Michael Mann, "Has Globalization Ended the Rise of the Nation-State?" *Review of International Political Economy* vol. 4, no. 3 (1997): 472–96, on p. 475.

generally considered part of the normal meaning of state democracy and does not need any exhaustive treatment here. But today not even the local dimension is independent of the external dimension. There is a growing number of organizations—both governmental and not—linking together communities and local governments that do not belong to the same state.[12] In some cases, geographic proximity encourages the birth of these organizations, which are often limited by well-defined functions. However, in other cases, these organizations pursue goals that overstep the functions assigned to them as subunits of a territorial state. Nation-states rarely decide to devolve their competencies on specific issues to interlocal institutions, even when the interlocal institutions are able to involve all the stakeholders. Let us take the case of the Danube, a river that flows through at least ten countries but involves each of those countries in different ways. The relevant policies are coordinated by an IGO, the International Commission for the Protection of the Danube River, which, although involving the various port authorities and members of civil society, is the result of a convention underwritten by thirteen states. In spite of this, it is no easy matter for the commission to hammer out common policies and ensure those policies are implemented.[13] Cosmopolitan democracy would suggest boosting the local government structure and, wherever necessary, setting up an ad hoc local government to solve problems involving separate parts of different territorial states. This approach would lend greater bargaining weight to the direct stakeholders and therefore make it easier to identify the policies most beneficial to the common good.

THE STATE DIMENSION

Although the democratic ideal has won converts among yesterday's adversaries, it is far from being established all over the world. The new democracies are in constant peril and are forced daily to overcome obstacles threatening their regime. Not even the more advanced democratic systems actually fully satisfy their own citizens' demands. Here the problem is not the expansion of state democracy, on which an abundant

12. For a review, see Chadwick F. Alger, "Searching for Democratic Potential in Emerging Global Governance," pp. 87–105 in *Transnational Democracy: A Critical Consideration of Sites and Sources*, ed. Bruce Morrison (Aldershot: Ashgate, 2003).
13. It is not surprising, therefore, that the exclamation most frequently heard in the Commission Secretariat is "Give us back the Austro-Hungarian Empire!"

literature is available,[14] but rather the extension of democracy to the transnational sphere. I view the state as both a laboratory and an agent of cosmopolitan democracy. It is a laboratory in the sense that nowadays one of the problems on the nation-states' agenda is to acknowledge the rights of individuals who are not normally considered citizens—for instance, refugees and immigrants. A great deal still remains to be done to ensure that these individuals have the same rights that native-born citizens have.[15] Democratic practice has to come to terms with the problem of who its citizens actually are. Are its citizens those who are born in a given community? Those living and paying taxes in the country? Those who would simply like to live there?

Even inside a given community, distinctions are beginning to be made among the rights of the various citizens and groups. One of the most significant developments in the modern theory of citizenship is the acknowledgment of the rights of communities that uphold different religious, cultural, and ethnic values. A democratic state is based not only on equality but also on the acceptance and indeed on the appreciation of these differences.[16] The principle of political equality is gradually beginning to be interpreted flexibly and creatively. However, acknowledging the differences among members of the same political community makes its limits much harder to determine. Indeed, one sometimes wonders about the logic behind the current dividing lines that sometimes group together individuals with few or no cultural, ethnic, and religious affinities into the same state while on other occasions separate individuals with strong affinities across different states. The need for a cosmopolitan approach based on the principle of inclusion no longer arises only at the frontier but also in the schools and neighborhoods that already accommodate the whole wide range of ethnic groups.

In addition to having an internal dimension, a state is characterized by being a member of the international community. What distinguishes a good member from a bad one? John Rawls pondered what the foreign

14. See, for instance, Shapiro and Hacker-Cordón, *Democracy's Edges*; April Carter and Geoffrey Stokes, eds., *Democratic Theory Today* (Cambridge: Polity Press, 2002); David Beetham, Sarah Bracking, Iain Kearton, Nalini Vittal, and Stuart Weir, eds., *The State of Democracy: Democracy Assessments in Eight Nations Around the World* (Dordrecht: Kluwer, 2002).

15. Rainer Bauböck, *Transnational Citizenship: Membership and Rights in International Migration* (Aldershot: Edward Elgar, 1994); Ruth Rubio-Marín, *Immigration as a Democratic Challenge* (Cambridge: Cambridge University Press, 2000).

16. Young, *Justice and the Politics of Difference*; Kymlicka, *Multicultural Citizenship*.

policy of a liberal state should be and noted several precepts that should unilaterally be followed by such a state.[17] We shall take his prescriptions as suggestions for guidelines for a democratic foreign policy. Rawls nevertheless left *agreements* between states in a residual role; this would allow the states—as in the pre–United Nations conception of international law—to autonomously determine their own external behavior. In the cosmopolitan democracy project, a liberal state must distinguish itself not only for the substance of its foreign policy but also because it follows a shared procedure. A nation-state wanting to be considered a worthy citizen of the international community should not only pursue a virtuous foreign policy (as suggested by Rawls) but also have the will to participate in the life of international institutions, to accept their procedures, and to respect their rules.[18]

THE INTERSTATE DIMENSION

The very existence of IGOs is an indication not only of the need to extend to interstate level at least some of the principles of democracy (formal equality among members, publicity of proceedings, rule of law) but also of the difficulties involved. It is not necessary to be an advocate of democracy and even less of cosmopolitan democracy to support the work of the IGOs: they have the aim of facilitating the functioning of states—both democratic and autocratic—as much as to restrict their sovereignty. Realists, idealists, functionalists, and federalists are all equally in favor of IGOs, even though each of these schools of thought envisages a different future for them. Are IGOs democratic institutions? If not, can they become so?[19] The concept of democratic deficit is applied increasingly not only to the EU but also to other organizations, starting with the UN (see chapter 6).[20] IGO members consist simply of governments accepted into the IGOs without having to pass any test of democratic legitimacy. Decisions affecting a number of countries may be

17. Rawls, *Law of Peoples,* pp. 10 and 83.
18. See the pioneering attempt by Andrew Linklater, "What Is a Good International Citizen?" pp. 21–43 in *Ethics and Foreign Policy*, ed. Paul Keal (Sydney: Allen & Unwin Keal, 1992).
19. A mentor of democratic theory, Robert Dahl, has provided a negative answer. See his *Can International Organizations Be Democratic? A Skeptic's View*, pp. 19–36 in *Democracy's Edges*, ed. Shapiro and Hacker-Cordón.
20. See, for example, Andrew Moravcsik, "Is There a 'Democratic Deficit' in World Politics? A Framework for Analysis," *Government and Opposition* vol. 39, no. 2 (2004): 336–63.

taken by bodies of which both democratic and autocratic governments are members. A democratic state may have well-grounded reasons for being reluctant to accept the majority principle, for example, if many of the representatives of intergovernmental bodies have not been democratically elected, and all the more so if the competencies are extended to include matters of internal relevance.

But even if IGO composition were limited to democratic countries alone, as happens in the EU, there is no guarantee that the decision-making process will respect the will of the majority of stakeholders. IGOs are based on the formal equality of the member states, and this means that the voting rights of each country are independent of its population and of its political or military power and degree of involvement in the decisions taken. Can a decision taken by the UN General Assembly by a majority vote be considered democratic when the vote of Malta is equal to that of India and that of Grenada to the United States? In theory, nation-states accounting for only 5 percent of the world population have a majority in the GA. Would a decision approved by only six states (China, India, the United States, Indonesia, Brazil, and Russia) be more democratic even if those six states account for more than half the world's population? What majority principle would lead to a greater degree of democracy?[21]

In the Security Council, the five-country right to veto is a breach of all conventional democratic principles; in the IMF and the World Bank, decision-making power is based on wealth. At G7 or G8 summits, although these organizations are not formally IGOs owing to the absence of a statute, a small number of governments make decisions on matters regarding the entire planet. The main contemporary military alliance, NATO, although today made up entirely of democratic countries, has on several occasions intervened in the internal affairs of individual member states in order to prevent allegedly pro-Soviet parties from gaining access to government through free elections. Much remains to be done in order to ensure the IOs accept the principles of democracy.[22] The participation

21. The issue is discussed in Derk Bienen, Volker Rittberger, and Wolfgang Wagner, "Democracy in the United Nations System: Cosmopolitan and Communitarian Principles," pp. 287–308 in Re-imagining Political Community, ed. Archibugi et al.; Richard Falk, Law in an Emerging Global Village: A Post-Westphalian Perspective (Ardsley: Transnational Publishers, 1998).

22. For an innovating attempt to define, quantify, and measure the level of democracy of several IGOs, see Thomas D. Zweifel, International Organization and Democracy: Accountability, Politics, and Power (Boulder, CO: Lynne Rienner Publishers, 2005). The ongoing Global Institutional Design project led by David Held, Mathias Koenig-Archibugi, Tony McGrew, and Paola Robotti

of individuals in IGO decisions is nonexistent or has only a decorative function. With the exception of the EU, which has an elected parliament, no other IGO sees the need to involve the people in discussing existing options. Only a small number of countries with more advanced political systems and generally of a small size allow their citizens to discuss the stance adopted by their own governments by the IGOs. In recent years, nongovernmental organizations have been consulted more often by the IGOs, albeit only in an advisory role.[23] We are still far from having achieved anything resembling a global legislative assembly.

Dahl is certainly right when he claims that it is not easy to come up with procedures that satisfy the requirements of democracy in the IGOs, although this should be used as an incentive to ensure the problem of their democratization is placed on the agenda.[24] There are numerous projects and campaigns aimed at the reform and democratization of both the UN and the other IGOs.[25] Let us examine choices that are political even more than theoretical. When it is a matter of demanding the abolition of the power of veto in the Security Council, of giving countries with a low quota in the IMF greater voting clout, of increasing the transparency of the World Trade Organization, where do the champions of democracy stand?

REGIONAL DIMENSION

Problems that do not fit into the nation-state dimension may be addressed at the regional level. In many cases the level of regional governance is more appropriate and effective for public policies. The most significant historical example of this is the EU, where the first six member states slowly but constantly developed a political system able both to strengthen itself and to strengthen its members' internal democracy. The capacity to associate first six, and then twenty-seven, and in the future an even larger number of countries, along with a parliament elected by universal franchise distinguishes Europe from all the other regional organizations. The

---

at the London School of Economics is investigating similar themes, but it also takes into account private and public-private governance initiatives and explores the effectiveness of international policies.

23. Steve Charnovitz, "Nongovernmental Organizations and International Law," *American Journal of International Law* vol. 100, no. 2 (2006): 348–72, advocates a more active role of NGOs in IGOs.

24. Dahl, *Can International Organizations Be Democratic?* p. 31.

25. For a review see Heikki Patomaki and Teivo Teivainen, *A Possible World: Democratic Transformation of Global Institutions* (London: Zed Books, 2004).

EU is without doubt the most sophisticated but not the only case of regional organization. The past decade has witnessed an increase in the number of regional organizations and a strengthening of their functions in all quarters, above all for commercial reasons. Not surprisingly many of those regional organizations look at the EU as a model to emulate.[26]

The regional dimension can be an important factor of stability in areas where the individual components are substantially less familiar with the procedures of democracy, where state political unity has often proved unable to retain the exclusive use of force within the state and to maintain peaceful relations without it. Let us take the case of the Great Lakes region in Central Africa: the formation of nation-states has been superimposed on older communities such as the village, the ethnic group, and race. Many of the conflicts in that area, such as the endemic conflicts between rival ethnic groups, could be addressed more effectively through a regional organization that, as well as including representatives of the states, would also incorporate some representatives from the various local communities. Others have suggested using the cosmopolitan democracy model to set up regional trade zones like Mercado Común del Sur.[27]

One interesting case is that of the East African Community,[28] which has endeavored to repeat some of the features typical of the EU even though the EAC's members have much weaker institutions and in some cases are on the brink of becoming "failed states." Already today the EAC issues passports, thus bypassing one of the monocratic powers claimed by the state, namely, to authorize its own citizens to go abroad and to decide who has the right to enter the state. There are plans to issue a common currency in 2009. It is hard to predict how far this process will go, and in all likelihood the elites will feel its influence more strongly than the masses: in Africa if you have a passport and currency you are already part of the elite. This could be a form of cosmopolitanism that is not necessarily open to the demos. This regional integration would still involve the transfer of competencies that had previously been

26. Mario Telò, ed., *European Union and New Regionalism* (London: Ashgate, 2001).

27. Heikki Patomaki and Teivo Teivainen, "Critical Responses to Neoliberal Globalization in the Mercosur Region: Roads towards Cosmopolitan Democracy?" *Review of International Political Economy* vol. 9, no. 1 (2002): 37–71.

28. Established in 1999. Present members are Burundi, Kenya, Rwanda, Tanzania, and Uganda. The source of my information on the EAC is Wanyama Masinde, Cosmopolitan Democracy as a Possible Framework for Understanding Political Transformations in East Africa (Ph.D. Draft, Birkbeck College, London, 2008).

the exclusive prerogative of the state to different institutions lacking powers of coercion. Unlike the EU, where consolidated nation-states gradually transferred competencies to the union, what is happening in East Africa shows that the process of integration can also take place between still-unconsolidated states. Such an integration can even be used as a policy to prevent the collapse of state institutions or to develop for the first time competencies hitherto not pertaining to the states.

THE GLOBAL DIMENSION

It is certainly hard to imagine how global decisions can be taken on the basis of democratic procedures. But let us begin by assuming that global governance actually exists and that international society is no longer, if it ever was, entirely anarchic.[29] Existing governance is highly imperfect, as it does not always succeed in achieving the set objectives and because in many cases it eludes all control. In the case of arms, financial flows, even of trade, the regulation planned by the various international regimes often fails to keep the various economic agents under control. And, more importantly, the existing controls are often not accountable. Is it possible to constrain global governance within democratic procedures? In a global dimension, citizens should have a voice and a political franchise in parallel to and independently of those they have inside the state. This proposal is perhaps less bold than it appears. For at least a decade the opinions of subjects not having any decision-making power have been aired at the various UN summits. On the other hand, a broader-based level of governance of the range of action of states, both individually and collectively, is gradually emerging. The UN itself and its specialized agencies, although retaining their essentially intergovernmental nature, have largely transcended these barriers.

The claim to a democratization of global governance has been advanced in numerous sectors: financial movements, migratory flows, environmental issues, defense of fundamental human rights, development aid.[30] This list could be continued at length. It is therefore not surprising that, in each

29. My understanding of global governance draws, among others, on Rosenau, *Along the Domestic-Foreign Frontier*; Robert O. Keohane, "Governance in a Partially Globalized World," *American Political Science Review* vol. 95, no. 1 (2001): 1–13; Held and McGrew, *Governing Globalization*; and Koenig-Archibugi, "Mapping Global Governance."
30. For a wide range of case studies, see Held and McGrew, *Governing Globalization*; Aksu and Camilleri, *Democratizing Global Governance*; David Held and Mathias Koenig-Archibugi, eds., *Global Governance and Public Account-*

of these regimes, there are initiatives and campaigns aimed at enhancing representativeness, transparency, and public assessment.[31] The various initiatives proceed independently, although each initiative is pushing in the direction of a greater democratization. However, it is equally important to indicate the direction in which these individual actions are nudging the international system. In this sense, cosmopolitan democracy merely sets out to offer a framework linking what the citizens and global movements are laboriously trying to achieve in so many different areas.

4.3 The Relations between Levels of Governance

FROM SOVEREIGNTY TO CONSTITUTIONALISM

The aims of cosmopolitan democracy thus take the form of the pursuit of democracy at different levels of governance that are mutually autonomous but complementary. At a time of increasing levels of governance and of the relative institutions, a question comes spontaneously to mind: how to distribute the competencies among the various bodies? Is there not a danger of creating fresh divisions among the bodies, in which each institution claims to be sovereign although none actually is? Could the existence of institutions with overlapping competencies, where each institution claims its own sovereignty, actually lead to new conflicts? Sovereignty is obviously the key concept on which the international legal system has been based since the Restoration.[32] It is sovereignty that has defined the competencies of nation-states and established that the limits of each one should coincide, at least formally, with its own borders. To abandon the universe

---

ability (Oxford: Blackwell, 2005); and Koenig-Archibugi and Zürn, *New Modes of Governance*.

31. Michael Edwards and John Gaventa, eds., *Global Citizen Action* (London: Earthscan, 2001); Glasius, Kaldor, and Anheier, *Global Civil Society*; David Held, *Global Covenant*.

32. It is often claimed that the modern concept of sovereignty was born with the Peace of Westphalia in 1648. In my view, it was only after the Congress of Vienna that the concept of nation-states as the sole actors of international politics was affirmed. The studies by Benno Teschke, *The Myth of 1648: Class, Geopolitics, and the Making of Modern International Relations* (London: Verso, 2003) and Andreas Osiander, "Sovereignty, International Relations, and the Westphalian Myth," *International Organization* vol. 55, no. 2 (2002): 251–87 provide sufficient material to challenge the conventional assumption. If it is considered that even the Congress of Vienna witnessed the participation of nonstate groups, such as, for instance, a delegation representing the Jews of Frankfurt, intergovernmental oligarchism could be considered an even more recent phenomenon.

of sovereign states would perhaps amount to a return to the so-called neo-medievalism that Bull has already warned us of, where the loyalty of the individuals and of the institutions would again have to be split between an emperor and a pope, between local and global powers.[33] Today this would mean that political agents would be under the authority of local authorities, national governments, IGOs, and nongovernmental associations and that any action would be subordinated to a variety of approvals. The fear is that all decision-making powers would be blocked, as decision-making capacity would no longer be linked to a legitimacy ensured by an effective power residing in sovereign states.

Cosmopolitan democracy is ideally part of that school of thought that, from Kelsen on, has considered sovereignty a dogma that must be superseded.[34] This idea is based on the assumption that it is incompatible with democracy to allow any political or institutional player to be not accountable. Whether a despot or a "sovereign" people, each political subject should be requested to come to terms with the other political subjects in the case of overlapping spheres of power. Historically, sovereignty has largely been an artificial creation, an "organized hypocrisy," that in only a small number of cases succeeded in limiting the extraterritorial interests of nation-states.[35] However, the problem arises of deciding what to replace sovereignty with, as even today the formal claim of sovereignty serves the purpose of curbing the domination of the weaker by the more powerful.

The tension between the concept of sovereignty and that of democracy demands that sovereignty be replaced, both within and between states, by constitutionalism, thereby subjecting every institution to rules, checks, and balances.[36] The idea behind this proposal closely resembles that of the vertical dispersion of sovereignty suggested by Pogge and of the cosmopolitan model of sovereignty proposed by Held.[37] Nevertheless, the very term *sovereignty*, at least from the normative point of view, seems incompatible both with the idea of democracy and with a level of legitimacy higher than that of the individual nation-state. This draws atten-

33. Bull, *Anarchical Society*, pp. 254–5.

34. Hans Kelsen, *Das Problem der Souveränität und die Theorie des Völkerrechtes. Beitrag zu einer reinen. Rechtslehre* (Tübingen: J.C.B. Mohr, 1920).

35. Stephen Krasner, *Sovereignty: Organised Hypocrisy* (Princeton: Princeton University Press, 1999).

36. I draw on the legal theory of Luigi Ferrajoli, *La sovranità nel mondo moderno* (Milano: Anabasi, 1995).

37. Thomas Pogge, "Cosmopolitanism and Sovereignty," *Ethics* vol. 103, no. 1 (1992): 48–75, on p. 62; and David Held, "Law of States, Law of Peoples: Three Models of Sovereignty," *Legal Theory* vol. 8, no. 2 (2002): 1–44, on p. 23.

tion to the need to redirect the conflicts of competence among the various levels of governance toward a global constitutionalism and to bring conflicts before jurisdictional bodies, as recommended by Kelsen, which would act in accordance with an explicit constitutional mandate.[38] The idea that global conflicts can be resolved by means of constitutional and legal procedures rather than by force is based on the conviction that rules may be enforced even in the absence of an ultimate power of coercion.[39] The cosmopolitan democracy project is thus seen to be much more ambitious—to transform international politics from a domain of antagonism to one of agonism.[40] In democratic states this process has gradually become established, and it is accepted as normal practice that the various institutions experience conflicts of competence.

REDEFINITION OF POLITICAL COMMUNITY CONSTITUENCIES

We have claimed that political communities of the disjunctive type based on dividing lines between the included and the excluded are not a suitable model of the democratic management of the *res publica* in the age of globalization. But while it is easy to find evidence of numerous repeated democratic deficits, it is much more difficult to identify what the ideal political community should be like. Who must decide what?[41] How many and which political communities must each individual belong to? We have stated several general principles that should inform democratic attitudes such as, for example, the inclination to participate of all persons involved in a decision-making process. But each person is involved to a different extent and with a different intensity. The broader the participation of stakeholders, the more important it is for each stakeholder's relative decision-making clout.

The levels of governance mentioned in the last section, although casting doubts on nation-state exclusiveness, are still based on geographic

38. Hans Kelsen, *Peace through Law* (Chapel Hill: University of North Carolina Press, 1944).
39. This line of research has been investigated by Friedrich V. Kratochwil, *Rules, Norms, and Decisions: On the Conditions of Practical and Legal Reasoning in International Relations and in Domestic Affairs* (Cambridge: Cambridge University Press, 1989); Ian Hurd, "Legitimacy and Authority in International Politics," *International Organization* vol. 3, no. 2 (1999): 379–408; William Scheuerman, "Cosmopolitan Democracy and the Rule of Law," *Ratio Juris* vol. 15, no. 4 (2002): 439–57.
40. Bobbio, *Future of Democracy*; Mouffe, *Democratic Paradox*.
41. The question is addressed by Carol Gould, *Democratizing Globalization and Human Rights* (Cambridge: Cambridge University Press, 2004), p. 159.

entities. The matter could be even further complicated by considering governance levels based on involvement. Carol Gould pointed out that political communities do not have to be defined solely and exclusively on a territorial basis; it would be possible also to have epistemic societies, linguistically fragmented communities, and even groups of individuals suffering from the same diseases.[42] So far, nonterritorial communities have been especially effective when targeted to avoid the authority of territorial states, as is the case of international criminal organizations or raw materials–trading cartels. But if specific communities have so far succeeded because they are motivated by the intention of eluding government's regulations, those communities can probably be even more successful if they receive appropriate delegation from public authorities to act on delimited areas of competence.

How can the ideal political community thus be delimited? On certain global issues, such as those related to the environment, safeguarding human rights, or future generations, there is no reason to depart from the "one person, one vote" principle. Even if each person is involved to a different extent, democratic theory assumes that individuals act as representatives of the political community. Even centenarians vote on environmental issues, the repercussions of which will be felt decades later. In a democratic political community, it is assumed that the judgment of individuals can contribute to the best decision for society regardless of whether the individuals are directly involved. However, the same principle does not hold for purely local issues, and so only the inhabitants of a given city are eligible to elect the mayor. When transplanting democratic principles at the global level, it is necessary to decide who is to wield the decision-making power. It is easy to find a Solomonic agreement based on the idea that everyone involved must be consulted, but in the end who actually decides? What is the composition of the specific decision-making bodies?[43]

42. Gould, *Democratizing Globalization and Human Rights*, p. 173.
43. The implications of the democratic principle according to which everybody affected in decision making should be consulted are explored in Hans Agné, "A Dogma of Democratic Theory and Globalization: Why Politics Need Not Include Everyone It Affects," *European Journal of International Relations* vol. 12, no. 3 (2006): 433–58 and Thomas Christiano, "A Democratic Theory of Territory and Some Puzzles about Global Democracy," *Journal of Social Philosophy* vol. 37, no. 1 (2006): 81–107. A possible way to tackle the reconfiguration of political communities is related to the paradigm of legal pluralism, especially in that it tries to match the specificities of communitarian (or particularistic) legal orders and the requirements of the discursive conception of dispute settlement—see Mariano Croce, *Spheres of Domination: Democracy and Power in the Global Era* (Roma: Università di Roma "La Sapienza," Ph.D. dissertation, 2007).

Let us return to the case of the Danube. How must the relative electoral weighting be decided in a reformed International Commission for the Protection of the Danube River? Under the existing system, Germany and Hungary have the same clout. In a reformed system, it is conceivable that an inhabitant of a city through which the river flows, such as Vienna, Budapest, or Belgrade, should have greater decision-making power than someone who lives in Berlin, Prague, or Sofia. As a first approximation, it is preferable for local matters to be self-regulated, because it is always better for the parties involved to be able to come up with institutional forms that can ensure that everyone is represented. This would entail an institutive process in which the various stakeholders decide on how decision making is to be regulated. Yet not always do the parties involved reach agreement. In the case of the Mururoa atomic experiments in 1996 (cf. § 3.2), the French state and the Pacific communities reached no agreement. In cases such as that, the parties should make recourse to other powers that are able to establish the relative weight of the various actors in decision making and to assign competencies. In democratic systems, this is the task assigned to the legislative assemblies and the constitutional courts. At the global level, similar institutions should also have the task of deciding on the decision-making clout of the stakeholders and of assigning competencies.[44]

4.4 What Type of Union of States?

The cosmopolitan project may be envisaged within the framework of the theory of unions of states. The theory of the unions of states takes in institutional relations and interactions among the various components. To accept the idea that the international system can converge on union means adopting a clear stance in favor of a specific form of global governance based on the legal coding of the interactions. Let us take the two principal models of existing state systems, confederation and federation, as our points of reference.[45] Confederation and federation will be described here as ideal models, not necessarily related to specific historical

44. Cf. Marchetti, "Global Governance or World Federalism?"
45. A classical definition of the juridical differences between a confederation of states and a federal state is given in Hans Kelsen, *General Theory of Law and State* (Cambridge, MA Harvard University Press, 1945), section V.D. For a theoretical and historical review of unions of states, cf. Murray Forsyth, *Unions of States: The Theory and Practice of Confederation* (Leicester: Leicester University Press, 1981). See also the stimulating essays by Martin Wight, *Systems of States* (Leicester: Leicester University Press, 1977).

experiences. Later, I will show how the cosmopolitan democracy model differs substantially from confederation and federation and how cosmopolitan democracy proposes a kind of meta-union among states. The salient features of the three models are summed up in table 4.1. The question is now to see to what extent the confederal and federal models satisfy the definitions of democracy in the following dimensions: (a) within states, (b) among states, and (c) global (for the sake of simplicity, the local and regional dimensions will not be addressed although they are nevertheless easy to infer).

THE CONFEDERAL MODEL

A confederation is an association of sovereign states that have underwritten a treaty to agree on given questions. Some confederations have come into being as coalitions to oppose rival states or unions of states and thus have an essentially military function. NATO is a case in point. Other confederations, such as Zollverein, the European Common Market, and the North Atlantic Free Trade Agreement were set up for commercial reasons. Some confederations, including several of the oldest, such as the Universal Postal Union and the International Telegraph Union, are virtually open to every state in the world, although they have only a limited scope. However, the confederations of interest here are those with universal validity and whose main objective is to prevent war and guarantee peace, such as the League of Nations and the United Nations.

a. Democracy within states. The confederal model may indirectly facilitate internal democratization, as it can lead to the removal of several of the obstacles placed in the way of internal political participation by a conflictual international system. However, the confederal model makes no provision for a channel of direct intervention to promote the democracy of states. The principle of noninterference prohibits the intervention of both the confederation and its individual member states in the internal affairs of another member. Not even in the most sensational cases of fundamental human rights breaches, such as genocide, does the confederation have the right to intervene in the internal affairs of a state. The only protection afforded to individuals in a confederation is that of their own governments. Even though the confederal model envisages a partial renunciation of external sovereignty, it does not entail any renunciation of internal sovereignty. Indeed, the very existence of a mutual institutional recognition among states may increase the stability of ruling governments even when these governments are not legitimated by any democratic mandate. Actually, the confederation makes external

Table 4.1
Three Models of Union of States: Confederation, Federation, Cosmopolitan Democracy

Distinctive Features	Confederal Model	Federalist Model	Cosmopolitan Democracy Model
Components	The members of a confederation are governments and not individuals.	The citizens are members of the federation and participate in the appointment of the federal government.	Both individuals and governments have their own representatives in the global sphere.
Citizenship	Individuals have neither rights nor duties vis-à-vis the confederation, except those envisaged by their own state.	Although the citizens are members of both individual states and of the federation, their duties vis-à-vis the former are secondary to those vis-à-vis the latter. The federation guarantees that the citizens' constitutional rights are respected in the individual states.	Together with their citizenship of the state, individuals also acquire a cosmopolitan citizenship. This envisages a minimal list of rights and duties vis-à-vis cosmopolitan institutions.
Membership criteria	Merits of the candidates' political constitution are not analyzed.	A federation is a union of states with politically homogeneous constitutions.	Admission to intergovernmental organizations is regulated by

(Continued)

Table 4.1 (Continued)

Distinctive Features	Confederal Model	Federalist Model	Cosmopolitan Democracy Model
	Accepted members are governments that have effective control of the territory whose membership is deemed advantageous to the other members.	The member states are called upon to respect the constitutional rules governing the federation.	the principle of effective control over a given territory, excluding only governments that violate fundamental human rights (for instance, genocide and apartheid). Cosmopolitan institutions accept only delegates deemed to be legitimate representatives of their respective peoples.
Decision-making criterion	There is formal equality among states, embodied in the principle of "one state, one vote."	Even though the formal equality between states is maintained, the principal electoral criterion of the federation is "one citizen, one vote."	1. Intergovernmental institutions are based on equality among the states, as guaranteed by the principle of "one state, one vote". 2. Cosmopolitan institutions are based on equality among citizens, as guaranteed by the principle "one individual, one vote."
Internal sovereignty	Internal sovereignty is held by the member states.	The member states devolve their internal sovereignty to the federation, which is competent in constitutional and fiscal matters.	The internal sovereignty of the states is limited by global constitutional rules and is aimed at ensuring effective self-determination.

Distinctive Features	Confederal Model	Federalist Model	Cosmopolitan Democracy Model
External sovereignty	External sovereignty is partially relinquished even though foreign and defense policy is the exclusive prerogative of state governments.	External sovereignty is firmly in the hands of the federal government, which controls both foreign policy and the armed forces.	The external sovereignty of the states is replaced by a global constitutionalism. The union has the task of solving conflicts by negotiation.
Powers of coercion	The confederation has no powers of coercion of its own. Its military actions rely on the armies of the member states.	The individual states can rely on autonomous police forces but have no armed forces, which are under the exclusive control of the federation.	The states retain their own armed forces. Humanitarian interventions to prevent acts of genocide are managed by cosmopolitan institutions.
Jurisdiction of states	No compulsory jurisdiction is envisaged. Any legal power that exists is more arbitrational than jurisdictional.	The federation's constitution provides for a compulsory jurisdiction regarding disputes between states and between a state and the federation. The executive power of the federation enforces decision execution.	The member states accept the compulsory jurisdiction of the international courts. Although the union has no means of coercion to enforce the decisions, it can use sanctions.

(Continued)

Table 4.1 (Continued)

Distinctive Features	Confederal Model	Federalist Model	Cosmopolitan Democracy Model
Criminal jurisdiction	Absent. Only the national courts have jurisdiction in individual crimes.	Individual states have their own autonomous criminal jurisdictions. In the case in which the constitutional rules have been breached, the federation can intervene and call criminal jurisdiction to itself.	A criminal court is envisaged which has compulsory jurisdiction and can intervene in the case of crimes not punished or pursued by national legislations.
Participation	The participation of member states is voluntary and revocable.	Secession from the federation is possible only in accordance with precise constitutional rules, and the decision of last resort is often in the hands of federal courts and legislative assemblies.	Participation is voluntary and revocable. It nevertheless requires consulting the citizens in addition to their governments. In cosmopolitan institutions, the union can resolve to accept citizens also representing states that do not intend to participate.
Territorial delimitation	The borders delimiting each state are accepted by all members and may be modified only on a consensual basis.	In disputes among states or within the state, the federation is competent to determine the territorial limits of individual states.	In the case of disputes among states or within the state, the territorial modifications are indicated by the union with a view to enforcing individual rights and self-government.

intervention on humanitarian grounds more difficult. Like individuals also the ethnic minorities of a state who seek their own self-determination, both internal and external, have access solely to the institutions of their own state and not to those of the confederation. The problem of internal democracy thus remains wholly removed from the international system.

b. Democracy among states. In the confederal model, nondomination is guaranteed by respect for the sovereignty and autonomy of the states. Nevertheless, a genuine interstate democracy is limited by the fact that both democratic and autocratic governments enjoy the same rights. It is actually possible to envisage a world order in which decisions are made quite democratically by the several governments even when all the governments are autocratic. This is an issue already addressed in chapter 3, namely the absence of any guarantee that an intergovernmental democracy will also translate into internal democracy.

c. Global democracy. As the confederal model makes no provision for any form of participation by individuals in international politics, the making of global choices is delegated to the relations among states, which are represented by their respective governments. The citizens have no direct say in global matters except through their own governments. Global democracy thus proves impossible. Even if all the members were democratic governments, the governments of the nation-states would not necessarily represent global interests, as they are called upon to represent the specific interests of their own constituency rather than the common interest. An example of this is the EU: the Council of Ministers on which the representatives of the individual governments sit is much more reluctant to support European solutions than a body elected by universal suffrage such as the European Parliament. The reason why the confederal model fails to satisfy the criteria for global democracy is that it is based on and reinforces intergovernmental oligarchism. This model provides no opportunity for constructing cross-links between civil societies in the individual states; the individual states have no institutional channels through which to communicate with each other and have the limitation of being represented by state political forces in matters that transcend state borders.

THE FEDERALIST MODEL

The federalist model has a much more rigid constitutional structure than the confederal model. The federalist model aims at implementing principles and rules that are valid for all the members of the federation.

107

The federalist model, which has its noblest theoretical foundations in the writings of Hamilton, Madison, and Jay, has been applied in numerous contemporary states, including the United States, Switzerland, and Germany.[46] These three nations grew up as confederations and gradually centralized their powers until they became constitutionally based federal states. Other earlier confederations such as the United Provinces of the Netherlands developed into a unitary state. In the important intellectual and political tradition that arose out of federalism, it is claimed that the problem of peace and democracy in the world can be resolved only by imposing strong limitations on the sovereignty of states and by giving rise to a process of centralization of power that leads to a world federal state.[47] In this tradition, it is considered that the subdivision of the world into nation-states is a transcendable historical legacy. Federalist thinking stresses the existence of human rights having universal values that may be safeguarded solely by setting up a corresponding political institution. Let us now examine whether this model of political organization satisfies the three criteria for democracy outlined above.

a. Democracy within states. When the federation is founded on the principles of democracy, democracy is necessarily extended to the individual members. In the case of conflict, the federal government has the authority and the necessary means of coercion to impose the respect of democratic principles on the individual nation-states. Conflicts among the various organs of a federation have been known to end in civil war. The most famous instance is the American Civil War, which led to the reinstatement of the union and the enforcement in all the states of a constitutional norm imposed by the federal government, namely, the abolition of slavery. The concept of democracy as an endogenous conquest (see § 2.2) gives rise to doubts as to whether a single model may be applied to all regions in the world. A prerequisite for the federal system is a unified system of rules among the various parties, which is unlikely to be compatible with existing cultural and anthropological differences in the world.

46. Hamilton, Madison, and Jay, *Federalist.* For a classical discussion, see Carl Joachim Friedrich, *Trends of Federalism: The Theory and Practice* (New York: Praeger, 1968).
47. A classical defense of federalism as a partial union among states was made by William H. Riker, *Federalism: Origin, Operation, Significance* (Boston, MA: Little, 1964). For an overview, see Lucio Levi, *Federalist Thinking* (Lanham, MD: University Press of America, 2008). A modern restatement of world federalism is provided by Myron J. Frankman, *World Democratic Federalism: Peace and Justice Indivisible* (Houndmills: Macmillan, 2004).

b. Democracy among states. In the narrow sense, democracy among states can no longer exist in a federation, as the sovereign states themselves have been abolished. Relations between the central authorities and the local authorities are instead regulated as conflicts of competence, as we learn from the history of existing federal states. The process of centralization giving rise to federal states has shown that the existence of external threats was what enabled different communities to accept a single sovereignty. The centralization of power that occurred in the Swiss Confederation, in the Dutch Provinces, and in the United States arose out of the need for defense against attack by other states.[48] The question is whether the same experiment is possible at the worldwide level in which there are no external dangers. It seems that, in the absence of any threat to survival, the desire to preserve local identity outweighs the desire to give rise to a centralized power. There is always the likelihood that one party will take control over the others using coercive means, creating a sort of federal empire. However, if a means such as war is used to set up such a model, there is no reason to believe that the institution's subsequent functioning would be based on the rules of democracy.

c. Global democracy. A centralized federal power would have the authority and the competence to address global problems on the basis of democratic principles. It is nevertheless likely that a number of problems would be addressed at the expense of individual communities. A government for the whole world, however democratic, would be the expression of a heterogeneous majority, while the minorities that were not part of the government would be even more heterogeneous. A government of this kind would therefore constantly be tempted to find technocratic solutions to problems. In a word, this kind of government would resemble Plato's government of guardians more than an authentically democratic government.

MODEL OF COSMOPOLITAN DEMOCRACY

Let us now examine the possibility of planning a union of states that is intermediate between the confederal model and the federalist one, that is, more centralized than the confederal model but less centralized than the federalist model. Unlike in the case of the first two models, no historically significant experiences of cosmopolitan democracy exist.

48. This is a point strongly emphasized by Riker, *Federalism*, p. 120.

The model that comes closest to cosmopolitan democracy is the result of transient experiences: confederations that took on the essential characteristics of cosmopolitan democracy in the move toward federal arrangements. However, the requirements of democratic management were much easier to satisfy in the past than in the present. In the contemporary world, the EU is passing through this intermediate stage: it is something more than a simple confederation but not yet a federal system. It is not known whether the EU will take the typical form of a federation or whether it will retain its distinctive features. The UN, as we shall see in chapter 6, already has some features that make it more sophisticated than a typical confederation.

Underlying the cosmopolitan model is the idea that it is preferable not to proceed beyond a certain degree of centralization of power, and in particular, of means of coercion, on such a large scale as that of the entire planet. When applied to the whole world, the cosmopolitan democracy model is not intended to be a temporary step toward a federal system but a permanent form of organization. Cosmopolitan democracy is therefore a project that aims to develop democracy at different levels of governance on the assumption that, although independent of each other, these levels may be pursued simultaneously. This model also shows that each level demands different procedures.

The cosmopolitan model sets out on the one hand to integrate and on the other to limit the functions of existing states by means of new institutions founded on the citizens of the world. These institutions would be competent to manage issues of global significance, such as the capability of interfering inside other states in cases of violation of human rights. The cosmopolitan system presupposes not only the existence of universal human rights protected by the states but also the formation of a hard core of rights that individuals can demand from global institutions. These rights are relevant, in the first instance, to the sphere of survival and to issues extending beyond state borders. Vis-à-vis these rights, the citizens of the world have certain obligations that should allow them, through global institutions, to perform a function of subsidiarity or of replacement with regard to the state institutions.[49]

---

49. The word *subsidiarity* has been transplanted from the language of the Catholic Church to political jargon since the Treaty of Maastricht instituting the EU in 1992. It identifies actions taken by European institutions that, however, do not contrast the will of member governments. It is one of the policy realities of the EU that cosmopolitan democracy wishes to expand in other regional and global dimensions.

a. Democracy within states. Unlike the case of the federalist model, the cosmopolitan democracy model can accommodate states with different political constitutions. This does not mean, however, blind acceptance of the principle of noninterference, as applies in the confederal model. Indeed, the cosmopolitan model has the declared aim of transmitting to and disseminating among the various political communities methods and tools of government and therefore of introducing and gradually developing democracy in all the members of the international community. However, the conception of democracy on which the cosmopolitan model is based seems to indicate that, in one form or another, differences in the political systems will continue to exist, which means that an IO must accommodate different systems. The idea of including states with autocratic regimes is grounded on two assumptions: on the one hand, there is nothing like the existence of common institutions to facilitate the development of democracy from within; on the other, the elimination or reduction of the threat of war deprives autocratic governments of one of their principal arguments for imposing their own internal dominion, that is, external threat.

Since intervention by one state in the internal affairs of another can be instrumental, the cosmopolitan model entrusts to the citizens, rather than to the national governments, the task of "interfering" in the internal affairs of each state. The aim of this interference is to increase political participation inside each state and to enforce recognized human rights. It arises out of the conception of democracy as outlined above (see § 2.5) that every nation in the world, although they are at very different stages of the democratic process, has something to gain from a critical analysis of its own political system performed in the light of existing experiences in other countries.

b. Democracy among states. Interstate relations are regulated by IGOs. Multilateralism is the instrument used to guarantee noninterference and to prevent individual states from performing hostile acts against other members of the international community. Should the arbitration performed by the intergovernmental institutions fail to achieve the desired result, disputes among states are sent before international judicial institutions, the mandatory jurisdiction of which is accepted by the states. Should a member state refuse to obey the decision of the judicial authority, the international community can take various kinds of coercive measures, including economic, political, and cultural sanctions. Military force is used solely as a last resort when all the other political and diplomatic measures have failed. It is placed under the direct control of the union's governing bodies and must be approved in advance by the institutions of world citizens (see chapter 7). It behooves the states participating

111

in an armed conflict to keep war victims on both sides to a minimum. One instrument used by the international community is to appeal to the citizens of the state having violated international law to overthrow its own government and replace it with a government that complies with international legality.

c. Global democracy. Issues deemed to be essentially global, such as environmental matters and those regarding humankind's survival, including the rights of future generations, are referred to transnational and not only to intergovernmental institutions. Global civil society is able to access political decisions on these matters through new permanent institutions. These institutions may be endowed with specific competencies (such as the environment, demographic issues, development, and disarmament) or with broader political mandates (such as the safeguarding of fundamental human rights and the safeguarding of future generations). Some of these topics may be addressed at the local or regional level by setting up ad hoc organizations. Other topics are entrusted to true global institutions. The global institutions are intended to supplement, not to replace, existing IGOs.

4.5 Between Functionalism and Federalism

Over the past sixty years, the sovereignty of states has been worn down substantially. It is not surprising that the de facto erosion is much more substantial than the de jure erosion. This erosion is further confirmation of the Marxist prediction that institutions respond much more slowly to changes in economic and social dynamics. Different schools of thought have tackled the problem of setting up an institutional framework that can handle the demand for international integration. These schools have included federalism, functionalism, and legal pacifism. The three schools of thought share the same objective—to increase integration and, at the same time, subject power to the rule of law and democracy. Despite sharing this objective, each of these schools of thought gives priority to different strategies.

Federalism emphasizes the idea that institutional quantum leaps must be introduced for the purpose of forcing political processes. Federalism requires that power should be concentrated in a single place from which a sophisticated system of democratic checks and balances can be deployed. The failure to concentrate power is attributed to the resistance of governments and the other state institutions, which would be the first to be stripped of their competencies and powers. Not always, however, is it the ruling classes that are responsible for the lack of integration. Let us take, for example, the case of the referendum to ratify the European Constitution in France and in the Netherlands of May 29 and June1, 2005. In these two countries, both founder members of the EU, governments and elites alike were in favor of ratification, while the people voted against it, thus showing how the transfer of power to IOs can be perceived by citizens as a leap in the dark. These cases show how pushing integration too hard may be counterproductive.[50]

The functionalist approach suggests more modest objectives should be pursued. This school of thought claims that it is more profitable to achieve the erosion of sovereignty as a spontaneous consequence of ongoing economic and social trends rather than by means of institutional forcing.[51] While transferring sovereignty from the state to the various organizations runs into strong opposition, the transfer of specific competencies serving the common interest is often much easier to achieve. These competencies may gradually be handed over to specific organizations, even in the absence of any clear-cut legitimation. The birth of many IOs, above all in the field of communications, has actually occurred thanks to the functionalist strategy, and even the most advanced regional organization, the EU, seems to owe more to the functionalist than to the federalist approach. Although abounding in wisdom, the functionalist strategy does not necessarily take the interests served into account. As we learn from the literature on international regimes, institutions that have no democratic legitimacy manage many functions today: the oil market, for instance, is managed "functionally" by a select group of multinational enterprises rather than by government or intergovernmental institutions capable of exerting control over them. Even when there is a deliberate transfer of functions to IOs, a gap is often opened in democratic control, and this gap has only partially been addressed in recent years.[52] Furthermore, if it lacks any institutional ties, integration can be reversible. Whenever

---

50. See Andrew Moravcsik, "What Can We Learn from the Collapse of the European Constitutional Project?" *Politische Vierteljaharesshrift* vol. 47, no. 2 (2006): 219–41.

51. For paradigmatic illustrations of functionalism, see David Mitrany, "The Functional Approach to World Organization," *International Affairs* vol. 24, no. 3 (1948): 350–63; Ernst B. Haas, *Beyond the Nation-State: Functionalism and International Organization* (Stanford, CA: Stanford University Press, 1964); and David Mitrany, *The Functional Theory of Politics* (London: Martin Robertson, 1975). For a contemporary reappraisal, cf. Mark Imber, "Functionalism," pp. 290–304 in *Governing Globalization*, ed. Held and McGrew.

52. Roland Paris, *Global Villagers at the Gates: Functionalism and International Democracy* (Portland: International Studies Association, February 2003).

common interests are disregarded, each state can go back to acting autonomously without feeling bound by any commitment.

Finally, legal pacifism aims at modifying the existing system by making the actions of individual governments and states accountable to international legal organizations.[53] This approach demands a unitary regulatory reference framework and a determination by the states to work out common rules. Legal pacifism has encountered considerable success in fostering the creation of institutions legally authorized to settle disputes among states (including international tribunals), even though those institutions are far from being capable of imposing a respect for legality on international politics.

Federalism sets out to replace state sovereignty with suprastate sovereignty by means of a constituent process, functionalism to wear it down slowly and progressively, and legal pacifism to subordinate it to the power of the court and the law. All three approaches have contributed in different ways to the process of international integration, and the cosmopolitan model owes much to these three traditions.

4.6 World Citizenship

A project as ambitious as that of cosmopolitan democracy also requires the availability of an innovative legal apparatus. Here we focus on two crucial aspects: citizenship and, in the next section, the global legal system.

The desire for a citizenship accommodating all human beings, such as to allow them to travel to, visit, and live in any corner of the earth, is an old and never satisfied one.[54] In recent times, this desire has taken on much more concrete features for increasingly large groups of individuals. Managers, rock stars, and football idols have become the symbols of a nonterritorial citizenship, but less privileged groups of individuals, whether they are immigrants, refugees, or tourists, also discover they are living in a metanational space. In the abundant recent literature on the subject, cosmopolitan citizenship is often interpreted more in a sociological than legal sense.[55] Cosmopolitan democracy is therefore aimed at

53. Kelsen, *Peace through Law*; Norberto Bobbio, *Il problema della guerra e le vie della pace* (Bologna: Il Mulino, 1984).
54. Its vicissitudes are described in Derek Heater, *World Citizenship and Government* (Basingstoke: Macmillan, 1996) and April Carter, *The Political Theory of Global Citizenship* (London: Routledge, 2001).
55. See, for example, Kimberly Hutchings and Roland Dannreuther, eds., *Cosmopolitan Citizenship* (Houndmills: Macmillan, 1999) and Nigel Dower and

representing the condition of the inhabitants of the Earth in the present era, marked by problems and interactions that transcend one's own local community.[56] One characteristic of this sociological dimension is the extent to which it varies among different groups of persons: each individual makes use of and consumes global space in a different way. Significant studies have focused specifically on particular groups that, because of their own personal and collective history, have an identity and membership status that coincide only partly or not at all with a specific territorial state. Ethnic minorities, refugees, and immigrants are but several examples of this.[57] In these cases, the specific social condition has drawn attention to the need for institutional instruments other than those made available by the more conventional forms of citizenship.

However, when speaking of citizenship it is useful to separate the sociological problem from the legal one, the analysis of the ongoing processes from the type of regulatory and institutional response required. This distinction, which would facilitate all studies on citizenship—even those addressing a single country—becomes essential when dealing with the transnational sphere. From the sociological point of view, we are all more or less, directly or indirectly, willy nilly, citizens of the world. The evidence outlined above shows how a significant and growing percentage of the world population no longer perceive as their principal identity that corresponding to their own nation-state (see § 3.6). However, this social feeling in no way shows that the rights and duties of world citizenship already exist.

The distinction between the sociological and the legal dimension could not actually be more clear-cut: while individual participation in global processes increases, legal rules still link rights and duties to the territorial states. These are not abstract problems: public administrations have to cope daily with controversial issues. Let us take, for example, e-business, which accounts for a significant and increasing proportion of business transactions. There is no longer a clear link between the place in which the service is performed and the place in which taxes are levied on the service (where paying taxes is considered one of the

John Williams, eds., *Global Citizenship: A Critical Reader* (Edinburgh: Edinburgh University Press, 2002).

56. Saskia Sassen, "The Repositioning of Citizenship: Emergent Subjects and Spaces for Politics," *New Centennial Review* vol. 3, no. 2 (2003): 41–66.

57. The problem has been stressed, among others, in Hannah Arendt, *The Origins of Totalitarianism* (London: André Deutsch, [1950] 1986); Kymlicka, *Multicultural Citizenship*; Seyla Benhabib, *The Rights of Others: Aliens, Citizens and Residents* (Cambridge: Cambridge University Press, 2004) and Bauböck, *Transnational Citizenship*.

citizens' duties). Similar problems arise in the case of different rights of citizenship: a growing number of persons, for instance, are entitled to or are denied health care in countries other than their own. In fields such as these, there is ample scope for IGOs actions directed toward harmonization.[58]

Can the existing gap between social and legal conditions be bridged? What are the conditions to generating a global commonwealth in which citizens would have explicit rights and duties? Cosmopolitan citizenship is appealed to as an instrument of participation in and of safeguarding human rights. By virtue of the Universal Declaration of Human Rights and the subsequent pacts, individuals have been endowed with positive rights that they can claim from their own states. In addition, the states have accepted to be mutually accountable for these rights. However, despite the complexity of the international regulations governing human rights, in which governments, IGOs, and NGOs are involved, the effectiveness of those regulations has so far been very modest. Ever since its inception, the UN and the other IOs have failed both to safeguard individuals and to mete out effective sanctions against states that violate human rights despite the frequency and extreme intensity of the abuses committed. This failure has opened up a chasm between recognized rights and enforcement. This situation is closely linked to the very nature of the current regime of human rights, which is only partially able to offset the principle of noninterference and the dogma of sovereignty. One reason why the regime of human rights is so weak is linked to the fact that this regime has been managed mainly within the framework of intergovernmental relations. Condemnation and acquittal have thus often become negotiating tools in the diplomatic contest, while the most effective sanctions are still found to be those applied through denunciation to public opinion. Individuals find themselves in a hybrid situation: they possess certain rights but have no direct extrastate access channels through which to exercise those rights. The projection of individuals into a global sphere has taken place without any adjustment being made to their legal status.

The concept of world citizenship may hopefully help to close the existing gap by obliging states to observe transparency and accountability in their actions vis-à-vis nonstate institutions. Cosmopolitan democracy is not intended to replace national citizenship with world citizenship. Such a replacement would lead back to the federalist option. World citizenship should not take on all the values of nation-state citizenship but rather be restricted to several fundamental rights. This would further

58. For a wide-ranging analysis of changes occurring in the traditional interstate system, see Andrew Linklater, *The Transformation of Political Community* (Cambridge: Polity Press, 1998).

mean that it is necessary to identify the areas in which individuals must have certain rights and duties insofar as those individuals are world citizens in addition to their rights and duties as citizens of secular states. In some cases the areas of competence may overlap and in others those areas may be complementary. The EU has shown that it is possible to accompany the citizenship existing inside the states with some form of transnational citizenship, and this experience is becoming an example for several other regional organizations.[59]

What spheres should world citizenship be invoked for? Let us take as our point of reference the Universal Declaration of Human Rights and the associated pacts. However sacred the principles enshrined in them are, they are so wide-ranging that it is impossible to imagine that the global institutions now being set up can manage to enforce them. Since they are not binding for anyone, the Universal Declaration has indicated such a vast array of principles that it may be considered a "book of dreams." It will be helpful to establish priorities on which world citizens hammer out an agreement to ensure that some core rights are enforced.[60] The first priority involves the sphere of survival. The second regards the respect of fundamental human rights and the possibility of each political community to govern itself and to share in the management of global problems.

Institutions and resources are required in order to achieve these goals. As far as institutions are concerned, these tasks should be entrusted to bodies that represent a direct expression of the citizens, regardless of and parallel to the institutions of their respective states. It is possible to envisage a world parliament expressing a secretariat that is called upon to act directly in cases of glaring need.[61] These cases would consist of natural disasters, famine, and any of the areas touching on survival. These institutions should be backed up by autonomous, albeit limited, resources that are not dependent on the member states. These resources could be funded by a small tax levy, for which numerous technical devices

---

59. Ulrich Preuss, "Citizenship in the European Union: A Paradigm for Transnational Democracy?" pp. 138–51 in *Re-imagining Political Community*, ed. Archibugi et al.

60. For an attempt in this direction, cf. Alessandro Ferrara, "Per una seconda dichiarazione dei diritti," *Filosofia e questioni pubbliche*, vol. 9, no. 2 (2004) 33–45.

61. The possibility of setting up a world parliament will be discussed in chapter 6. The proposal has now been put forward by a growing number of persons—cf., for instance, Richard Falk and Andrew Strauss, "Toward Global Parliament," *Foreign Affairs* vol. 80, no. 1 (January–February 2001): 212–20 and George Monbiot, *The Age of Consent: A Manifesto for a New World Order* (London: Harper Perennial, 2003).

have been suggested, for instance, international taxes such as a surcharge on air tickets and financial transactions.[62] Only when survival is at risk because of conflicts would these institutions be entitled to request the intervention of the states, as the states have a much more powerful secular arm (see chapter 7). However, in addition to direct intervention, world citizenship should imply a political role of intervention in global affairs backed up by a mandate adequately covering the whole range of the Universal Declaration. A world parliament would have the authority to perform these tasks. Although lacking any concrete means for carrying out direct intervention, a world parliament would still be performing a politically burdensome role, particularly for the more democratic states. These interventions would actually no longer be bound by the principle of noninterference, as they would not now be promoted by a state but by a body representing world citizens.

A contract of citizenship characterized by basic rights and minimum duties opens up the way to a global commonwealth of citizens, which could take thicker forms for certain groups of persons in conditions of extreme need. Groups of persons deprived of their national citizenship rights could find protection in a more comprehensive world citizenship in which the institutions in charge perform several administrative functions such as the issue of passports, hitherto the exclusive competence of the states.[63] Refugees often live in conditions of extreme poverty and are certainly not members of any elite. Today they number about twenty million, often living in makeshift camps, who have to fight to survive. If these persons were provided with the status of world citizenship, they could become the first group to benefit from the "right to have rights" ensured by cosmopolitan institutions and denied them by their states of origin (see § 6.6 for the action taken by the UN High Commissioner for Refugees). If refugees were granted certain rights associated with world citizenship, such as a guaranteed income and a chance to stay in a free port while awaiting repatriation, a significant discrepancy would arise between the social group to which the rights were granted and the social group having the duties. If the contributions needed to fund world citizenship were to come, as some have suggested, from taxes levied on air travel or financial transfers, it would be the elites who bore the brunt,

62. See Inge Kaul and Pedro Conceição, eds., *The New Public Finance: Responding to Global Challenges* (Oxford: Oxford University Press, 2006).
63. As is the case, de facto, for refugees, cf. Pierre Hassner, "Refugees: a Special Case for Cosmopolitan Citizenship?" pp. 273–86 in *Re-Imagining Political Community*, ed. Archibugi et al.

while the beneficiaries of the rights would be groups, such as refugees, in conditions of extreme hardship.[64]

Another significant case is that of immigrants, although this case leads to the opposite prescription. Immigrants have to live and work in countries different from their original one; they pay taxes but have fewer rights than members of the state in which they now live (for example, immigrants do not have the right to vote). If it is considered that the vast majority of immigrants gravitate toward the richer and more developed countries, it would be counterproductive to safeguard immigrants by means of a world citizenship, the legal and political strength of which would inevitably be weaker than that of the nation-state. It would seem in this case that the idea of world citizenship is more useful if used to request that the host states incorporate into their own system the extension to aliens of rights hitherto reserved to natives of these countries. In this sense, world citizenship would become an instrument for exerting pressure on the states to convince them to become champions of cosmopolitanism in their own territorial area by granting rights and duties to those who de facto participate in the life of their community.

4.7 Toward Cosmopolitan Law

The idea of cosmopolitan law—introduced by Kant in his well-known essay *Perpetual Peace*—has been brought back into fashion in an attempt to seek a legal framework for the demand for a generalized enforcement of human rights.[65] From the standpoint of legal construction, possibly Kant's greatest contribution is related to the subdivision of public law into three branches: public, interstate, and cosmopolitan. These

64. Also in a national context there are often discrepancies between the communities of duty-holders and right-holders (for example, very affluent groups may pay with their taxes a substantial part of welfare benefit to groups with a high unemployment rate). Within a national context, a common identity makes the two groups permeable, also because, at least in principle, any individual can potentially move from one group to the other. The rights and duties associated with a world citizenship are more likely to belong to separate groups. Obligations will therefore need to be based on solidarity rather than on identity.

65. Daniele Archibugi, "Immanuel Kant, Peace, and Cosmopolitan Law," *European Journal of International Relations* vol. 1, no. 4 (1995): 429–56; Pavlos Eleftheriadis, "Cosmopolitan Law," *European Law Journal* vol. 9, no. 2 (2003): 241–63; Jürgen Habermas, *The Divided West* (Cambridge: Polity Press, 2006), pp. 80–81; Seyla Benhabib, *Another Cosmopolitanism* (Oxford: Oxford University Press, 2006).

branches correspond to the three organization levels that the philosopher himself had referred to in the three definitive articles of his hypothetical peace treaty. The first article was dedicated to internal constitutional law and acknowledged the republican constitution as a device that favored peace. The second article was dedicated to interstate law, inviting nation-states to form a free federation. The third article was dedicated to cosmopolitan law, observing that "the peoples of the earth have thus entered in varying degrees into a universal community, and it has developed to the point where a violation of rights in one part of the world is felt everywhere."[66]

Unfortunately the Kantian season in legal doctrine was short-lived. First the Napoleonic wars and then the Restoration were destined to support a rigid dichotomy between internal public law and interstate law. This is clearly expressed in Hegel's philosophy, to the extent that in his *Philosophy of Law* the very term *international* was replaced by the concept of external state law.[67] After the Napoleonic frenzy, during which making and unmaking states had become a party game between one battle and the next, Hegel expressed the need to bolster internal sovereignty, the negation of which had been the cause of so much bloodshed for nearly twenty years. Sovereignty was gradually reinforced in European law during the nineteenth century, becoming the legal doctrine inherited by the twentieth century. However, ever since the foundation of the UN, states are increasingly obliged to account for their actions to other states, to IOs, and even to the world public opinion. The result has been a surprising expansion of the range of action of international law: today international law includes fields that actually lie outside the purview of relations among states. Environmental law, humanitarian law, the rights of future generations, and even the right to democracy are constrained within too narrow a framework in the field of interstate relations and would deserve a different position.

What is the most appropriate response that legal doctrine can give? Is it preferable to push back the frontiers of international law to incorporate these new developments or rather to found a new branch of law? In accordance with the levels of governance outlined above, the cosmopolitan project aims to reinvigorate the three-way division of law suggested by Kant. This means making a distinction between the rules governing relations among states and the rules directly involving citizens of the world. The subdivision of competences is no easy matter. But if truly cosmopolitan institutions were to be set up, the current legal framework would be reductive. Indeed, international law would frame regulations

66. Kant, "Towards Perpetual Peace," pp. 107–8.
67. Hegel, *Philosophy of Law*, § 330, p. 262.

and organizations even when the substance of the matter no longer involved the states exclusively. This leads to the need to distinguish regulations that govern interstate relations and that have their place in international law and regulations that refer to individuals and global problems and that should be included, as Kant had already suggested, in cosmopolitan law.

This reappraisal of competencies raises an important objection and a corollary. In the first instance there is indeed a danger that commitments undertaken on global issues that today are inappropriately but sometimes effectively addressed by international law will vanish and be taken over by cosmopolitan law. One example is the Kyoto Protocol on climate change: states have entered into undertakings with other states, which can enforce the agreements through a battery of instruments that would not be available to newborn cosmopolitan institutions. Should the states be accountable for their actions in environmental or human rights matters to institutions representing the citizens of the world, the states would have a counterpart that was formally endowed with greater legitimacy but that lacked the clout to drive home its point. This objection may be countered in various ways. First, it is likely that the denunciation of rights violations would be more effective if it did not come from other governments but from institutions acting in the interest of all citizens, as these institutions are perceived as objective and therefore more authoritative. This type of effect is certainly greater in countries with a vibrant public opinion. We would expect democratic governments to become more reluctant to violate given rules if this were dictated by cosmopolitan law rather than by international law, and that the opposite would be true for autocratic governments. Second, the existence of cosmopolitan law in no way means that the states should disregard these problems. Indeed, we should hope that the democratic states will be willing to act as the "secular arm" of cosmopolitan law and institutions. Third, we should hope that direct instruments of pressure, such as sanctions applied directly by the citizens (economic boycotting, investment strikes, tourism strikes, and so on), take on a more significant role as a result of the granting of cosmopolitan citizenship that also imposes obligations vis-à-vis individuals.

The implementation of the legal project originally called for by Kant does not imply that cosmopolitan law should ultimately absorb international law.[68] Should international law evolve and become cosmopolitan law, the legal corpus for interstate relations would diminish. This result will introduce a new internal/cosmopolitan dichotomy in law that would

68. This hypothesis is hinted at in a recent essay by Habermas, *Divided West*, p. 149, which I otherwise share.

lead toward a federal system rather than toward a cosmopolitan democracy because the lack of a body of law regulating interstate relations would imply the dissolution of individual states into a world state. Conversely, adding cosmopolitan law to the already existing bodies of public law and international law will lead to an overall cosmopolitan legal system subdivided into three branches. As outlined above, conflicts of competence are likely to occur among the three levels of law, although these conflicts can be addressed with the instruments proper to law.

Chapter 5
Critical Debate on Cosmopolitan Democracy

The idea that democracy can regulate international politics has contaminated current political language. Political leaders, journalists, and intellectuals make increasingly frequent reference to this hope, which appears in the party platforms, official declarations by IOs, and the slogans of the global movements. Unfortunately a stark gap still exists between rhetoric and reality: even if claims that the intention is to democratize world politics increasingly mark intergovernmental summits, there is still no trace of those radical changes that many had expected.

In academe, an increasing number of reflections have been made on this topic. In political theory, international relations, sociology, and many other subjects, a lively debate is now under way, which has often opened up new research horizons. "Democracy in a single country" it held to be increasingly less satisfactory, ensuring the introduction of a plethora of prefixes (beyond, post-, supra-, inter-, trans-, across) required to enlarge the national sphere. Much of the literature comes from young researchers,[1] which authorites us to hope that today's ideas can

1. See, for instance, Antonio Franceschet, *Kant and Liberal Internationalism: Sovereignty, Justice and Global Reform* (Houndsmill: Palgrave, 2003); Andrew Kuper, *Democracy beyond Borders: Justice and Representation in Global Institutions* (Oxford: Oxford University Press, 2004); Patrick Hayden, *Cosmopolitan Global Politics* (Aldershot: Ashgate, 2005); Michael Goodhart, *Democracy as Human Rights: Freedom and Equality in the Age of Globalization* (London: Routledge, 2005); Terry Macdonald and Kate Macdonald, "Non-electoral

become tomorrow's reality, that the academic debate will also affect the political framework. At least one visible consequence has been achieved: it is no longer a taboo to extrapolate the principles and values of democracy beyond state borders. In table 5.1 I have attempted to define the various acceptances also in light of their use so far in the literature. Usage is anything but homogeneous and coherent, but it emerges from the comparison that the term we prefer, *cosmopolitan* democracy, tends to incorporate all the other terms as subsets.

There has been no lack of criticism leveled at the idea of extending democracy beyond the state. Although varied, this criticism may be divided into four main streams. The first stream is represented by the realist approach, which censures the naïveté of the cosmopolitan project. Moreover it suggests that, whether we like it or not, this project could become a kind of "useful idiot" of the current U.S. political hegemony. A second stream of Marxist tendency, stresses the importance of economic interests in defining the rules of world politics. Then there is the critical stream, according to which a more integrated global system can dilute and even empty the democracy painstakingly constructed inside the states, whereby global democracy ends up clashing with the local form. Communitarian and multiculturalist authors share this concern. Next, some emphasize the need for a more accurate definition of the relationship between the rule of law and democracy beyond the state. Finally, albeit rapidly, I mention the debate on cosmopolitan justice: ethical cosmopolitanism is virtually the twin brother of the institutional cosmopolitanism to which this book is dedicated. As sometimes happens, relatives often tend to ignore each other when they are too close.

On the other hand, no consideration will be given to those who, by opposing democracy, are also against its global dimension. This stance is actually theoretically consistent: one has no reason to be favorable to an extension of democracy beyond the borders when one is against democracy inside the state. The enemies of democracy today seem to be irremediably condemned by history, but as we shall see, several of the arguments used for centuries against democracy reappear today in a different form in order to criticize the expansion of democracy into another domain.

Accountability in Global Politics: Strengthening Democratic Control within the Global Garment Industry," *European Journal of International Law* vol. 17, no. 1 (2006), 89–119; Raffaele Marchetti, *Global Democracy* (London: Routledge, 2008); and Terry Macdonald, *Global Stakeholder Democracy*.

Table 5.1

Qualification of Democracy among Separate Political Communities

Qualification of Democracy	Main Acceptance	Typical Authors
Postnational	Inclusion of agents outside the state in democratic procedure Development of integration at regional level, above all in Europe	Habermas; Sbragia[a]
International	Democratic regulation of relations among sovereign states	Inter-Parliamentary Union; Dahl; Youngs[b]
Multinational or Plurinational	Mode of coexistence among different ethnic groups inside the same state	Gagnon and Tully; Keating[c]
Transnational	Democratic regulation of relations between separate communities, in particular when the areas of competence overlap Legitimization of nonterritorial political communities	Dryzek; Thompson, Anderson; McGrew; Morrison; Gould; Bohman[d]
Global	Extension of principles of democracy in international organizations and problems of humanity (such as the environment)	Boutros-Ghali; Strauss; Holden; Patomaki and Teivenen; Cohen and Sabel[e]
Cosmopolitan	Application of values and norms of democracy at different levels, from local to global	Archibugi; Held; Falk; Kaldor; Franceschet; Hayden[f]

[a] Jürgen Habermas, *The Inclusion of the Other: Studies in Political Theory* (Cambridge, MA: MIT Press, 1998); Jürgen Habermas, *The Postnational Constellation: Political Essays* (Cambridge, MA: MIT Press, 2001); Alberta Sbragia, "La democrazia post-nazionale: una sfida per la scienza politica?" *Rivista Italiana di Scienza Politica* vol. 34, no.1 (2004): 43–68.

[b] *Universal Declaration on Democracy* of the Inter-Parliamentary Union adopted in Cairo on September 16, 1997, www.ipu.org/cnl-e/161-dem.htm; Robert Dahal, *Can International Organizations Be Democratic? A Skeptic's View*, pp. 19–36 in *Democracy' Edges*, ed. Ian Shapiro and Casian Hacker-Cordón (New York: Cambridge University Press, 1999); Richard Youngs, *International Democracy and the West: The Role of Governments, Civil Society, and Multinational Business* (Oxford: Oxford University Press, 2004).

(Continued)

125

Table 5.1 (*Continued*)

^c Alain-G. Gagnon and James Tully, eds., *Multinational Democracies* (Cambridge: Cambridge University Press, 2001); Michael Keating, *Plurinational Democracy: Stateless Nations in a Post-Sovereignty Era* (Oxford: Oxford University Press, 2001).

[d] John S. Dryzek, *Deliberative Democracy and Beyond* (Oxford: Oxford University Press, 2002); Dennis F. Thompson, "Democratic Theory and Global Society," *Journal of Political Philosophy* vol. 7, no. 2 (1999): 111–25; James Anderson, ed., *Transnational Democracy: Political Spaces and Border Crossings* (London: Routledge, 2002); Anthony McGrew, "Transnational Democracy: Theories and Prospects," pp. 267–94 in *Democratic Theory Today*, ed. April Carter and Geoffrey Stokes (Cambridge: Polity Press, 2002); Bruce Morrison, ed., *Transnational Democracy: A Critical Consideration of Sites and Sources* (Aldershot: Ashgate, 2003); Carol Gould, *Democratizing Globalization and Human Rights* (Cambridge: Cambridge University Press, 2004); James Bohman, *Democracy across Borders* (Cambridge, MA: MIT Press, 2007).

[e] Boutros Boutros-Ghali, *An Agenda for Democratization* (New York: United Nations, 1996); Andrew Strauss, *Taking Democracy Global: Assessing the Benefits and Challenges of a Global Parliamentary Assembly* (London: One World Trust, 2005); Barry Holden, ed., *Global Democracy: Key Debates* (London: Routledge, 2000); Heikki Patomaki and Teivo Teivainen, *A Possible World: Democratic Transformation of Global Institutions* (London: Zed Books, 2004); Joshua Coehn and Charles Sabel, "Global Democracy?" *NYU Journal of International Law and Politics* vol. 57, no. 4 (2005): 763–97.

[f] Daniele Archibugi and David Held, eds., *Cosmopolitan Democracy: An Agenda for a New World Order* (Cambridge: Polity Press, 1995); David Held, *Democracy and the Global Order* (Cambridge: Polity Press, 1995); Richard Falk, *On Human Governance: Towards a New Global Politics* (Cambridge: Polity Press, 1995); Mary Kaldor, *New and Old Wars* (Cambridge: Polity Press, 1999); Antonio Franceschet, *Kant and Liberal Internationalism: Sovereignty, Justice and Global Reform* (Houndsmill: Palgrave, 2003); Patrick Hayden, *Cosmopolitan Global Politics* (Aldershot: Ashgate, 2005).

5.1 Does Political Power Grow out of the Barrel of a Gun? Realist Criticism

POLITICAL REALISM

When it is explicitly normative, political theory runs the risk of producing sermons. This is a danger run also by an ambitious project such as that of cosmopolitan democracy, above all because it proposes an institutional transformation that does not follow the existing distribution of power. It is no coincidence that the bitterest critics of a democracy extended beyond the state borders also include the realist theoreticians. These critics point out that force and vested interests are ultimately the main elements governing international relations. Consequently, any attempt to bridle world politics by means of institutions and popular participation is purely utopian and often doomed to cause more harm than good.[2]

I do not deny the importance of force and vested interests in politics, particularly in international politics, although to hazard the claim that states' interest is the only driving force behind world changes is simplistic, especially in contemporary historical conditions. The conventional paradigm of realism in international relations, illustrated in such masterly fashion by Hans Morgenthau, was applied in a context in which the main actors on the world political stage were the states.[3] That hypothesis corresponded more closely to the international situation prevailing in the mid-twentieth century than to the present one. When new actors appear on the world political scene, interests become more complex and harder to reduce to a univocal strategy expressed exclusively by the actor-states. Today each state expresses and represents a multitude of interests: majorities and minorities, central government and local administrations, enterprises and trade unions, social movements and ethnic groups—each of which has its own agenda and direct connections beyond the frontier. It is more difficult and sometimes impossible to identify a univocal position that corresponds to the interests of all the subjects belonging to a state. A plurality of players increases agreements and disagreements, makes coalitions less stable, and induces those advocating specific interests to create transnational alliances.

For this reason it is incorrect to assert that the main actors in world politics are unanimously opposed to a democratic management of power. It would seem more appropriate to claim that opposing interests exist and there is tension between them: on the one hand, strong drives toward management of world affairs in the hands of a few may be identified (a few governments, a few military centers, a few large corporations); on the other hand are those who demand greater participation.[4] Those who demand to have a greater say—whether peripheral states, global movements, or national industries—are not necessarily the pure

---

2. Pier Paolo Portinaro, *La rondine, il topo e il castoro. Apologia del realismo politico* (Venezia: Marsilio, 1993), chapter 9; Danilo Zolo, *Cosmopolis: Prospect for World Government* (Cambridge: Polity Press, 1997); Geoffrey Hawthorn, "Running the World through Windows," pp. 16–26 in *Debating Cosmopolitics*, ed. Daniele Archibugi (London: Verso, 2003).

3. Hans Morgenthau, *Politics Among Nations: The Struggle for Power and Peace* (New York: Alfred A. Knopf, 1948).

4. For an attempt to identify these contesting interests in specific areas, see the chapters in Held and Koenig-Archibugi, *Global Governance and Public Accountability*, and Koenig-Archibugi and Zürn, *New Modes of Governance in the Global System*.

in heart. They are subjects who are defending their own interests, which often clash with those of other powers. If these interests originate from those subjects who wield less power, these interests will necessarily be antihegemonic and therefore better protected in a system in which power is distributed among several institutions. The intention to give these interests an institutional representation, as in the cosmopolitan project, is no longer a theoretical issue but a political choice.

The realists are right when they claim that the interests of those wishing to gain access to the center of world power are anything but univocal. The interests of the great multinational corporations, for instance, are quite different from the interests of the global movements. The WEF and the WSF are in many respects antagonistic. Davos and Porto Alegre may be taken as two paradigmatic examples of transnational lobbies that often have different agendas. Yet WEF and WSF do have one thing in common: both demand to participate in global choices and are not content to delegate exclusively national governments to represent them in world politics. On the other hand, anyone who has followed the work of the WEF or the WSF knows perfectly well that neither at Davos nor at Porto Alegre will a univocal vision ever emerge and that both places act as clearinghouses (*fora* in the true sense of the term) for multifarious and often opposed interest groups. It would therefore be anything but useless if these groups, together with others, whether represented or not, addressed and resolved their differences in accordance with democratic rules.

The cosmopolitan democracy project is criticized by realists as being not only unfeasible but also undesirable.[5] Desirability should not be confused with feasibility, as instead is often the case in this line of criticism. However, the problem of whether the cosmopolitan project is desirable or not obviously must be addressed, as some fear that this project can legitimize the concentration of power in just a few sites, which would inevitably lead to a more irresponsible use of force. In a realist paradigm, this would mean legitimizing the use of violence by the stronger against the weaker. In such a view, rather than concentrating force, it would be much more useful to retain the conventional balance of power.

On this point, however, realist thinking misconstrues the cosmopolitan project. The cosmopolitan project in no way aims to concentrate force but rather to distribute power and increases the procedures re-

---

5. Portinaro, *La rondine, il topo e il castoro*, chapter 9; Zolo, *Cosmopolis*; Hawthorn, "Running the World through Windows"; David Chandler, "New Rights for Old? Cosmopolitan Citizenship and the Critique of State Sovereignty," *Political Studies* vol. 51, no. 3 (2003): 332–49.

quired to legitimize the use of force. Rather than rely on a balance of power that is by nature unstable, cosmopolitan democracy is based on a contractualization of power.[6] Despite what certain critics claim, cosmopolitan democracy is not a project for world government but a project for a voluntary and revocable union of government and metagovernment institutions, where the final coercive power is distributed among the several actors and subjected to the judicial control of existing and suitably reformed international institutions.[7] The implicit repulsion between realism and cosmopolitan democracy therefore lies in a more fundamental difference of viewpoint regarding the possibility of taming power. While realism views politics essentially as an instrument of dominion and is therefore skeptical about the chances of regulating it, cosmopolitan democracy considers that politics can be transformed into an instrument of service and that, since power has been successfully harnessed in the internal sphere, power can likewise be harnessed in the external sphere.

AMERICAN HEGEMONY

The reason why so many realists are so bitterly opposed to the cosmopolitan project is probably their disenchanted analysis of force in the contemporary world. Today, the planet is dominated by a hegemonic bloc led by a state wielding overwhelming power—the United States—that defends concentrated economic interests.[8] This hegemony ranges from the economy to politics and, in the final analysis, is consolidated also in military force. The same authors point out that many IOs—such as the IMF, World Bank, WTO, and NATO—are often functional to the defense of the interests of the new hegemonic bloc. These

6. Already in 1793 Kant noted, "For a permanent universal peace by means of a so-called European balance of power is a pure illusion, like Swift's story of the house that the builder had constructed in such perfect harmony with all the laws of equilibrium that it collapsed as soon as a sparrow alighted on it." See "On the Common Saying: 'This May Be True in Theory, but It Does Not Apply in Practice,'" pp. 61–92 in *Kant: Political Writings*, at p. 92.
7. Those who misunderstood the cosmopolitan democracy project include Zolo, *Cosmopolis* and, even more, Ingeborg Maus, "From Nation-State to Global State or the Demise of Democracy," *Constellations: An International Journal of Critical and Democratic Theory* vol. 13, no. 4 (2006): 465–84; and Helen Dexter, "The 'New War' on Terror, Cosmopolitanism and the 'Just War' Revival," *Government and Opposition* vol. 43, no. 1 (2008): 55–78.
8. Chandler, "New Rights for Old?" Peter Gowan, "The New Liberal Cosmopolitanism," pp. 51–66 in *Debating Cosmopolitics*, ed. Archibugi.

129

authors and consider that a project aimed at increasing the coordination of state policies can only lead to a reduction in the autonomy of the several states and to the reinforcement of the existing hegemonic power. During the very years in which some idealist thinkers were caressing the idea of reforming the UN and were discussing global governance, the more powerful countries made use of military force, often using a terminology that, linguistically speaking, dangerously resembled that used by all those who sought to achieve a world order based on the values of legality and democracy (this will be further discussed in chapter 8). The universality of the democratic principle runs the risk of becoming an improper rhetorical means for justifying the use of war.

That a new political and military hegemony centered around a single actor, the United States, has now become a commonly accepted opinion. Realists and cosmopolitans agree that the internal democratic control over a national government does not guarantee that the power available to the national government will be used in the defense of disseminated interests. The problem is, which strategy is the most effective for defense against the new hegemony? For left-wing realists, who are stubborn opponents of the new American hegemony, it is necessary to retain and perhaps boost the old panoply of sovereignty. However, it does not seem at all likely that the juridical category of sovereignty is able to stand up to any hegemony: the breaches of sovereignty in the course of history have been as numerous as the petitions of principles in its defense.[9] In fact, sovereignty has been used more often to allow governments to abuse their citizens than to protect a weak state from the greedy designs of a more powerful state. If the aim is not only to parry a specific hegemony but also to avoid abuse of power, sovereignty has proved to be powerless.

Power may be balanced in many ways. The conventional way is to have several forces in perpetual conflict among themselves. According to some realists, the present American hegemony could be curbed more effectively by means of a heterogeneous coalition than by an unlikely democratization of international relations. History has shown us many cases of hegemonic onslaughts that have been countered by coalitions among the opposing forces.[10] A heterogeneous alliance appeared on the political scene before the Iraq War in 2003: an unusual and motley front, comprising democratic governments (France and Germany), intermediate governments (Russia), and autocratic governments (China) and allied with a very active world public opinion, endeavored to prevent the war

---

9. Krasner, *Sovereignty*.

10. See the classic book by Ludwig Dehio, *Gleichgewicht und Hegemonie. Betrachtungen über ein Grundproblem der neueren Staatengeschichte* (Krefeld: Scherpe Verlag, 1948).

waged by George W. Bush and Tony Blair. When the chips were down, however, the alliance proved not to have the power to prevail. Furthermore, the arguments on which this alliance was based were not the most solid. The states concerned invoked the respect of the abstract principle of noninterference and sovereignty. Rather than put forward a proactive strategy ("what are the legitimate and effective strategies for changing a despotic regime?"), the alliance tried to set itself up as a force of interdiction ("no to the invasion"). More authoritative global institutions would instead have rendered international legality more rigorous because those institutions would have simultaneously challenged the internal legitimacy of the Iraqi regime and the international legitimacy of an invasion. Politically speaking, the democratization of the global system therefore represents a more solid and farsighted antihegemonic project.

5.2 "No More Enemies, No More Frontiers": The Marxist Critique

THE DOMINATION OF THE ECONOMY

It is often pointed out that the hegemonic domination of the United States and its closest allies is intimately related to the existing international economic regime.[11] If it concentrated on the institutional features characterizing the world order and neglected economic dynamics, cosmopolitan democracy would be ignoring the central points of power and focusing merely on the superstructure. Marxist-leaning authors such as Görg and Hirsch again propose the ancient dilemma: does the economic structure depend on the institutional superstructure or vice versa? If the causal nexus is believed to run from the economy to politics, rather than the contrary, is it not necessary to transform the economic order to modify the politics? International democracy as an exclusively institutional project would therefore be impossible, while only a new economic regime could lead to the transformation of world political relations.[12]

In this view, a strong causal nexus is identified between politics and the economy, which is perceived as much more blurred, above all in the world panorama, which is dominated by corporations operating in many countries and whose relations with governments are certainly complex. Many economic interests are more than satisfied with the present-day relative lack of control systems (suffice it to consider the financial markets) and

11. Gowan, "New Liberal Cosmopolitanism."
12. Christoph Görg and Joachim Hirsch, "Is International Democracy Possible?" *Review of International Political Economy* vol. 5, no. 4 (1998): 585–615.

have no interest in increasing democratic control over capital flows or international trade. However, a comparable number of economic interests, perhaps more widely spread, are pressing for increased control.[13] Financial speculation benefits a few groups but stands in the way of others, and many economic powers today hope for a change in the architecture of the international financial system. Several of the most interesting proposals aimed at limiting the damage of the globalization of the financial markets come from George Soros himself; if he is not to be written off as a case of schizophrenia, it must be inferred that not only univocal interests exist.[14]

INTERNATIONALISM OR COSMOPOLITANISM?

Again, in Marxist circles it is sometimes believed that an improper use has been made of the term *cosmopolitan*. For instance, Brennan deems the term *internationalism* more appropriate to describe such a project.[15] What is obviously the essential point are the concepts and not the words. But I continue to consider the qualification of democracy as cosmopolitan to be more meaningful than calling it international. The word *international* has several different acceptances.[16] The modern meaning introduced in the eighteenth century by the Abbot of Saint-Pierre and by Jeremy Bentham was to become canonical in international law and refers to the relations among sovereign states. In this context, reference is made to a form of organization with a two-tiered level of representation: in the first level, the definition of a government within the states, and in the second level, the formation of an international (or better still, interstate) society, whose members are the governments themselves. Of course, this kind of internationalism is quite different from the one we are defending here.

This acceptance of the term is not exclusive, however. Some think in terms of an internationalism involving other traditions that are "transversal" to states rather than "between" states.[17] These authors are refer-

---

13. Some of these cases are discussed in Aksu and Camilleri, eds., *Democratizing Global Governance*; see also Dieter Kerwer, "Governing Financial Markets by International Standards," pp. 77–100 in *New Modes of Governance*, ed. Koenig-Archibugi and Zürn.

14. See George Soros, *On Globalization* (New York: Public Affairs, 2002).

15. Timothy Brennan, "Cosmopolitanism and Internationalism," pp. 40–50 in *Debating Cosmopolitics*, ed. Archibugi, on p. 76.

16. Perry Anderson, "Internationalism: A Breviary," *New Left Review* second series, no. 14 (March–April 2002): 5–25.

17. Cf. Gilbert, *Must Global Politics Constrain Democracy?* Brennan, "Cosmopolitanism and Internationalism."

ring to the internationalism of the workers' movements and of the various international associations of workers in the nineteenth and early twentieth centuries. The same term was applied to the spate of peace congresses held in the early nineteenth century, where individual participants from different backgrounds joined together to avert war, the principal responsibility for which was attributed to the national governments. These congresses saw the participation, side by side, of Victor Hugo and Giuseppe Garibaldi, revolutionary activists and fervid religious believers, pioneering trade unionists and captains of industry anxious to expand trade.[18]

The emblem of the internationalist spirit of the workers' movement was announced in the famous slogan "Workers of the World, Unite!" In this meaning of the term, internationalism no longer referred to the representatives of states but rather to political subjects within the state who were in conflict with their own governments, which were considered to be an expression of the adverse social class, the bourgeoisie. In the Marxist view it is assumed that the proletariat of the various countries has shared interests such that the conflicts between their own states of origin may be considered as superseded. These feelings are captured in the song *"Bandiera rossa"* (Red Banner), which runs: "No more enemies, no more frontiers, only red banners at the borders." This kind of internationalism was based on the idea that after the proletariat had abolished social classes, conflicts between nations also would disappear, and no community (dominated by the workers) would want to subjugate any other. Consequently it would no longer be necessary to envisage a form of international political organization to arbitrate and resolve disputes, simply because there would no longer be any need. Sovereignty itself would be dissolved together with its bearing structure, the bourgeois state.

However, the political platform of proletariat internationalism is no longer suited to the contemporary age. In particular, cosmopolitan democracy no longer relies on a single class to interpret the interests of each individual. Indeed, cosmopolitan democracy proposes the creation of institutions and channels of representation for all citizens. The aim is no longer to do away with class distinctions but more modestly to ensure that the citizens' demands, whatever their class, are directly represented in global affairs. This means establishing that discussion of global issues is a matter for the majority of citizens and not just for one class. However, cosmopolitan democracy draws from proletarian internationalism the idea that common sentiments and interests exist among

18. Sandi E. Cooper, *Patriotic Pacifism: Waging War on War in Europe, 1815–1914* (Oxford: Oxford University Press, 1992).

133

citizens that are not reflected in the policies of their respective governments. Paraphrasing the *Communist Manifesto*, Ulrich Beck thus made the following appeal: "Citizens of the world, unite!" in order to point out that the common interests of individuals can, in many cases, prevail over the divergent and antagonistic interests of their respective governments.[19]

The perspective of a world citizenship is not aimed at abolishing conflict among social classes but simply at providing institutional places where conflicts can be addressed, above all when, as already outlined in Marxist tradition, those conflicts take place across state borders. If a prolonged civil war in Sierra Leone is also linked to diamond traffic and if it is deemed that traders in Antwerp, Moscow, or New York are involved in fomenting the hostilities, what institutional channels can be used to remedy the situation? In all likelihood, policies implemented by international institutions—such as the introduction of a certificate of origin for the diamonds—are able to ease the conflict, while exclusively local policies would fail to do so.[20] In some cases, transnational campaigns have successfully influenced political subjects called upon to make decisions, and their efficacy could be even further increased if they were able to make use of institutional channels.[21]

5.3 Global Governance against Democracy?

CAN INTERNATIONAL ORGANIZATIONS BE DEMOCRATIC?

Skepticism vis-à-vis the cosmopolitan project has been expressed not only by realist theoreticians but also by unflagging and incisive advocates of democracy. Let us examine in particular what one of the main theoreticians of democracy in the contemporary age, Robert Dahl, has written on the subject.[22] Dahl claims that IOs cannot ever be as demo-

19. Ulrich Beck, "The Cosmopolitan Manifesto," chapter 1 in Ulrich Beck, *World Risk Society* (Cambridge: Polity Press, 1999), p. 18.
20. See Andrew J. Grant and Ian Taylor, "Global Governance and Conflict Diamonds: The Kimberley Process and the Quest for Clean Gems," *The Round Table* vol. 375 (July): 385–401.
21. For a review of some of these campaigns, see Edwards and Gaventa, *Global Citizen Action*; Mike Prokosch and Laura Raymond, eds., *The Global Activist's Manual* (New York: Thunder's Mouth Press, 2002).
22. Dahl, "Can International Organizations Be Democratic?" Robert A. Dahl, "Is Post-national Democracy Possible?" pp. 35–45 in *Nation, Federalism and Democracy*, ed. Sergio Fabbrini (Trento: Editrice Compositori, 2001), on p. 38.

cratic as the individual states have now become. He therefore asserts that the idea of postnational democracy is misleading. Dahl has made a list of minimum criteria for assessing the democratic status of a state system, as set out on the left-hand side of table 5.2. He comes to the conclusion that it is unrealistic to think that these criteria can also be applied to IOs.

Table 5.2

Dahl's Criteria of Democracy and Their Extension to International Organizations

Criteria of Democracy Indicated by Dahl	Possible Extension to International Organizations
"Final control over important government decisions is exercised by elected officials."	For some areas it is possible to envisage elected officials (for instance by means of a world parliament). Administrators may also be elected for IGO activities carried on in the field (health care, food, refugees). However, any generalization of the principle would lead to a world federal state.
"These officials are chosen in free, fair and reasonably frequent elections."	The electoral principle may be applied at various levels. But other forms of democratic participation may also be envisaged, including consultation with a random sample of statistically representative world citizens.
"In considering their possible choices and decisions, citizens have an effective right and opportunity to exercise extensive freedom of expression."	As freedom of expression is often repressed by authoritarian governments, IGOs should protect individual and collective freedom of expression and make available the means of exercising it.
"Citizens also have the right and opportunity to consult alternative sources of information that are not under the control of the government or any single group of interest."	Access to information is today substantially guaranteed inside the states. Attempts to form a regionally based (as in the case of Europe) or global public opinion have so far only been sporadic. However, the globalization of the mass media and of the new information technology is leading to the generation of a global public sphere.

(Continued)

135

Table 5.2 (*Continued*)

Criteria of Democracy Indicated by Dahl	Possible Extension to International Organizations
"In order to act effectively, citizens possess the right and opportunities to form political associations, interest groups, competitive political parties, voluntary organizations and the like."	National associative life may be extended also to the transnational level. International associations (parties, trade unions, movements) already exist that have so far expressed a range of different positions. Reinforcement of the global institutions could also lead to a reorganization of the representation of interests.
"With a small number of permissible exceptions, such as transient residents, all adults who are subject to the laws and policies are full citizens who possess all the rights and opportunities just listed."	The Universal Declaration of Human Rights has already confirmed the existence of individual universal rights. Cosmopolitan citizenship would have to extend the equality of the inhabitants of the world as far as a minimal list of rights and duties is concerned.

Sources: Robert A. Dahl, "Is Post-national Democracy Possible?" pp. 35–45 in *Nation, Federalism and Democracy*, ed. Sergio Fabbrini (Trento: Editrice Compositori, 2001), on p. 38 [left column]; Author's text [right column].

If the possible extension of these criteria to the global sphere is considered, as we have attempted to do on the right-hand side of table 5.2, it is easy to understand Dahl's skepticism. It actually seems difficult, at least in the short term, for the constituent principles of democracy to become an integral part of IOs and, to an even lesser extent, of a global order. Dahl's criteria correspond to what we today expect from a democratic system: extending democracy beyond the state cannot be achieved simply by following the beaten track. It is necessary to make an assessment of Dahl's criteria and compare those criteria with the criteria set out in section 2.3 (table 2.1). From this comparison, it emerges that Dahl's criteria do not encapsulate the core of democracy, but only a few of the means of achieving conditions of nonviolence, popular control, and political equality. To simply duplicate the criteria indicated on the left-hand side in the case of the IOs or the global sphere would mean shifting toward a federal type of world state (cf. § 4.4). From an analytical point of view, the federal model is in no way different, except for its scale, to the representative democracy practiced today in many states.

Cosmopolitan democracy, on the other hand, raises the issue of a transmogrification of democracy to render it able to respond to global challenges, at the same time retaining its decentralization. Let us therefore return to the basic principles set out in § 2.3 and verify the extent to which they have already been applied or are applicable in the area of IOs that already exist or are being set up (cf. also § 3.2). All three stated criteria—nonviolence, public control, and political equality—already lie at the heart of existing IOs, while the principles of mediation and the applications are already substantially different from those now applied in individual states. Dahl, therefore, rightfully claims that no absolute symmetry exists between the democracy in individual states and the democracy to be introduced into the IOs, nor should symmetry be sought. However, if the proposed objective is to *increase* democratic participation, particularly when many complain of its absence, it becomes essential to find more satisfactory feasible applications. In table 5.3 the three principles are linked to IOs.

Dahl does not seem to be against IOs, nor does he deny that it is desirable to increase their transparency and allow IOs to be evaluated. However, he considers the use of the term *democracy* incorrect. If we accept the idea that decisions that cross state borders must be taken by ad hoc institutions and that those decisions must at least satisfy the criteria of transparency, representativeness, legality, and control by stakeholders, the difference becomes largely terminological: we could, for example, refer to "more democracy" or "democratization." One wonders to what extent the champions of democracy are opposed to the concrete reforming of IOs, such as the creation of a parliamentary assembly at the UN or the compulsory jurisdiction of the ICJ.[23] The situation should be avoided in which, in view of the difficulty of attaining democracy at the international level, we neglect to act to increase the legitimacy of the global decision-making process in those areas in which it would be possible.

THE DANGER OF GLOBAL TECHNOCRACY

But there is always a lurking fear that a level of governance above that of the state can ultimately void the democratic contents painstakingly built up inside it. A clear warning of this came from the referendum on the European Constitution held in two founder members of the EU—France

23. Cf. Falk and Strauss, "Toward Global Parliament." For a wider set of proposals of IOs' democratization, see Patomaki and Teivainen, *Possible World*; and Zweifel, *International Organizations and Democracy*.

Table 5.3
Democratic Principles and International Organizations

Basic Principles	Existing International Organizations	Democratic Reform of International Organizations
Nonviolence	Member states' commitment to settle disputes peacefully and to use force only in self-defense	Reinforcement of the principle of nonviolence through the following: i. Compulsory competence of international jurisdiction ii. Individual criminal responsibility for the crime of aggression iii. Safeguarding by means of humanitarian intervention of individuals at risk of suffering massive political violence
Public control	Control exercised by member governments	Extension of control to the citizens through a world parliament
	Publicizing and transparency of proceedings	Right of access to international organizations for demands from global civil society and nongovernmental organizations
	Codification of norms in treaties, statutes, and international pacts	Control by cosmopolitan institutions over the exercise of power in the member states
Political equality	Principle of formal equality of states	Equality of states considered from the substantial and not the formal point of view
	Equality of rights of individuals guaranteed by the Universal Declaration of Human Rights	Equality of citizens established on the basis of minimum rights and duties guaranteed by a cosmopolitan citizenship Direct participation of individuals through representative elected to a world parliament

and the Netherlands—on May 29 and June 1, 2005. It was voted out by 61.6 and 54.8 percent of voters. These figures are even more revealing when it is recalled that the governments of these two countries implemented policies favoring greater integration: the ruling elites were disavowed by their own citizens. Not even European integration, even though it is taking place exclusively among democratic countries and allows a wide range of popular control over actions and policies, is necessarily accepted by the respective peoples.

The same fear of international integration may be perceived in small communities that have a high level of participation, which are often reluctant to become members of IOs. Switzerland—Rousseau's homeland, the birthplace of the Red Cross, and headquarters of the League of Nations and of many UN agencies—joined the UN only in 2002 and has maintained its independence from the EU even though it is now completely surrounded by it. The Norwegians twice rejected membership of the EU, and the Swedes and Danes have stubbornly retained their monetary sovereignty and refused to change to the euro. In order to retain the image of the kings and queens on their coins, Swedes and Danes pay a daily price in terms of purchasing power. Here it is not so much a matter of judging these attitudes as of trying to understand them, above all because these attitudes are displayed by peoples who, in terms of democracy, have a lot to teach us. Nor can these resistances be attributed to an indifference to problems lying outside the communities. The Scandinavian and Benelux states are persistently and generously committed to the solution of global problems, for instance in the form of generous development aid donations.

How does one account for this resistance to international integration displayed by small communities with a high level of self-government? One hypothesis is that the hostility arises out of the fear that governments could use the obligations stemming from international institutions to restrict popular sovereignty.[24] The tactic does not seem to favor any specific government; in democratic countries, governments remain in power for shorter periods than those envisaged in international agreements. Those who do benefit are rather the elites (the establishment and dominant economic groups), which can exploit international agreements to impose their choices against the will of the demos. In a word, IOs could become a Trojan horse that would allow technocracy to elude internal democratic control. In Europe, the Maastricht parameters have

24. Klaus D. Wolf, "The New Raison d'État as a Problem for Democracy in World Society," *European Journal of International Relations* vol. 5, no. 3 (1999): 333–63, on p. 343.

become a dogma that has compelled various governments to curb public expenditure; the IMF directives have influenced wage policy in many developing countries and indeed affected their chances of attaining democratization.[25] IOs can even limit the autonomy of political communities without it being clear what the prevailing mechanisms of democratic accountability are. This frequently arouses reluctance in the population to delegate powers that are too broad to IOs that are difficult to control.

Does this lack of international integration mean that these communities can retain a higher degree of autonomy and that the people can exert their control? Let us take the case of three neighboring countries, Finland, Sweden, and Norway. Vis-à-vis the EU, Finland is fully integrated, Sweden did not adopt the euro, and Norway is not an EU member. Can it be said that for this reason Norway has greater political autonomy than Finland? It would not seem that in vital issues such as financial flows, immigration, and the environment Norway is more autonomous than Finland. Norway is often compelled passively to accept European directives in order to avoid being marginalized in international integration, while Finland has at least the chance to express itself in the European institutional fora. Today, Norwegian political autonomy seems to be at greater risk than that of Finland. Membership of supranational bodies helps preserve democracy in nations much more than it hinders it. To refuse to extend democracy to decision-making echelons beyond the state does not simply leave them in limbo but also endangers democracy within the state.[26]

THE COMMUNITARIAN/MULTICULTURALIST OBJECTION

Greater international integration not only conjures up the technocratic specter. Some also fear that extending democracy to the global sphere can threaten the very identity of individual political communities. Communitarian and multiculturalist thinkers believe there could not be a

25. Jan Aarte Scholte, *Civil Society Voices and the International Monetary Fund* (Ottawa: North-South Institute, 2002); Devesh Kapur and Moisés Naím, "The IMF and Democratic Governance," *Journal of Democracy* vol. 16, no. 1 (2005): 89–102.

26. Michael Zürn, "Democratic Governance Beyond the Nation-State: The EU and Other International Institutions," *European Journal of International Relations* vol. 6, no. 2 (2000): 183–221.

close link between democracy and cosmopolitanism, claiming that a political system may be one or the other, but not both.[27]

It is not denied that new problems are raised by the global society. Kymlicka, for example, exhorts the democratic state to address new issues such as migration, financial flows, multiethnic communities, and minority rights and, at the same time, to make a positive contribution to rendering global society more humane, for example, by strengthening the international protection of human rights and boosting development aid. To exonerate the state from these responsibilities in the name of a newly forming and undefined world order is hazardous, as it would create a void between the existing state political system that, however inadequate, could be extended and a still-nonexistent global system. Although agreeing on the need to find institutional mechanisms that can tackle the political problems accompanying globalization, Kymlicka is of the opinion that these responsibilities can be more satisfactorily shouldered by the existing states rather than by new and newly forming institutions based on world citizens.[28] I shall certainly not be the one to deny that each state has the possibility of contributing to the political management of new problems. In addressing environmental and immigration issues, development aid, and scientific research, each state can become a workshop of cosmopolitanism. The global institutions proposed herein have no intention of exonerating from their cosmopolitan responsibilities other actors such as the state or indeed the individual, but rather to reinforce them.

Some fear that extending the boundaries of a political community will lead to the loss of solidarity that is needed to maintain the cohesion of any society.[29] The smaller a community, the stronger the participation and mutual support. I am aware of the risk that indiscriminately extending solidarity to all the inhabitants of the Earth will ultimately deprive everyone of it. On the other hand, the feeling of solidarity does not seem to be geographically circumscribed or disjunctive, either sociologically or even less from the regulatory standpoint. To express solidarity for distant groups of persons does not mean denying it to those who live in our own neighborhood.

The redistribution of income, which the workers' movement succeeded in achieving by transforming the guardian state into a welfare state,

27. See Craig Calhoun, "The Class Consciousness of Frequent Travellers," pp. 86–116 in *Debating Cosmopolitics* for the former and Kymlicka, *Multicultural Citizenship* for the latter.
28. Will Kymlicka, "Citizenship in an Era of Globalization: Commentary on Held," pp. 112–26 in *Democracy's Edges*, ed. Shapiro and Hacker-Cordón, on p. 117.
29. Calhoun, "Class Consciousness," p. 112.

represents one of the central features of social solidarity. Some doubt whether a cosmopolitan democracy could achieve a comparable degree of income redistribution at the world level.[30] Focused as it is on the institutional plane, cosmopolitan democracy cannot indeed be the exclusive heritage of those who are favorable to a redistribution of income, and it would be a good thing if both liberals and socialists supported the institutional proposals, albeit with programs having different contents. Held and McGrew, for example, presented a cosmopolitan *social*-democratic program that included specific objectives related to defense of labor.[31] Nothing would prevent a cosmopolitan *liberal*-democratic program—for example, one based on the free circulation of goods, capital, and workers—from being opposed to this program. The neoliberal program has been under way for some years, although in the absence of any democratic accountability. For this reason, any extension of the institutional framework in which the various options could confront each other would inevitably benefit the weaker components. One of the reasons why a significant part of today's world does not reap the benefits of the wealth generated elsewhere is that its voice is not heard. Giving the masses political rights also means increasing their bargaining clout as far as the redistribution of income and wealth is concerned.

THE QUEST FOR THE GLOBAL DEMOS

It is often reiterated that a cosmopolitan democracy could not be democratic owing to the lack of a global demos.[32] In effect, today no global demos exists that can be compared with that which exists within nations. Global civil society, often referred to as representing the global demos, is still composed of minorities and elites, of a small percentage of privileged persons who are able to travel and are capable of communicating in several languages. But it is also unthinkable that the demos

30. Calhoun, "Class Consciousness," p. 112.
31. David Held and Anthony McGrew, *Globalization/Anti-globalization* (Cambridge: Polity Press, 2002), p. 132.
32. Calhoun, "Class Consciousness"; Nadia Urbinati, "Can Cosmopolitical Democracy Be Democratic?" pp. 67–85 in *Debating Cosmopolitics*; Winfried Thaa, "Lean Citizenship: The Fading Away of the Political in Transnational Democracy," *European Journal of International Relations* vol. 7, no. 4 (2001): 503–23; Glyn Morgan, "Democracy, Transnational Institutions, and the Circumstances of Politics," pp. 173–90 in *Transnational Democracy*, ed. Morrison. The problem is discussed from an opposite perspective by Zürn, "Democratic Governance Beyond the Nation-State" and Habermas, *Postnational Constellation*, chapter 5.

precedes the institutions entirely. In many cases, the institutions create the demos. The American demos is today single also because—more than two centuries ago—some colonists fought for the United States of America, in spite of their different ethnic and religious origins. If this subjective choice had not been made, we would probably have had different states, each proud of its own identity, just as there are different identities in the United States and Canada. To think that the demos is independent of the institutions is like claiming that it is independent of history.

The same critics claim that without the demos there is no democracy, and the very etymology of the word prevents us from disagreeing. But it does not appear that other shared criteria exist to decide which elements are required for a multitude of persons to be considered a demos. Peoples may be the inhabitants of a village, of a city, of a country. Peoples are those who belong to a race or to the same religious faith or who even identify themselves through the same rituals (see chapter 9). The bonds of solidarity required to ensure the survival of a community do not necessarily coincide with a territorial state. It would seem more useful to consider which elements bring individuals together, and this question leads us to assert that in many functional areas the *demoi* are different and not always clearly delimited within the confines of a territorial state. While the communities of fate overlap, the static anchorage of a political community to a "people" is not the best way to achieve an effective administration of their problems.

Others have detected an elitarian tendency in cosmopolitanism.[33] Cosmopolitans may be defined as those who know the world and feel at ease anywhere in it. Webster's dictionary, for example, defines *cosmopolitan* as "composed of people from or at home in many parts of the world; especially not provincial in attitudes or interests." This brings to mind the old criticism made by nationalist thinkers of "rootless cosmopolitans,"[34] who for this reason are at home everywhere and thus have no solidarity for anyone. Yet Kant's and Condorcet's philosophy of history contains a conception of cosmopolitanism that not only refers to the individual destiny of a privileged few but also represents a goal for the whole of humankind. Marrying the cosmopolitan ideal with the concept of democracy is an attempt to make this destiny explicit. Indeed, it is reassuring to see that empirical research seems to disprove

33. Brennan, "Cosmopolitanism and Internationalism"; Calhoun, "Class Consciousness"; Urbinati, "Can Cosmopolitical Democracy Be Democratic?"
34. Eleonore Kofman, "Figures of the Cosmopolitan," *Innovation* vol. 18, no. 1 (2005): 83–97. See also Chris Rumford, ed., *Cosmopolitanism and Europe* (Liverpool: Liverpool University Press, 2007).

that elites are more likely to support cosmopolitan values than the population at large: this is the outcome of an empirical survey based on a World Values Survey.[35] The construction of a global demos is based on the assumption that it is possible to develop a sense of responsibility in the citizens not only *of* the world, but also *for* the world.[36]

5.4 Globalize the Rule of Law or Democracy?

The need to tame globalization and bring it back under political control may be addressed by means of different strategies, which are not necessarily in agreement among themselves. Many believe, for example, that it is more realistic and satisfactory to pursue a strategy aimed at globalizing the rule of law rather than democracy.[37] The modern concept of democracy includes the rule of law and not just the majority principle.[38] However, as soon as it is attempted to transfer these concepts from the state level to the global level, it is useful to accept the invitation, for analytical purposes, to separate the principle of the rule of law from the democratic principle.

Dahrendorf claims that to plead the cause of the creation of a global democracy is like "barking at the moon."[39] In addressing the same problems, he suggested that it would be much better to attribute greater weight and jurisdiction to institutions that were less easily influenced by the demos, such as those in which membership is permanent and where membership is top-down rather than bottom-up. Dahrendorf cites as examples of institutions to be reinforced the central banks, the American Supreme Court, and the British House of Lords (although he spares us the Assembly of Cardinals). Dahrendorf's vehement attack on global

35. See Peter A. Furia, "Global Citizenship, Anyone? Cosmopolitanism, Privilege and Public Opinion," *Global Society* vol. 19, no. 4 (2005): 331–59.

36. Jeremy Waldron, "What Is Cosmopolitan?" *Journal of Political Philosophy* vol. 8, no. 2 (2000): 227–43.

37. Ralf Dahrendorf, *Dopo la democrazia*, interview ed. Antonio Polito (Roma-Bari: Laterza, 2001); Scheuerman, "Cosmopolitan Democracy and the Rule of Law"; Urbinati, "Can Cosmopolitical Democracy Be Democratic?" Morgan, "Democracy, Transnational Institutions"; and Slaughter, *New World Order.* The English term *rule of law* is, in this context, much more appropriate than the German, French, and Italian equivalents of "state of law" precisely because it does not imply the existence of a state power of last resort.

38. See, for example, the essay by Jürgen Habermas, "On the Internal Relation Between the Rule of Law and Democracy," pp. 253–64 in Habermas, *Inclusion of the Other.*

39. Dahrendorf, *Dopo la democrazia*, p. 9.

democracy is nevertheless accompanied by biting criticism of democracy as such. Dahrendorf would like to modify the distribution of power, shifting functions from the elected bodies to technocratic organs inside the states themselves. While Dahl's doubts are associated with the risk that the global dimension can weaken democracy as we know it today in the states, those of Dahrendorf are opposite in sign, as they refer to democracy itself. Without embarking on the old debate on the governance of the custodians, we should question if a reinforcement of the rule of law and the institutions for safeguarding it would be capable of responding to the new global problems.

The rule of law at the international level may be deemed satisfied as soon as the states respect the obligations contracted in the treaties and other international covenants. The states themselves should then enforce respect for the obligations by the actors that lie within their jurisdiction, even when that jurisdiction is not exclusive (as in the case, for instance, of multinational corporations which, by definition, operate in more than one country and therefore are bound by various national regulations and authorities). This competence would correspond to a reinforcement of the confederal model (see § 4.4), with the states mutually agreeing to respect common rules and likewise to enforce their respect by the subjects under their jurisdiction. Indeed, there are a growing number of areas in which interstate agreements, often implemented by administrative and bureaucratic structures, manage to operate quite effectively.[40] If airliners can take off and land, if we can receive mail, if we can communicate via telephone and email, it is because of a dense network of international agreements underwritten by national administrations and implemented in the absence of any ultimate power of coercion. Even when the agreed rules and standards are not the most convenient for a given state, having them is nevertheless convenient. Since exclusion from participation would in itself be a heavy sanction, the states tend to respect the agreements undertaken.

These international regimes are able to operate as they are *functional* to everyone's interests. This is not all. These regimes often enjoy direct participation by all the subjects involved: the telephone companies participate in the definition of the rules and standards of the International Telecommunications Union to no lesser extent than the governments. Yet there is no democratic filter regulating to whom, why, and with what right participation in these regulatory functions is granted. Customers and employees, for example, are the weakest link in the chain and often

40. Slaughter, *New World Order*; Sabino Cassese, "Administrative Law without the State? The Challenge of Global Regulation," *NYU Journal of International Law and Politics* vol. 37, no. 4 (2005): 663–94.

are not represented at all in these bodies.[41] It may pragmatically be assumed that the issue of legitimacy is of secondary importance provided that telephones work. But when regulation becomes more intrusive in the sphere of internal power, as in the case of the regime of human rights, states become much more jealous of their own autonomy and the stated objectives are far from being attained. Even when the rule of law is accepted de jure, it is often eluded de facto, without even the democratic states displaying greater respect for international law than the autocratic ones.[42]

It is certainly no surprise that, in the absence of sanctions, international law is less respected than national legislation and that the more demanding and costly it is for a state to respect it, the less willing the state is to enforce it. For this reason, although I agree with those desirous of strengthening the rule of law, as far as both its legislative and its judicial components are concerned, it seems necessary to base the rule of law also on an enhanced political legitimacy. The institutions that promote and enforce the rule of law—whether the UN General Assembly or the International Court of Justice—need to be legitimized by a more direct popular mandate. Only if the legitimacy of the rules is enhanced will it be possible to ensure that the depositaries of force will "voluntarily" obey them. Direct participation by citizens in world political life seems to be the principal modality for increasing the legitimacy of the rules. Without legitimization and without powers of coercion, the rule of law runs the risk, as is the case today, of remaining mere moral preaching. The judicial organs themselves, unless incorporated into a democratic order, can be turned into a new juridical oligarchy or worse and may act solely when their action is in harmony with the will of the more powerful states.[43]

The observations made concerning the prevalence of law nevertheless suggest an appealing way forward: can the rule of law precede democracy? In the development of liberal states it often happened that the law

41. Nayef H. Samhat and Rodger A. Payne, "Regimes, Public Spheres and Global Democracy: Towards the Transformation of Political Community," *Global Society* vol. 17, no. 3 (2003): 273–95, discuss how these regimes may be transformed into a bottom-up nonterritorial democratic management.
42. As discussed, for example, in Falk, *Law in an Emerging Global Village* and Held, "Law of States, Law of Peoples."
43. Antoine Garapon, *Des crimes qu'on ne peut ni punir ni pardonner: pour une justice internationale* (Paris: O. Jacob, 2002); Hans Köchler, *Global Justice or Global Revenge? International Criminal Justice at the Crossroads* (Wien and New York: Springer, 2003); and Danilo Zolo, *La giustizia dei vincitori* (Roma-Bari: Laterza, 2006) have warned against this risk in the case of the new international criminal justice.

courts preceded the parliaments. Before a clear-cut separation was achieved among executive, legislative, and judicial powers, the law courts occasionally seized also the coercive power required to enforce their decisions. In some cases, the courts succeeded in this enforcement even in the absence of coercive powers of their own and even against the executive power.[44] Ever since the time of Kelsen, juridical pacifism has entertained hopes that a similar pathway could be followed in international relations.[45] Although lacking coercive power, the judiciary can play a decisive role in the international system in conditioning the actions of the main actors.

It may be objected that the rule of law at the global level has already been legitimized by the fact that norms are implemented by the individual states and that the larger the number of democratic states, the greater the indirect popular legitimization. This is an important channel of legitimization but one that is often insufficient for the reasons illustrated above (see § 3.5). Democratic states, which were also the promoters of the UN and of the majority of IOs, periodically violate international law and hinder the judiciary. These violations of the law would probably be more difficult if the rule of law were still anchored to democratic institutions established by the world citizens. The governments of the democratic countries would at least experience some embarrassment in explaining to their own electors why they ask their electors to respect the law when they, the governments themselves, do not respect international laws.

5.5 Global Ethics and Cosmopolitan Democracy

I have already said that the debate on global ethics is a thread that runs parallel with that of cosmopolitan democracy.[46] The former is part of ethical cosmopolitanism, the latter of institutional cosmopolitanism.

44. Luigi Ferrajoli, ed., *Diritti fondamentali* (Roma-Bari: Laterza, 2001).
45. Kelsen, *Peace through Law* and, in the same spirit, the proposals made by Grenville Clark and Louis Sohn, *World Peace through World Law* (Cambridge, MA: Harvard University Press, 1958) and by Richard A. Falk and Cyril E. Black, eds., *The Future of the International Legal Order* (Princeton: Princeton University Press, 1969).
46. The problem of cosmopolitan ethics has been dominated by the attempt to extend John Rawls' theory of justice to the global level. See Charles Beitz, *Political Theory and International Relations* (Princeton: Princeton University Press, 1979) and Thomas Pogge, "An Egalitarian Law of Peoples," *Philosophy and Public Affairs* vol. 23, no. 3 (1994): 195–224. These more audacious approaches were, however, cooled down by Rawls himself in his *The Law of Peoples*, pp. 116–19.

Unfortunately, the two research programs have interacted only to a limited extent, while it would be extremely useful to compare them more attentively.[47] The debate on ethics has shed light on the rights and duties of individuals and states outside their borders. One of the central problems that has been analyzed is the distribution of world resources and the theoretical justification of responsibility, both individual and statal, vis-à-vis external agents. This debate has nevertheless focused less on institutional instruments attempting to determine the extent of resource distribution or of the modes of transfer.

Substantial objectives, for instance a redistribution of income between rich and poor countries, also demand the existence of ad hoc institutions. The welfare state was not the outcome of compassion expressed by the well-to-do classes but only the result of social struggles leading to the introduction of equal political rights for individuals. Only when workers had achieved political clout was it possible to guarantee economic and social rights. Today a similar problem exists at the international level: to establish the responsibility of the rich (and democratic) countries versus the poor (and often nondemocratic) countries also entails finding (possibly democratic) institutional channels to link the two areas. A fundamental difference exists with reference to what has taken place within individual states: on the interior, rich and poor are part of the same community and the richer part would not be able to organize society without the contribution of the poorer part. One way or another, the various components would thus be obliged to coordinate their efforts inside a system as, in the absence of these interactions, the community itself would collapse. As far as the subdivision of the contemporary world is concerned, the northern countries can survive even if they slam the door in the face of the southern ones, and this considerably reduces the bargaining power of the South.

This makes it even more urgent to develop cosmopolitan ethics and institutions.[48] But until such time as the rich states are able to decide unilaterally to devote part of their own income to development aid, such aid will be limited and reversible. It is alarming to note that, after the fall of the Berlin wall, development aid in the democratic countries was reduced, while the inequality among countries and within countries

47. For an overview of this flourishing debate, see Thomas Pogge, ed., *Global Justice* (Oxford: Blackwell, 2001) and Simon Caney, *Justice Beyond Borders* (Oxford: Oxford University Press, 2005).
48. Nancy Fraser, "Reframing Justice in a Globalizing World," *New Left Review* no. 36 (November–December 2005): 69–88.

increased.[49] This casts a sinister light on the motives underlying western solidarity: it would appear to be a generosity dictated by the need to contain the Soviet enemy.

5.6 An Open Project

In spite of the ambitions of the cosmopolitan project, the criticism the project has received has been substantially benevolent. Much of this criticism is useful in better directing the sense and implications of cosmopolitan democracy, and the obstacles pointed out are anything but abstract; they are problems that have to be faced on a daily basis by political reality. Cosmopolitan democracy has no intention of setting itself up as a closed theoretical project; quite the contrary, the only source of vitality available to cosmopolitan democracy is drawn from intellectual debate and the experiences of political and social life acquired in the contemporary world. The second part of this book examines how the principles of cosmopolitan democracy can be applied in concrete situations.

49. Statistics are available in World Bank, *World Development Indicators* (Washington, DC: World Bank, 2007), on pp. 26 and 58.

PART TWO

THE PRACTICE OF COSMOPOLITAN DEMOCRACY

Chapter 6
The Central Importance of the United Nations

6.1 Everyman's Home

The UN was born to be everyman's home, the home of all peoples, as is forcefully stated in the first line of the preamble to the charter: "We the peoples of the United Nations." Yet ever since the UN's foundation, its profile has remained much lower than originally expected. The explanation for this is not hard to understand: on the one hand, the governments have jealously retained the privilege of being exclusive representatives of the interests of those they govern. Governments have appropriated the right to be the only international political subjects, to the extent that the intergovernmental oligarchy has actually been glorified by the charter itself. On the other hand, a specific regime, that of the Cold War and nuclear terror, foiled all attempts to transform the organization into an arbitrator of international politics. There was even the suspicion that a contingent interstate system—the Cold War—was excogitated on purpose by the dominant classes in order to preserve their own oligarchic power.[1]

Many have hoped that it would be possible for the UN headquarters to be reconstructed on the rubble of the Berlin wall for the purpose of coordinating the more important political decisions. While all over the

---

1. The state of the UN during the Cold War is well described in Adam Roberts and Benedict Kingsbury, eds., *United Nations, Divided World* (Oxford: Oxford University Press, 1988).

world the ends of so many dictatorships were being celebrated and millions of persons were being allowed to vote for the first time, expectations were that a similar upheaval would take place at the UN. On January 31, 1992, for the first time in history, all the members of the UN Security Council were represented by their own heads of governments. Was this not a sign that the will existed to use the institution to make strategic decisions?

It is not surprising that in the 1990s we saw a flourish of projects to reform the UN and the other international organizations. Inveterate dreamers and retired politicians gave free rein to their reforming fantasies, proposing bold changes in the practice and even the constitutional structure of the UN.[2] These projects often ignored existing power relations in world politics, and, if anything, constitutional engineering strove to make the UN more representative, more effective, and even more democratic. This reforming frenzy contaminated the UN institutions on several occasions, and a number of working groups were set up to assess the proposals made by diplomats, experts, or nongovernmental organization.[3] UN reform thus became a small manufacturing business whose products seem doomed to early demise.

There have been a series of symbolic dates: 1995, when the first fifty years of the organization were celebrated in great pomp and ceremony; 2000, at the beginning of the new millennium; 2005, when the justly soft-pedaled sixtieth-anniversary celebrations were held. In no case were any significant modifications made to the UN structure. The hopefuls were disappointed. Conversely, perhaps because of the high expectations raised, many commentators began to speak perversely of the death of the UN—during the siege of Sarajevo, in the midst of the genocide perpetrated in Rwanda, in the wake of the Srebrenica massacre, when the Twin Towers were destroyed, when the Iraq War began.

The UN has not only had to come to terms with its own powerlessness to address the hurly-burly of world politics. Today the UN is faced with

2. Cf., for instance, Commission for Global Governance, *Our Global Neighbourhood* (Oxford: Oxford University Press, 1995). For a relatively realistic overview of what could be reformed, see Paul Kennedy, *The Parliament of Man: The Past, Present, and Future of the United Nations* (London: Allen Lane, 2006). For a review of more daring proposals, see Richard Falk, "Reforming the United Nations: Global Civil Society Perspectives and Initiatives," pp. 150–86 in *Global Civil Society 2005/6*.

3. For the more recent, cf. UN, *A More Secure World: Report of the Secretary General's High Level Panel on Threats, Challenges and Change* (New York: UN, 2004), at www.un.org/secureworld and UN, *We the Peoples: Civil Society, the United Nations and Global Governance* (New York: UN, 2004), at www.un.org/reform/civilsociety.

a much more serious problem: its most influential member has done its best to throw a spanner in the works. Under the administration of George W. Bush, the United States—the hegemonic nation of the twenty-first century and main single source of UN funding—has displayed a marked estrangement not only from the organization conceived of by its thirty-second president, Franklin Delano Roosevelt, but also from the multilateral system set up by its twenty-eighth president, Woodrow Wilson. George W. Bush's vision of the international system is the opposite even of his father's.[4] And so, paradoxically, the attempt to reinforce the UN as the central forum of world politics is being stymied not by authoritarian states but by the democratic state to which the UN owes its creation. This will be a difficult legacy to overcome in the next years.

Realist theoreticians have no reason to be surprised. Considering the present distribution of world power, realist theoreticians have no reason to expect that the more powerful countries will agree to devolve a substantial part of their own power to the UN and the other international organizations. The idealists are obliged to retreat and to admit that the internal regime is not a good indicator for predicting the willingness to embark on multilateral options. But not even the grand international relations theories can predict the future path of the UN or the role the UN will play in future society. The explanatory capacity of the theories must also be able to cope with a variety of new factors: the growing importance of soft power, the role of legitimization, and the proliferating number of actors. We live in an age in which the events are outstripping theory and the UN's future is related more to the political struggle than to academic predictions.

Although nowadays we are forced to reconsider the present and future of the UN, it must not be overlooked that the UN expresses an activism and a visibility that it did not have in the past. One indicator is enough to show this: in the forty-five years elapsing between 1946 and 1989, the Security Council passed 646 resolutions, an average of 15 per year, while from 1990 to 2006 it passed 1,092, more than 68 per year. In cases where there was no agreement among the principal governments, as for the invasion of Iraq, the different positions were publicly debated before the SC rather than in the secret closets of diplomacy.[5] This led to a clear-cut contradiction between the decision to use the UN to debate whether it was necessary to take up arms and then to begin the

4. As noted by Habermas, *Divided West*, pp. 102–4.
5. For an assessment of the role played by the SC, see Ian Hurd, *After Anarchy: Legitimacy and Power in the United Nations Security Council* (Princeton: Princeton University Press, 2007).

war without its approval. This has become the symbol of the current destiny of the UN: there is an increased willingness to use the UN as a forum for debate and discussion without allowing it to direct the much-invoked global governance.

6.2 The Democratic Discourse at the United Nations

The cosmopolitan democracy project views the UN as the pivot of the entire world judicial and political system. In human memory, the UN is the most ambitious international organization ever to be established. It is not only unrealistic but also absurd to imagine that the UN can be bypassed for the purpose of establishing a new world order. Indeed, it is necessary to reclaim the UN and use it to perform the task for which it was founded. But is it possible to make the UN democratic or at least *more* democratic?

Several principles underpinning democracy are already present, although one must daily weave one's way through the ambiguities. In the first place, the UN was set up to avert war and ensure peace and was supposed to demonstrate the will of the various member states to accept the preemptive nonaggression pact that represents the prerequisite for the development of democracy. Instead, the number and ferocity of the wars waged after the foundation of the organization, in which its more influential members gaily participated, are sufficient to show that this is a formal principle that is not upheld in practice. In the second place, the UN has been inclusive to the highest degree and has succeeded in welcoming among its members practically every country in the world, including all the former colonies as they gradually gained independence. In spite of this, the UN has remained an essentially intergovernmental institution, but not only. It has constantly taken care in its actions not to trample the principles of state sovereignty and noninterference. If in practice interference was the order of the day and if several member states were governed by a puppet government placed in power by other states, these represented problems to which the UN has continued gladly to turn a blind eye. In the third place, the UN has endeavored to be sensitive to the expressions of civil society—NGOs, businesses, national parliaments, religious denominations, trade unions, and so on—although relegating them to a purely decorative function.

The discourse on democracy has been rendered misleading by numerous acts of hypocrisy of the North, South, West and East. The first hypocrisy comes from the western democracies: although the United States, the United Kingdom, and France genuinely believed that they could use the UN as an instrument for extending their own constitutional forms to the international sphere, they had no compunction about appropriating the right to block any decision regarding security, attributing to themselves the imperial privilege (in the literal sense of the term) of being members of the SC with the power of veto. The Soviet Union was certainly more consistent, preventing the very word *democracy* from being included in the Universal Declaration of Human Rights.[6] The directory of great powers formed by the authoritarian states is a brutal fact but not a contradiction. That the democratic countries should be part of this is both brutal and contradictory.

The second hypocritical act comes from the governments of the developing countries. Although they constantly accuse the UN of not being sensitive to the needs of the weaker nations, the majority of these governments have failed to apply democratic principles within their own countries. Harassment and in some cases the actual massacre of their own citizens have thus often accompanied their anticolonial and anti-imperialist rhetoric. The representatives of these governments were certainly not credible when they stood up in the UN assembly to demand for the organization the democracy they denied in their own backyard.

It was not only the hypocrisy of those sitting physically in the institutions of the organization that tarnished the democratic discourse. There is also a conceptual problem that has been ignored for decades: what is the significance of applying democracy in international organizations? And even when certain fundamental principles have been agreed upon, is it perhaps conceivable that the member governments will comply with a rational plan that does not reflect the existing power relations? The architects of the UN deliberately chose to create an organization whose members could be both democratic and nondemocratic countries because they assumed that this would provide a vital contribution not only to international peace but also to the enforcement of human rights. Since the start of the Cold War, many politicians and scholars argued that it was impossible to democratize the UN if a large proportion of its members, and until quite recently the majority, were ruled by unelected governments.[7]

6. On the role played by the various states in the foundation of the UN, see Stephan C. Schlesinger, *Act of Creation: The Founding of the United Nations: A Story of Superpowers, Secret Agents, Wartime Allies and Enemies, and Their Quest for a Peaceful World* (Boulder, CO: Westview Press, 2003); Evan Luard, *A History of the United Nations*, 2 vols. (Houndsmill: Macmillam, 1982–89); and Joseph P. Baratta, *The Politics of World Federation: United Nations, UN Reform, Atomic Control*, 2 vols. (Westport, CT: Praeger, 2004).
7. See John Bolton, "The Creation, Fall, Rise, and Fall of the United Nations," pp. 45–62 in *Delusions of Grandeur: The UN and Global Intervention*, ed.

In fact, the simultaneous pursuit of the democratization of the UN (as well as of the other international organizations) and of the member states can only be mutually reinforcing. The UN has made an important, albeit insufficient, contribution to international peace and has thus also favored democratization in many of its members.[8] We are at a decisive political, institutional, and above all theoretical crossroads based on what has been postulated in chapter 3: to claim that an organization that accepts authoritarian governments can be an instrument of global democracy is based on the hypothesis of a causal link between external and internal. That is, the claim is based on the assumption that the simultaneous presence of democratic and authoritarian governments in the same institution puts pressure on the latter and, in the final analysis, helps wear down authoritarian regimes to a greater extent than if the authoritarian governments were excluded.

It is true, however, that the beneficial effects may be slow to come and may not be straightforward. In the case of the Soviet Union and of the other eastern European countries, included among the founder members of the UN as early as 1945, the authoritarian institutions survived until 1989. In other words, there are no surefire recipes to guarantee a timely democratization. But what happened in Europe is linked to the Cold War, which was fomented in order to avoid allowing the European peoples to more vocally demand the rights that were being denied them. And it also depended on the fact that the range of action of the international organization was restricted to the member governments. The acceptance of diversity among regimes need not necessarily become passive complacence but should, on the contrary, be accompanied by political, social, and cultural pressure. This pressure is all the more effective when exerted by nongovernmental subjects.

At this point a distinction may be made between *static* and *dynamic* policies pursued by democracies in mixed international organizations. A *static* policy accepts the principles of sovereignty and noninterference and limits itself to regulating the relations among states without attempting to modify the internal regimes. The relations among states

---

T. G. Carpenter (Washington, DC: Cato Institute, 1997) and, in a longer historical perspective, see Luard, *History of the United Nations*, vol. 1.

8. The beneficial effect of IOs on internal democracy has been investigated: cf. Jon C. Pevehouse, "Democracy from the Outside-In? International Organizations and Democratization," *International Organization* vol. 56, no. 3 (2002): 515–49 and Kristian S. Gleditsch and Michael D. Ward, "War and Peace in Space and Time: The Role of Democratization," *International Studies Quarterly* vol. 44, no. 1 (2000): 1–29.

may even be conflictual, but the nature of the conflict is more likely to involve external considerations, such as areas of influence and access to strategic resources, than the way power is exercised on the interior. This leads to the exclusion of nonstate actors from world politics, as they are considered to be a hindrance to the strategists' action. A *dynamic* policy pursued by the democracies accepts as a necessary evil the participation of authoritarian regimes in international organizations but at the same time favors contacts among civil societies, supporting and encouraging alternative leaders with the aim of isolating and eroding the legitimacy and internal power of autocratic regimes. Strategic considerations come second, and the champions of democracy can also make available resources and means as incentives to obtain a change of regime.

One wonders, however, if talking about democratizing the UN still makes any sense in the present political situation. After the Gulf War, would it not have been more productive to focus on reaffirming what was already written in the charter, namely, to reiterate the principle of the nonuse of military force except in self-defense? Would it not be necessary, rather than challenge the present constitution, to safeguard the principles of noninterference and self-determination? In my view, to reiterate what is valid in the charter does not necessarily mean running counter to the reform of the organization. Those opposed to multilateralism have a recurrent need to decry the UN for its inefficiency, the lack of democracy of the member states, and, of course, the fact that it does not meekly rubber stamp all the choices of the powers that are dominant today. It is only too easy to claim that the UN is not sufficiently democratic, but those that protest are often the same powers that do all they can to hinder reforms in that direction. The issue of the democratic reform of the UN thus has a political significance, as it shows that democracy may be achieved in the organization provided that there is a sufficient will to do so.

Proposed reforms have come from several different quarters. Ever since the beginning, a reforming frenzy has raged at the UN, which has so far borne very little fruit. In reviewing this now vast literature, let us attempt to appreciate the extent to which each of the proposed reforms approaches the conceptual model of cosmopolitan democracy. Here let us examine only four aspects of the multifaceted debate on UN reform: the SC, the judiciary, citizens' participation, and the safeguarding of human rights. These issues have been addressed not only and not so much in diplomatic fora, but above all by NGOs, independent researchers, and global movements. The principal recent proposals include the following:

1. The report tabled by the then secretary-general Kofi Annan at the 60th GA[9]
2. *An Agenda for Democratization,* the document that the then Secretary-General Boutros Boutros-Ghali presented on the very last day of his mandate, December 30, 1996 and that has never been properly debated.
3. The High-Level Panel on *Threats, Challenges and Change,* set up by the then Secretary General Kofi Annan, composed of sixteen members and chaired by the former prime minister of Thailand Anand Panyarachun.[10]
4. The High-Level Panel on UN-Civil Society set up by the then Secretary-General Kofi Annan, composed of twelve members and chaired by the former Brazilian president Fernando Enrique Cardoso.[11]
5. The Commission for Global Governance report chaired by Ingvar Carlsson and Shridath Ramphal.[12] Although dated, this report has been widely debated and still represents an authoritative position of liberal thinking.
6. The Socialist International "Position Paper," which, among other things, appealed to the party members in the government to support the proposals at the UN itself.[13]
7. The report of the "World Federalist Movement-Institute for Global Policy."[14]
8. The international campaign "Reclaim Our UN," coordinated by the Peace Round Table—Peoples' Assembly and developed as part of the World Social Forum.[15]
9. The proposals discussed and presented at the symposium "Envisioning a More Democratic Global System," Widener University School of Law, April 2006.[16]

9. UN, *In Larger Freedom: Towards Development, Security and Human Rights for All*, Report of the Secretary-General Kofi Annan (New York: UN, 2005).
10. UN, *More Secure World.*
11. UN, *We the Peoples.*
12. Commission for Global Governance, *Our Global Neighbourhood.*
13. Socialist International, *Reforming the United Nations for a New Global Agenda* (London: 2005) at www.socialistinternational.org/6Meetings/Council/MidEast-May05/Documents/English/UNReform-E.doc.
14. World Federalist Movement-Institute for Global Policy, *A Call for International Democracy* (New York, 2005), at www.globalpolicy.org.
15. Peace Round Table–Peoples' Assembly, *Reclaim Our UN* (Perugia: 2005), at www.reclaimourun.org.
16. "Envisioning a More Democratic Global System," *Widener Law Review*, special ed. Andrew Strauss, vol. 2, no. 13 (2007): 243–446.

I have listed together official documents, the works carried out by influential and authoritative commissions, and the proposals made by independent civil society organizations and academic scholars. All these initiatives combined proposals that lie halfway between formal reforms and informal ones. Formal reforms at UN level are often very difficult to achieve even though it is possible to make significant changes in practice and consuetudinary law. In fact, except for the enlargement of the elected members of the SC in 1963, further changes in the structure of the UN were achieved more in practice than by constitutional modification.

6.3 The Security Council

The SC represents the most extreme form of intergovernmental oligarchism. Inaccessible to any political subject that is not a government representative, the SC is dominated by five countries that, thanks to the dual privilege of being permanent members and of having the right to veto, actually succeed in monopolizing the organization's agenda. While it is true that the use of the power to veto has been substantially reduced since the end of the Cold War (it was used nearly 5 times per year between 1945 and 1996, but only 1.7 times per year over the past decade), the fact that the five permanent members can always throw down this singular trump card on the table does affect the position of the other members.[17] Moreover, the coexistence in the SC of permanent members and elected members violates one of the two basic principles of the UN and of IOs, namely, equality among members.

Although the SC functions were modeled on those of a state executive, the SC's composition makes the body quite different. Not even in an ideal type confederal model it is conceivable that the guarantee of peace and security should be entrusted to a small number of governments that are not requested to consult those who are directly involved. In a federalist model, the members of an executive would not be selected from among limited territorial authorities (no federal state has an executive composed exclusively of regional governors), but rather from agents representing all political players. Accepting that SC members are states is now a necessity because they are the actual depositaries of force. However, this does not mean that access should be denied to any other voices. A different composition of the SC could substantially change its

17. This has been defined as the "hidden veto"—cf. James Paul and Céline Nahory, *Theses Towards a Democratic Reform of the UN Security Council* (New York: Global Policy Forum, July 13, 2005).

authoritativeness. However necessary it may be the presence of states, including the most powerful ones, a counterweight of moral power is also needed. This requires the SC to include representatives who represent and can speak in the name of the general public, even though they can wield no force.

In whose name do the members of the SC act? The charter states that the SC "shall act in accordance with the Purposes and Principles of the United Nations" (art. 24, para. 2), although the charter does not specify the individual responsibility of each member. Some members claim that in the SC they must act exclusively to safeguard their own interests and those of their allies, so that one hears periodic references to "our nation's vital interests." It would instead be important to state clearly that in the SC each member must act in the general interest and not just in its own. Although only a formal aspect, from the terminological viewpoint such a statement would help clarify that the members are called upon to exercise a global responsibility. Theoretically, this approach would mean applying one of the primary principles of democracy, namely, that anyone holding office must act in the name of not only those whom they represent or who have elected them but of all members of the political community.

For the past fifteen years, the debate on reforming the UN has centered mainly around the possible enlargement of the SC. UN members have risen from the original 51 to the current 192. The first SC enlargement in 1963, when the elective seats were increased from six to ten, bringing the total number of seats to fifteen, has now become insufficient to guarantee efficiency and representativeness. Moreover, the relative strength among countries has changed considerably sixty years after the end of World War II. Japan and Germany not only have a larger population but pay into the organization's coffers much larger contributions than France and the United Kingdom (respectively, 18.9, 8.4, 5.9, and 5.9 percent of the ordinary budget). It is not surprising therefore that, discreetly but insistently, Japan and Germany have put in a request to have a permanent seat in the control room.

However, further enlargement to two northern countries would make the presence of the South in the UN even more marginal. It would be hard to justify on purely financial grounds the reason why India, with its one billion inhabitants, should be left out and Japan and Germany allowed in. If India's application were accepted, two entire regions would be left out, Africa and Latin America, and of course each would demand a permanent seat. Inside these regions, however, no agreement exists on the candidature of a single state. Brazil, for instance, although the largest country on Latin America, is also the only Portuguese-speaking rather than Spanish-speaking country and is somewhat frowned upon by the other Latin American countries. It is an even more difficult task to find a candidate that will satisfy all the peoples of Africa. In general the candidature of individual states is vigorously opposed by neighboring countries, rivals in the past, present, or future. The candidature of Japan aroused the hostility of China, that of Germany the opposition of Italy, that of India the refusal of Pakistan. Keeping everybody happy would mean turning the SC into such a huge organization that its operative capacity would be paralyzed. It is therefore not surprising that not even the high level commissions charged with implementing a proposal have been able to reach an agreement. A permanent seat on the SC has thus become a special kind of Figaro: everyone wants it but no one has got it. This is not necessarily bad news; the admission of new states having the power of veto would indeed likely paralyze the organization even more strongly.

Can the much-hoped-for occasion of SC reform enhance the representativeness and democratic nature of the UN? The criteria on which the democratic reform of the SC could be based may be summed up as follows:

- Each member must act not only in compliance with UN regulations and international law but also in the interest of all and not just of his own state.
- Although it is quite unrealistic to demand the abolition of the power of veto, it is advisable to restrict it to certain issues and to require that the countries that continue to make use of it pay a corresponding political price. As a first step, the charter should be applied in cases concerning (a) abstention from the vote when the members are involved parties (art. 27, para. 3) and (b) nonapplication of the right to veto on procedural questions (art. 27, para. 2).
- As far as the method of enlargement is concerned, the only feasible proposals are those that attract a very broad consensus. One of the most interesting and original proposals was made by Italian diplomacy in 1994. Probably intended to block the cooptation of Japan and, above all, Germany, Italy, encouraged by Ambassador Paolo Fulci, suggested enlarging the SC by creating a new category of ten "more frequently rotating" seats elected by the GA but reserved for a group of twenty countries.[18] These countries would be selected from among the more populous and those that

18. See Paolo Mastrolilli, *Lo specchio del mondo. Le ragioni della crisi dell'Onu* (Roma-Bari: Laterza, 2005), pp. 79 et seq. and Andrea De Guttry and Fabrizio Pagani, *Le Nazioni Unite* (Bologna: Il Mulino, 2005), pp. 153 et seq.

contribute more generously to the organization. This selection would facilitate an extremely necessary integration and political coordination at the local level. At the same time, the remaining ten seats would be available for the smaller countries, thus increasing those countries' chances of gaining access to the SC.

• Even though the principal members of the SC are the states, this does not mean that they should be exclusive members. In keeping with the intention to break with or at least limit intergovernmental oligarchism, it is more than ever necessary to attempt to open the SC up to other actors, such as the regional organizations. The EU is a natural candidate for a seat on the SC (the President of the European Commission has for many years been a participant at the G7 and now G8 summits). At a time in which the EU is moving toward a common foreign policy, it is hard to see why there are some EU members of the SC who vote in a different way (even though this problem concerns the EU and not the UN). In the future, the SC would open up to the other regional organizations, for instance, the Arab League, the Association of South-East Asian Nations, the African Union, Mercosur, and the North American Free Trade Agreement. This openness would allow two birds to be killed with one stone, as it would boost regional stability and at the same time increase the representativeness of the SC. Regional organizations would become permanent members as soon as they attained a certain degree of political and institutional cohesion, which would allow them to express a common foreign policy. There is no request to give the power of veto to the regional organizations, and it would already be an important achievement if the SC gave regional organizations merely a consultative vote.[19]

• It is not surprising that proposals made inside the UN, originating from government diplomatic representatives, have focused only on enlarging the SC to take in other states. The most radical proposal, however, involves the idea of opening the SC up to nongovernmental subjects. Global public opinion could make a useful contribution if it were successful in finding autonomous representation channels. It would be very useful if government choices could come to terms with the will of individuals, whose power would act as a counterweight to the power of governments. How can the voice of the citizens of the world have an institutional role? The royal road would consist of setting up a world parlia-

19. More radically, Paul and Nahory, *Theses Towards a Democratic Reform*, suggest that the SC could be more effective if all its members were regional organizations.

ment (see § 6.6), the executive organs of which had access to the SC. Secondarily, it could be envisaged that nongovernmental organizations recognized by the GA could elect their own representatives.

• The SC should also request more frequent consultative opinions, particularly when coercive instruments are involved, from the ICJ.

6.4 The Judiciary

The constitutionalists that drew up the UN Charter envisaged, albeit only *in nuce*, the separation of powers, as for constitutional states. Consequently, the SC was to represent the executive, the GA the legislative, and the ICJ the judiciary. As we have already seen in chapter 4, the cosmopolitan democracy model reserves a central role for the judiciary and, although it is still inconceivable that the executive should be subordinated to the judiciary, as is the case inside the various states, it is more than ever desirable that the judiciary should be reinforced. In compliance with this model, the juridical institutions of the UN, if suitably transformed, can help subject world politics to the scrutiny of legality.

It is not surprising that arbitration has become much more frequent in recent years. The Project on International Courts and Tribunals jointly promoted by New York University and the University of London has surveyed a large number of international judicial bodies plus eight different types of quasi-jurisdictional procedures, subdivided into extinct, dormant, existing, and proposed.[20] Many of these courts are competent for specific aspects and the contracting parties are not exclusively states. A wealth of arbitration mechanisms have been developed on the basis of functional interests, a kind of international administrative justice, to make up the judicial network of global governance.[21] Yet these arbitration mechanisms manage to be effective even without possessing an ultimate coercive power, perhaps because they do not affect the states' vital interests. In these cases, compliance with international administrative judicial power can be explained by the fact that reputation is an asset to

20. Basic information on this project can be consulted at www.pict-pcti.org. See Philippe Sands, Ruth Mackenzie, and Yuval Shany, *Manual on International Courts and Tribunals* (London: Butterworths, 1999) and Cesare Romano, Laurence Boisson de Charzournes, and Ruth MacKenzie, eds., *International Organizations and International Dispute Settlement: Trends and Prospects* (Ardsley, NY: Transnational, 2002).
21. As emphasized by Slaughter, *New World Order* and Sabino Cassese, "Administrative Law without the State?"

be safeguarded. In short, this is one of those cases in which exclusion is itself a powerful deterrent.

Here we are focusing on judicial power of a more specifically political nature. Let us continue to observe the distinction between the three spheres of judicial power (cf. § 4.4): (a) inside the states, (b) among states, and (c) global issues. I envisage an internal jurisdiction that remains the same except in the case in which the crimes committed are so egregious that the international community, by means of ad hoc instruments, decides to take judicial power into its own hands. In the case of disputes among states it is a matter of reinforcing the powers and jurisdiction of the international courts and, in the first instance, of the ICJ. Crimes that in size or nature are an offense against humankind instead come under the jurisdiction of global institutions such as the ICC. Currently the ICC can intervene solely in the case of individuals and only when the state judiciary systems have proved incapable or unwilling to open criminal proceedings. In this three-way split, disputes among states belong to the sphere of international law, while disputes concerning global issues are assigned to another sphere of law, cosmopolitan law.

REFORM OF THE INTERNATIONAL COURT OF JUSTICE

The ICJ statute follows that of the old Permanent Court of International Justice of the League of Nations, showing that at the end of World War II the innovations suggested in the doctrine by thinkers such as Hans Kelsen and others were not applied.[22] In the first place, the competence of the ICJ has continued to be limited to relations among states. In the second place, the ICJ has retained the old arbitration style structure and not introduced a jurisdictional structure. Although different modes of activating the court exist, current regulations mean that the ICJ can be competent only when the states are willing to accept its jurisdiction. Only sixty-five states have accepted the compulsory jurisdiction of the court. The fact that the activation of the court depends on the willingness of states to submit a case, and more precisely of a state to submit a case and of another state to accept jurisdiction, has obviously reduced the scope of the court's jurisdiction.

It is sufficient to glance through the eighty decisions and twenty-five consultative opinions handed down by the court since 1946 to realize that the ICJ's role has been completely marginal. Those decisions and opinions only touch upon completely secondary aspects of the political history of the past sixty years. The court expressed no opinion on the

22. Kelsen, *Peace through Law.*

legitimacy of atomic weapons, the wars in Indochina and Vietnam, or the invasions of Hungary, Czechoslovakia, and Afghanistan, nor did the court intervene in the invasion of Iraq. In some cases, the court must even reproach itself for not having taken a stance when it could have: in 1999, for instance, in the wake of the war waged by NATO against Serbia to combat the risk of genocide in Kosovo, the Yugoslav Federation called to account the various NATO countries. Included among the NATO countries were various western European countries that accepted the jurisdiction of the court a priori. The court, however, upheld—unanimously, to tell the truth—a procedural loophole, namely, the fact that the Yugoslav Federation had not adhered to the court under its new name, "Serbia and Montenegro."[23] It is one of those cases that confirm it is often not even necessary to make formal changes to the institutions; a little courage is often enough to make the court more active, particularly in view of the fact that the court itself decides whether or not it has jurisdiction. The impartiality of individual judges is also often questioned. Some statistical analysis of the voting patterns of the ICJ's judges has also indicated that the judges favor the states that appoint them and those close to their own states in terms of political systems and income levels.[24] These behaviors seriously undermine the authority of the court.

Over the past fifteen years, debate on reforming the international judicial system has been directed principally toward the establishment of the criminal court, consequently pushing the need for ICJ reform onto the back burner. What needs to be done instead is to bear in mind the role that a more aware judicial system can play. The main reform to be introduced is a fairly simple one that requires no change to be made in the UN charter or the ICJ statute; it is enough for all the member states of the organization to be obliged to accept the ICJ's jurisdiction. The court would therefore be able to make a decision whenever a state lodges a complaint without any objection by the opposite party succeeding in preventing the procedure. To increase the number of states that accept the automatic jurisdiction of the ICJ thus becomes the first step toward a more sophisticated international judicial system. More radically, it would be useful to overhaul the way the court is activated. Currently the court acts at the instigation of the states, while it should have a compulsory

---

23. Decisions of December 15, 2004 on the *Legality of Use of Force*, Serbia and Montenegro versus the majority of the EU's members of NATO. This decision was strongly criticized on both legal and political grounds. See, for example, Michael Mandel, *How America Gets Away with Murder* (London: Pluto Press, 2004).

24. Eric A. Posner and Miguel F. P. de Figueiredo, "Is the International Court of Justice Biased?" *Journal of Legal Studies* vol. 34, no. 2 (2005): 599–629.

jurisdiction and thus be activated whenever it deems the rules of international law have been violated.

It would be necessary to extend ICJ jurisdiction to include also non-state subjects such as collective groups, liberation movements, and insurgents. This extension would mean that the ICJ could treat all the disputes between collective groups with judicial instruments. As usual, what is at stake is that the opening of judicial channels to deal with disputes should lead to a reduction in the use of force. Likewise, the ICJ could at least condemn the unlawful use of force. The ICJ's role could be much greater if its judges decided to interpret their mandate more broadly. This leads us to the classic case in which consuetudinary law could, if accompanied by a little more courage, achieve as much as a formal reform.

What could a radical reform of the ICJ achieve? Such a reform could enable the ICJ to come up with decisions that declare when states' behavior is illegal and when acts of reparation are required. But even when the ICJ has handed down a decision, one cannot expect that the opposing parties will rush to comply with it, and the deliberations of the ICJ might well have no effect. The charter calls upon the states to accept the decisions of the ICJ (art. 94, para. 2); otherwise the coercive measures envisaged in chapter 7 will be meted out. This means that enforcement can be decided upon only by the SC. It is a known fact that numerous resolutions of the SC have remained a dead letter, and it is probable that the same thing will happen to the ICJ's decisions. However, those decisions would still consist of authoritative judicial statements that would affirm the rule of law over that of force. Above all, in countries with governments subjected to scrutiny by public opinion, the periodic violation of the dictates of the judicial authority would at least cause some embarrassment.

INTERNATIONAL CRIMINAL JUSTICE

With the encouragement of the United States, the World War II victors decided to prosecute a small number of persons responsible for crimes of aggression and crimes against humanity at Nuremburg and Tokyo. This prosecution entailed overturning the principles according to which no one can be held responsible for acts committed on behalf of a state or because the defendant was merely obeying orders. But another principle was violated with these tribunals, that of *nullum crimen nulla poena sine lex certa* (no crime, no punishment without a previous certain law), and the international community was expected to introduce suitable laws and instruments at least ex-post. The International Law Commission was charged to codify the norms emerging in the post–World War

168

II legal order, and as early as 1949 the commission approved the Nuremburg Principles, which were not, however, incorporated into new judicial institutions. Since the end of World War II, the cases of judicial proceedings started by national courts against those responsible for crimes against humanity, war crimes, and the crime of aggression committed outside their territorial jurisdiction have been relatively few and far between and their judicial legitimacy often controversial.[25] In the last decade, national courts became more active in an attempt to prosecute those responsible for crimes committed in other states (as in the case of General Augusto Pinochet).[26]

The SC's creation in 1993 and 1994 of two special tribunals for crimes against humanity in the former Yugoslavia and in Rwanda represented a fresh start. That the SC, an executive body, should establish ad hoc judicial bodies is an anomaly repeatedly pointed out by jurists. These ad hoc decisions have introduced a form of selectivity (why set up tribunals for the former Yugoslavia and Rwanda rather than for Iraq and East Timor?), which is in clear contradiction with the principle of equality before the law. An international criminal court could have been set up much earlier, and it would have been the logical consequence of approving the Nuremburg Principles. However, the states, including the permanent SC members, have made this kind of development impossible. The idea of introducing a criminal judicial power during the years of the Cold War was mere wishful thinking.

The political climate prevailing in the 1990s, however, finally allowed the establishment of the ICC, with the signing of the treaty in Rome in the Hall of the Horatii and Curiatii, on July 17, 1998. This was a historic event as, for the first time by means of an international treaty the member states accepted the principle of a possible criminal jurisdiction applicable to internal affairs. Of course, the progress of the court has been marked by setbacks. One hundred twenty states have so far signed the founding treaty, but those states that have not (yet?) include powerful countries like China, Russia, and the United States. However, the required ratification has proceeded with unexpected speed, and the judges

25. For an analysis of some of these cases, see Antonio Cassese, *Human Rights in a Changing World* (Cambridge: Polity Press, 1990) and Garapon, *Des crimes qu'on ne peut ni punir ni pardoner.*
26. The Pinochet case has been widely debated by jurists and public opinion. For a review, see Michael Byers, "The Law and Politics of the Pinochet Case," *Duke Journal of Comparative and International Law* vol. 10 (2000): 415–41. No less than Henry Kissinger, "The Pitfalls of Universal Jurisdiction," *Foreign Affairs* vol. 80, no. 4 (2001): 86–96, has attacked a supposed judicial tyranny.

were elected to the court on March 11, 2003, thus enabling the court to function with more than 100 participating states so far.

It is still too early to take stock of the action of the ICC, although it must be emphasized that the establishment of the ICC is the only significant constitutional reform introduced in the new international climate. The ICC was made possible by the combined efforts of courageous jurists and political leaders from developed and developing countries, but above all by the pressure exerted by global public opinion through numerous NGOs.[27] The question is why many governments of non-democratic countries or with recent or fragile democratic institutions (including, for example twenty-seven African states) have decided to subscribe to the court, while a longstanding democracy like the United States has opposed the court or exercised a kind of passive resistance.[28] The attitude of many unstable democracies is perhaps understandable: precisely because they are countries at greater risk of suffering a *coup d'état* and are places where massacres have taken place even in recent times, the ICC represents a preventive external protection against violent upheavals and atrocities. In other words, the ICC is aimed to protect the citizens from abuses committed by their current rulers but also government members themselves in the case of possible violent and unconstitutional regime changes.

It is less justifiable that the United States, the country that imposed the Nuremburg and Tokyo tribunals, that urged that *ad hoc* tribunals be set up for the former Yugoslavia and Rwanda, and that on numerous occasions backed up its national courts when they tried dictators and torturers in the developing countries, should refuse to participate in the

---

27. See Glasius, "Expertise in the Cause of Justice" and, more comprehensively, Marlies Glasius, *The International Criminal Court: A Global Civil Society Achievement* (London: Routledge, 2005).

28. During the Clinton administration, the United States had linked its acceptance to several pejorative amendments to the original statute, for example, by leaving the crime of aggression undefined and therefore not prosecutable. Subsequently, however, the Clinton administration signed the Rome Treaty on December 31, 2000. The Bush administration changed tack completely as anticipated in John R. Bolton, "The Risks and Weaknesses of the International Criminal Court from America's Perspective," *Law and Contemporary Problems* vol. 64, no. 1 (2001): 167–80. The American Servicemembers' Protection Act (August 2, 2003) codified opposition to the ICC. The Bush administration subsequently asked a growing number of countries, especially those benefiting from U.S. military assistance, to sign bilateral immunity agreements safeguarding its citizens from the possibility of being referred to the ICC. The position of the U.S. government on the ICC is monitored and discussed by the Global Policy Forum at www.globalpolicy.org.

ICC from the outset. Until the ICC's performance is assessed, it seems essential that the number of member states should be increased. Also the bilateral immunity agreements that nullify the Court's work ought to be considered illegitimate.

At the theoretical level, should the ICC be considered part of interstate law or of cosmopolitan law (see § 4.7)? From the formal point of view, the ICC corresponds totally to an institution of interstate law: it was established by a treaty signed by sovereign states, even outside the UN system. Any amendment to the existing statute can only follow in the same direction. The member states have therefore delegated a considerable portion of their own sovereignty to another organization. But because of the court's independence and the fact that it is called upon to judge individuals, the ICC appears as an institution inspired by cosmopolitan law, aimed at defending and even repressing violations of legality wherever they occur. The ICC is the judicial instrument that gives material effect to the principles of Nuremburg, thus allowing the repression of crimes committed in many states. It is certainly a logical contradiction that the first effective institution governed by cosmopolitan law should be established by the states while its main function is precisely to judge any unpunished breaches of law within the states. Conceptually, cosmopolitan law should receive its own legitimacy from a worldwide legislative assembly. However, politics does not follow a logical path and it is difficult to imagine the ICC being set up in any other way: no institutions exist for citizens of the world, and even if they did they would not have sufficient powers to oblige the states to collaborate. All we can do is acknowledge that cosmopolitan judicial power is today in advance of the legislative and executive powers. This reinforces the idea that the states can act as champions of cosmopolitanism.

6.5 World Citizens at the United Nations

Calls have often been made for the voice of the citizens of the world to be heard in an independent and parallel fashion with respect to their representation in their own states. The most suitable institution in which world citizen's voices can be heard is precisely the UN, which would thereby finally be able to fulfill the promise expressed in the preamble to the charter, "We the peoples of the United Nations." The absence of any direct channels of contact among individuals means that the life of the UN is even further removed from the life of the people, to the point that the people are totally misinformed as to the functions, tasks and costs associated with the organization. In order for the UN to become the fulcrum of cosmopolitan democracy, it is necessary to bring world citizens closer to the life of the organization. The very idea of democracy is based on the principle of those who are governed participating in the choice of those who govern and until such time as the UN hears the peoples' voice in making its decisions there will be a deficit of legitimacy.

Whereas the confederal model does not require any direct citizen participation, in the federal model the citizens are expected to contribute and to express a legislative and executive power. The aims of the cosmopolitan model are more limited and directed towards providing the citizens with a channel of autonomous representation that is characterized by a vast jurisdiction but limited powers. Many proposals have been made in this sense (see § 6.2) some resting on a major constitutional reform, others trying to progressively modify current institutions and practices. Also, in this case a global commonwealth is more likely to be the result of progressive reforms than the consequence of a single rational plan. The fundamental incremental steps that could be taken to attain this aim are set out in the following section.

FOR A WORLD PARLIAMENTARY ASSEMBLY

The dream of an elected WP directly representing the peoples of the world rather than their governments is as old as it is ambitious. Electing a WP is an idea that has been championed for decades by the federalist movements, and has received widespread support from NGO's and even from the European and Canadian parliaments and this idea has come back into fashion in recent years.[29] A world parliamentary assembly would solve the problems of representativeness and legitimacy encountered by any global democracy project, as it would again place decision-making power directly in the hands of a body representing all the inhabitants of the Earth. But which functions and what jurisdiction should be attributed to such a body are still a moot point. The more ambitious the tasks envisaged, the less likely it is that the proposal will be implemented, as it would inevitably lead to a redistribution of authority,

29. Clark and Sohn, *World Peace through World Law*, designed a WPA on the ground of an ambitious constitutional reform of the UN. Recent advocates include the Socialist International, *Reforming the United Nations*, Falk and Strauss, "Toward Global Parliament"; Monbiot, *Age of Consent*; and a wealth of NGOs for global justice and democracy. See Saul H. Mendlovitz and Barbara Walker, eds., *A Reader on Second Assembly and Parliamentary Proposals* (Wayne, NJ: Center for UN Reform Education, 2003). The Committee for a Democratic UN is currently promoting a world campaign; see the Web site www.uno-komitee.de.

legitimacy, and power. Assigning to a WPA all the powers and functions normally associated with the national parliaments would mean taking a decisive step toward a federalist model. Such a step, it has been argued, is not only unrealistic but perhaps not even desirable.

Even without being able to express executive power, a WPA would have to have a very wide jurisdiction and represent a forum where the main world problems such as economic and social development, the defense of human rights, the promotion of political participation and the safeguard of the environment, could be discussed. The WPA could begin by advising the GA, the SC, the UN specialized agencies and other IOs. The WPA's main function would be orientation and policy setting. Even if it had no effective power, the WPA would be the visible and tangible demonstration of the institutionalization of a global commonwealth of citizens. The WPA should aim, however, at increasing its powers, albeit only in substantially limited areas, and at being able to have direct powers in emergencies and exceptionally serious situations only. These WPA powers should be focused on three areas:

1. Protection of fundamental human rights, also with the possibility of deciding on humanitarian intervention in matters of survival.
2. Proactive capacity—in the case of disputes—to redefine the boundaries and jurisdiction of the various political communities.
3. Identification of the most appropriate level of governance in the case of cross-border problems involving political communities. As pointed out in section 4.3, this action would entail the capacity to define the decision-making role played by the various stakeholders. For example, the WPA should have the power to indicate the decision-making authority and the forms of representation of the cross-border organizations.

Who should take part in the election of deputies to the assembly? Mention has already been made of the utility of leaving the intergovernmental bodies open to nondemocratic states (see § 4.4) But the same principle is not valid for a parliamentary assembly. In this case, priority would have to be given to the criterion of legitimacy rather than to that of efficacy. Autocratic governments would thus have the option of allowing free elections, albeit only to elect their own delegates to the WPA, or else of not being represented in the WPA and therefore increasing their own isolation. For its part, the WPA could decide to invite to its own work as observers representatives of the civil society of countries ruled by autocratic governments.

A WP could be set up by a demanding constitutional reform or, more directly, by the GA as its subsidiary body. The existing charter (art. 22) states that "the General Assembly may establish such subsidiary organs as it deems necessary for the performance of its functions." More realistically, Strauss has suggested following the same pattern that has successfully led to the making of the ICC, namely, a treaty signed by a group of like-minded states, in the hope that other states will follow if the venture is successful.[30]

What could such a WPA look like? It might be instructive to review some of the proposals made. Monbiot proposed a parliament composed of some six hundred members elected by the inhabitants of the planet using a proportional system.[31] A perhaps more realistic proposal was made over fifteen years ago by Jeffrey Segall, the tireless champion of the Conferences for a More Democratic United Nations.[32] His proposal envisaged a parliamentary assembly comprising some six hundred deputies, but one in which a more than proportional representation was accorded to the smaller countries and a less than proportional one to the larger countries. Segall suggested assigning one seat to all countries with a population of fewer than one million, while the most populous country, China, would have thirty-one seats. Segall's criterion obviously attributes much greater clout to the smaller countries, thus offsetting the excessive influence that might otherwise be wielded by a few countries with very large populations. This could be justified by the fact that, as they exist today, countries represent historical entities reflecting the planet's diversity.[33]

The most significant case of an international parliament is of course the European Parliament, which today comprises deputies elected in twenty-seven member countries. Although having only limited powers, the European Parliament provides a platform for debate and for the organization of cross-border interests. National MPs belong to different groups of different political color, which engenders debate that does not principally reflect the national interests but rather different values. It is

30. See Strauss, *Taking Democracy Global*, which also contains a discussion of the advantages and disadvantages associated with the various options.
31. Monbiot, *Age of Consent*, p. 133.
32. Jeffrey Segall, "A UN Second Assembly," pp. 93–109 in *Building a More Democratic United Nations*, ed. Frank Barnaby (London: Frank Cass, 1991).
33. Already in the eighteenth century, the Abbot of Saint-Pierre observed that the smaller states, precisely because they wield less power, are more favorable to a balanced international politics and therefore that it will be advantageous for the stability of the international order to grant them a more than proportional electoral weight. Charles Irénée Castel de Saint-Pierre, *Project pour render la paix perpétuelle en Europe* (Paris: Fayard, [1713–1717] 1986), pp. 187–91.

also interesting to note that on many occasions the European MPs are more in favor of European proposals than their colleagues in the same party and the same country but elected in the national parliaments. This confirms that, in this case, clothes do make the man, and membership of a given institution also modifies the political priorities.

The current proposals follow the idea that the electoral constituencies, as in the case of the European Parliament, should be situated in the territorial states. But nothing prevents the electoral constituencies from being intended for different types of political community and that, for example, areas inhabited by the same people but split by several frontiers can come together to elect their own representatives. Or to decide which border areas in conflict belong to the same electoral constituency. Or to reserve some seats for nonterritorial communities such as the Roma people, immigrants, or even communities linked by specific joint vital interests.

TRANSITIONAL STEPS

The prospect of a WPA is now discussed at Porto Alegre and in other global gatherings and is increasingly the subject of academic debate. However, practically all traces of this prospect have faded away in the diplomatic corridors, which goes to show that, at the present state of affairs, the idea is still shrouded in the misty reign of utopia. But there are a number of ongoing initiatives that should be mentioned. There are also several, and not necessarily conflicting, transitional steps that may be taken to make the voice of the people heard in world politics.

One significant experiment was attempted by the Assembly of Peoples of the United Nations organized by the Italian peace movement since 1995, on the occasion of the commemoration of the first fifty years of the UN. This was an event with a high symbolic value, to which the organizers invited representatives of critical situations: marginalized ethnic groups, stateless peoples, and members of NGOs. Argentina was represented by the "Madres de Plaza de Mayo," the association of relatives of the *desaparecidos*; the Kurdish people by representatives of Turkish, Iraqi, and Iranian nationality; the United States by a Harlem community. There were many representatives of peoples without a state: Roma, Palestinians, Tamils, Berbers, and Chechens. Other Assemblies of Peoples were held biannually. These assemblies heard the cry for help from persons representing millions and millions of individuals who do not have access to the GA or whose official representatives follow agendas in contrast with their interests. Concrete proposals emerged for a different way of managing the planet and for a reform of the economic institutions and of the UN itself. Can these assemblies be considered "dress rehearsals" for a forthcoming WPA? Perhaps. Nevertheless, two issues remain unresolved. The first issue refers to the representativeness of those participating in the assemblies. The second issue is the capacity of so many proposals to attain shared solutions. To be against the dominant system is enough to express an alternative proposal but not necessarily to convene toward such a project a sufficiently broad consensus to achieve it.

The UN has already acknowledged that civil society has an important role to play. Ever since the 1992 Rio de Janeiro Summit, international NGOs have always participated actively to the summits.[34] Before many other IOs, the UN has played an important role in transposing the NGOs from the streets to the corridors, and from the corridors to the debating assembly rooms. It is important today to take one further step and to formalize the role played and the tasks involved. In the last few years, decisive steps in this direction were taken precisely at UN headquarters. For example, the GA has already demanded an "Informal Hearing of the General Assembly with non-governmental organizations, civil society organizations and the private sector," which was held prior to its sixtieth session in New York (June 23–24, 2005). An informal hearing may not seem to be very much, especially if those involved in the hearing have not themselves received any legitimization from "the peoples of the United Nations." But the fact that the governments represented in the GA feel the need for such an initiative is perhaps a sign that the time is ripe for more radical reforms. It is a pity that this initiative has not become a regular feature and that currently there is no intention to repeat it.

A first step could be to increase participation of the national parliamentary institutions. The WPA could initially be set up as a "second tier" parliament, the members of which are nominated by the national parliaments, following the procedure already successfully tested in the European Parliament until election by universal suffrage was introduced in 1979. This step would have the advantage of bringing not only the majorities but also the minorities closer to the life of the organization and could lead to a subdivision into parliamentary groups not necessarily along geographic but along political lines. A large number of IOs, including the Council of Europe, NATO, and the Organization for Security and Co-operation in Europe, already have among their bodies parliamentary assemblies composed by Members of Parliament chosen by the respective national parliaments.[35] And it is certainly sur-

---

34. See Pianta, *UN World Summits and Civil Society.*
35. For a review of these "transnational parliamentary assemblies" and an assessment of their effective role in the governance of international organizations, see Stefan Marschall, "Neoparlamentarische Demokratie jenseits des Nationalstaates? Transnationale Versammlungen in internationalen Organisationen," *Zeitschrift fur*

prising that the wider IO, the UN, has no direct link yet with national parliaments.[36]

The second step involves aiming at a reinforcement of the institutions of civil society and thereby extending political representativeness with respect to the way in which civil society is expressed in the internal politics of the states. It has been suggested, for example, that an assembly composed of the approximately six thousand NGOs recognized by the UN be set up, thus making NGOs' participation in the UN permanent, which has thus been rendered visible in the case of the various thematic summits, in the case of the Millennium Assembly (2000), and on numerous other occasions. In practice, it would be a question of institutionalizing the informal Consultation held in the run up to the sixtieth GA. This would leave open, however, the problem of the representativeness of such an assembly.

The third transition step consists of organizing a WP symbolically outside the UN with the resources of global civil societies. Such an independent parliament may acquire legitimacy only if a substantial number of players in world politics (political parties, global movements, and other associations) are committed to the venture. If such an initiative were to gain authoritativeness, it would become more difficult to oppose the making of a more institutional WPA.[37]

WHAT STATES CAN DO

States can autonomously, and without necessarily obtaining the approval of the other states, bring their own citizens closer to the UN. Indeed, the way ambassadors to the UN are nominated is exclusively the prerogative of the national state. Whenever a state wishes to enlarge the representativeness of the delegation, nothing prevents the state from

---

Parlamentsfragen vol. 37, no. 4 (2006): 683–97. Their existence is one of the criteria employed by Zweifel, *International Organizations and Democracy*, to assess the relative level of democracy of the various IOs.

36. A significant experiment in this direction is represented by the attempt to link elected members of national parliaments through the Web. See the venture E-parliament in Action at www.e-parl.net. See Robert C. Johansen, "An E-Parliament to Democratize Globalization," pp. 93–117 in *A Reader on Second Assembly and Parliamentary Proposals*, ed. Mendlovitz and Walker.

37. Bruno S. Frey and Alois Stutzer, "Strengthening the Citizens' Role in International Organizations," *Review of International Organizations* vol. 1, no. 1 (2006): 27–43, suggest increasing people's participation in IOs by choosing a random sample of citizens. They could act as trustees and express their opinion on the various choices faced by the IOs.

working to obtain representativeness on the inside. There are many possible ways of doing this. One way is to make the nomination of ambassadors the responsibility of the parliament rather than of the government, so as to involve both government and opposition parties. It has also been proposed to make at least one of the five representatives of each country at the UN an elected office. A process of election would bring the peoples closer to the action of the UN, and the election campaign itself could become a way to advertise issues for which the UN is competent. Election of representatives would also allow government and opposition to be involved and thus extend the representativeness of the delegation. These proposals are based on an implicit assumption: conventional diplomacy in IOs and at the UN in particular is now old fashioned. Life at the UN would reap a benefit from having a diplomatic corps with a more active function than that of mere representation, and having a stronger participation than that provided by the government could facilitate the attainment of this goal.

6.6 Defense of Human Rights

THE HUMAN RIGHTS COUNCIL

One of the main contradictions of the UN is that on the topic of human rights the UN utters solemn and pompous declarations followed by weak and slow procedures and inconclusive and clumsy instruments.[38] The 1948 Universal Declaration of Human Rights and the 1966 Pacts dedicated respectively to civil and political rights and economic, social, and cultural rights confirm an extremely wide range of norms. However, the teeth and claws that the UN can use to defend them are not strong enough. This weakness is the result of the constitution of the UN itself and the great reverence in which the principle of sovereignty is held. The bulk of the UN human rights regime is, in fact, based on the assessment of members' situations, an assessment mainly carried out by other members.

It is therefore a shared opinion, to quote Kofi Annan, that on the subject of human rights, the UN must finally move on from the era of legislation to that of their implementation. It is inconceivable that greater elements of democracy can be introduced into the UN if, at the same time, the UN does not become more effective in promoting and protecting

---

38. A broad overview of the international dimension of human rights is provided in Jack Donnelly, *Universal Human Rights in Theory and Practice*, 2nd ed. (Ithaca, NY: Cornell University Press, 2003).

individual rights inside the states. The ICC does not have the task or the possibility of becoming a higher tribunal for the protection of human rights; the ICC can only concern itself with contingent and exceptionally serious violations. For this reason, it is essential for the UN to continue assessing the national systems, reinforcing this assessment, and denouncing those regimes that are inadequate overall, not just in individual cases. This is a dual strategy: on the one hand, the UN must continue to monitor the extent to which human rights, defined in the broad sense according to existing legislation, are effectively safeguarded in each state; on the other, the UN must concentrate its direct executive on the criminal prosecution of exemplary cases and on protecting groups exposed to major violations.

In the UN, the system adopted for assessing the human rights regime is complex and clumsy. The member states sitting on the Commission on Human Rights often committed blatant violations at home, discrediting the whole organization, the experts, and the NGOs that were fighting to obtain tangible results. Only recently, on March 15, 2006, did the GA approve the formation of a Human Rights Council to replace the preceding commission whose forty-seven members are elected directly by the GA rather than by the Economic and Social Council. The most significant novelty is that the member states are supposed to be chosen for the capacity they demonstrate to protect human rights internally and, during their mandate, agree to be subjected to a review of their own internal situation carried out by the council itself. This is supposed to discourage states that systematically violate human rights in their own backyard from being candidates and to guarantee that the states that are members of the council are exemplary models.

It is still too early to decide whether the new Human Rights Council will succeed in taking more decisive action than its predecessor. However, two aspects already indicate that the new institution has inherited the weaknesses of the preceding organization. The first aspect is its composition, which is still exclusively intergovernmental. Nongovernmental actors can participate, but only at the invitation of a government. As a result, it is no longer possible to reserve seats for institutions such as Amnesty International, Human Rights Watch, and the International Peoples' Tribunal, which have previously displayed competence, impartiality, and passion in defending human rights. In the present situation there is no guarantee that the assessment of human rights will come within the sphere of the negotiations conducted by the diplomacy of the states. The second aspect is related to the fact that very few instruments continue to be available to the council. Condemnation and culpability are not followed up. If human rights are to be defended, credible incentives are needed. The EU obtained tangible results when it linked membership of the new states to the respect of human rights and the introduction of democratic institutions. The incentive—participation in the common market—was sufficiently strong to convince the respective governments to undertake radical transformations. Unfortunately, the UN is unable for the time being to offer such significant incentives.

What incentives could the UN use? One idea is to link the instruments of the financial institutions, such as the IMF and the World Bank, to the respect of human rights. The financial institutions impose a number of conditions before granting their loans and aid, although these conditions are conventionally economic. Coordination between the council and the economic development agencies could provide a way to couple recommendations with tangible incentives.

The time has also come for the UN no longer to stop short at assessing the existing human rights regime in each country but to begin to take also the efficacy of its democratic institutions into account. Human rights violations represent the pathological side of a political system; the system's democratic institutions make up its physiology. And there is nothing better than a sound physiology for reducing and restricting pathological degeneration. For this reason, at the UN it has become urgent to assess existing constitutional systems on a consensual basis by extending the practice of making recommendations, as is the rule in the human rights field. The work done so far on a voluntary basis by NGOs (cf. § 2.5) would gain in authoritativeness if it were carried out within the UN.

THE PROTECTION OF REFUGEES

Among the many activities carried on by the UN, one is of particular importance as regards the topic of cosmopolitan citizenship—that on behalf of refugees. Through its High Commission for Refugees, the UN provides assistance for about nineteen million persons, some nine million of whom are international refugees and the others displaced persons who have had to abandon their place of residence but continue to live inside their own country. Through the United Nations High Commissioner for Refugees, assistance and protection are provided for displaced persons and refugees. Aid distribution affords the refugees material survival, and at the same time the commission endeavors to shelter them from risk factors such as wars and conflicts. This entails a huge effort, and the UNHCR alone provides protection for about half the individuals living in these conditions. It often happens that the UNHCR has to shoulder all the responsibility for refugee assistance without, however, being given the necessary powers. In a world of sovereign states it is the governments that allow displaced persons to cross their frontiers, and it is again the governments that set the duration and place of hospitality accorded to refugees on their own territory. Numerous obligations are imposed on the states by international treaties, but the UNHCR has no way of ensuring those treaties are enforced.

Refugees are the classic problem that everyone would like to offload onto others. Except in the case of natural disasters (which are generally accompanied by a temporary status), the states of origin have little desire to see their citizens repatriated. The abandonment actually takes place as a consequence of a (political, ethnic, or some other kind of) conflict that has to all intents and purposes made these groups of persons undesirable inside their own state. Likewise, the host states are often obliged to accept these populations out of necessity, in conditions of total precariousness, and for an uncertain duration. Moreover, in many refugee camps there are armed groups that represent a threat to security for the host state. The risk of having to receive masses of refugees is distributed randomly: states with unstable neighbors have a greater likelihood of receiving undesirable refugee flows. The 1951 Convention relating to the status of refugees imposes the obligation of providing assistance in the case of need but not the obligation for the load to be spread among all the members of the international community. The neighbor of a country torn by civil war is more at risk than a desert island. It is therefore not fair that some states should have to devote greater energy and resources than others to assisting refugees.

Refugees are economically and socially vulnerable categories. They are persons who have had to abandon their homes and their network of social and professional contacts, often at a moment's notice. The fact that refugees find themselves in a situation of uncertainty regarding their own future (When, if, and under what conditions will they be able to return to their customary place of residence? In which part of the world will they have to begin a new life?) paralyzes their chances to begin a new existence. For these reasons, refugees are the group most in need to exercise the rights of citizenship they have lost de facto if not de jure in their country of origin and that they cannot exercise de jure in the host country.[39] In reforming the UN it would be important to guarantee security and rights to these groups of persons more fully by performing that role of subsidiarity vis-à-vis state citizenship that lies at the heart of the cosmopolitan democracy project. One possibility would be for the UN to issue these nine million inhabitants of the planet (only 1.5 per thousand of the total population) a true cosmopolitan citizenship.

39. See Hassner, "Refugees: A Special Case for Cosmopolitan Citizenship?" in *Re-Imagining Political Community*, ed. Archibugi et al. and, more broadly, Benhabib, *Rights of Others*.

This would mean giving refugees certain rights (for instance, that of holding a passport and therefore of being able to move internationally) and at the same time regulating their right to receive the assistance that they already receive from the UNHCR and other UN agencies.

The practical problems that issuing refugees with cosmopolitan citizenship would create cannot be passed over in silence. The states, both those of origin and the host states, might envisage washing their hands of the matter by passing the problem of accepting refugees and their ultimate accommodation to another institution, tasks that currently lie outside UN powers. Indeed, it is precisely the case of refugees that spells out the sense of cosmopolitan citizenship: it is not a matter of replacing state citizenship, but merely of supplementing it. This approach should not lead to an elimation of the obligations of the states of origin toward their own citizens but indeed lead to an acceptance that the international community can act in defense of individuals. During a transition period, cosmopolitan citizenship would provide the judicial instrument for allowing the UNHCR to manage the flows of refugees toward the host countries and, if necessary, to divide the refugees among several different countries. Establishing cosmopolitan citizenship for refugees would ultimately allow the refugees to return and live in safety in their own country. To shoulder this new international responsibility, the UN must also increase its own capacity to deal with the internal problems underlying this issue.

It is often said that cosmopolitan citizenship is something elitist, a privilege for privileged groups who travel and have a network of social connections in several countries. This concept of cosmopolitan citizenship is essentially dependent on its sociological rather than judicial dimension. But if the first to obtain cosmopolitan citizenship as a judicial title were the refugees, who can justly be considered the "damned of the Earth" of our era, cosmopolitan citizenship would be an instrument to protect the underprivileged. In the future cosmopolitan citizenship could be envisaged to extend to other needy categories: after the refugees, immigrants would be a category that could benefit from it.

6.7 From Criticism to Reform

In this chapter I have concentrated solely on a few of the proposed UN reforms. I have focused attention on the ideas that are more directly associated with the cosmopolitan democracy project in order to set up a conceptual link between the model presented in part one and the principal contemporary IO. No space has been devoted to the essential reform of specialized agencies, including financial institutions.[40] Although equally necessary for the purpose of achieving a more stable, transparent, and responsive global governance, these reforms are less directly linked to the constitutional aspects of a cosmopolitan democracy.

I am fully aware that it might appear odd to propose such bold reforms at a time in which the UN is under daily attack. All possible means have been employed to diminish the UN's authority. The UN has been accused of being inefficient, and yet whenever a natural disaster looms, or an epidemic, a genocide, or a war, all responsibility is offloaded onto its shoulders. The UN is said to be too expensive, overlooking the fact that its total budget amounts to only $13 billion a year, less than what the city of New York alone spends on education. The UN is blamed for too much red tape, when it has only sixty-one thousand employees, fewer than the Italian Tax Police. The UN is also accused of being undemocratic, which is true. But all those who believe that democracy is the most efficient way of managing power should not dodge the issue of trying to apply democracy to the functioning of the UN. As far as democracy is concerned, it is not simply a matter of transposing the state dimension onto that of the IOs. The proposals for reform presented in this chapter show that nothing stands in the way of applying democratic methods and values to the UN.

40. Cf. Patomaki and Teivainen, *A Possible World*; Zweifel, *International Organizations and Democracy*. For a critical overview, see Held, *Global Covenant*.

Chapter 7
Cosmopolitanism and Humanitarian Intervention

7.1 The Cosmopolitanism of Survival

In July 1995, during the final phases of the bloody civil war in the former Yugoslavia, fighting raged on in the Bosnian enclave of Srebrenica, which was populated by Muslims but claimed also by the Serbs. The town had been declared a "safe haven" by the UN Security Council on April 15, 1993 (Resolution 819), like other cities under siege in Bosnia-Herzegovina such as Sarajevo, Tuzla, Mostar, and Zepa. The UN had thus sent an unequivocal political message to the Bosnian Serbs led by Radovan Karadžić and General Ratko Mladic and indirectly to the Serbian government of Slobodan Milosevic. In the event the promised protection was much weaker than guaranteed and the other cities with a majority Muslim-Bosnian population were periodically attacked by Bosnian Serb soldiers. Ambushes, summary executions, and rape were the daily fare of the civil war.

Despite the siege, many displaced Muslims, also on the strength of the Security Council commitment, sought refuge in Srebrenica, which was considered safer than other localities. The presence outside the city, in the Potočari area, of some four hundred Dutch blue helmets under the command of Commander Tom Karremans, represented a protection that was not only military but above all political. On July 11, 1995, following a fiercer attack than usual, the weakened defenses collapsed completely and the Bosnian Serb irregular troops entered the city. In the preceding days NATO air forces had attempted to dissuade the attack by carrying out a number of low-level flights but, not having received the order to open fire, which could come only from the UN High Command, and in particular from the French general Bernard Janvier, they did not appreciably deter the attackers. On the day of the attack, NATO aircraft destroyed a couple of Bosnian Serb tanks, but then operations had to be called off for reasons of poor visibility and above all owing to the possible reprisals to which the Dutch blue helmets would be exposed. After the front collapsed, between twenty and twenty-five thousand now-unarmed Muslims gathered at Potočari, around the blue helmets' camp, pleading to be saved. A Dutch soldier told the population that they could not protect them and invited them to disperse. None of the blue helmets gave them any precise information as to where to go and how to get there.

General Mladic entered the city, intoxicated with joy, and immediately had some Muslim signs taken down and went to parley with Commander Karremans. They smoked a cigarette together, had a drink, and discussed the differences between soldiers and politicians. They then negotiated the withdrawal of the blue helmets. In the meantime, in the area around the camp, witnesses were talking of piles of dead bodies, cases of rape, and even children's throats being cut in front of their parents. A few thousand Muslim men decided to try to escape into the woods; others put themselves under the protection of the blue helmets. The day after, the Bosnian Serb occupiers separated women and children from the men who had stayed behind. Women and children were loaded onto buses brought in from Sarajevo and transferred to a camp hastily set up in Tuzla, beside the airport runway. Many of the fleeing men were captured, while those who stayed behind in Potočari were taken prisoner. Soon after this they were murdered and buried in mass graves. Their fate became known only after U.S. intelligence sources produced aerial photographs showing mounds of fresh earth that were believed to be possible mass graves. It is estimated that over 7,800 unarmed men were murdered.

The Srebrenica massacre represented a turning point in the Bosnian affair. Such was the shame felt by the international community that the UNPROFOR (UN Protection Force) mission was terminated forthwith and replaced by the much more robust IFOR (Peace Implementation Force) mission under NATO command, making it quite clear that a second massacre would not be tolerated. However, the Srebrenica enclave had now been lost by the Bosnian Muslims, and this was taken into account in dividing up the territory among the different ethnic groups. It was one of the largest massacres to take place in Europe since the end of World War II and one of the gloomiest pages in UN history. In other parts of the world—in Cambodia, in Rwanda—even larger massacres than the Srebrenica one had taken place, but there had been no explicit UN commitment to protect the civilian populations that had been disavowed, with unarmed men actually being abandoned in the hands of those who were to murder them only a few hours later. In April 2002, following the publication of several film sequences shot by Bosnian Serb soldiers and of a special investigation, the Dutch government led by Wim Kok resigned as a result of the way its troops had behaved.

KOSOVO 1999

Four years later, after the war in Bosnia had been brought to a laborious close, new conflicts broke out in neighboring Kosovo, where a precarious coexistence had been established between the Serb-speaking population of Greek Orthodox religion, which represented about 10 percent of the population, and the Albanian-speaking majority of Muslim faith. While the Albanian population was demanding independence and backing up its claim by means of guerrilla operations, the Yugoslav state intervened in defense of the Serb population, often by carrying out indiscriminate reprisals. A number of mass killings took place, mostly of Albanians. NATO placed the region under its control as a precise consequence of the Srebrenica massacre and held a series of talks in February 1999 at Rambouillet castle (Paris) with Kosovo separatists and the Yugoslav government. After considerable pressure had been exerted, the agreement was signed by the Kosovo separatists but not by the Serbs. Russia considered that too much had been demanded of Serbia, and also NATO countries such as Italy and Greece deemed the requests presented not a fair basis for an agreement.

As the winds of war gathered, the atrocities committed by both sides increased, initially directed mainly against the Albanian population. This period marked the beginning of the Albanian exodus from Kosovo, which involved as many as 850,000 persons (out of a total of about two million inhabitants). In March 1999, NATO began heavy bombing of Serbia and Kosovo, hitting not only military targets but also civilian targets. There were numerous errors, which caused a number of civilian victims estimated at between 1,200 and 5,000 persons. The use of fragmentation bombs increased the number of civilian victims, while the use of depleted uranium munitions led to a still-to-be-quantified increase in the incidence of tumors, which affected also NATO troops even though they had spent only a limited period in the area.

Many of the mass graves found at the end of the war could be traced to massacres having occurred after the end of the negotiations and during the NATO air strikes. Even though official sources have attempted on numerous occasions to minimize the number of civilian victims, it would appear that more victims were caused by aerial bombardments than by ethnic cleansing. Even the chairman of NATO Military Command, General Naumann, expressed dissatisfaction with the effectiveness of the intervention: "Promised on humanitarian needs, it was difficult to defend the NATO intervention logically and politically when it was initially causing damage but did not prevent the expulsion of Kosovars. That a huge outflow of refugees followed the initial bombing was, embarrassing, to say the least."[1] At the end of the acute phase of the conflict, the same type of intimidation and violence was inflicted on the new Serbian minority.

TOO MUCH AND TOO LITTLE

I have compared two well-known and tragic events that apparently encapsulate contradictory ethical issues. Only a few years after these events the general impression is that, in both cases, the international community should have done more and better. However, the crimes with which the international community has besmirched itself are quite different and indeed opposite. In the first case, it was guilty of indifference, as it did not have the courage to stick its neck out enough to avoid a massacre and, more in general, to avert a bloody civil war. In the second, possibly in the grip of guilt feelings at not having intervened effectively on the previous occasion, it became involved in a violent intervention that probably did more harm than good. In the first case, it intervened too little and too late; in the second, too much and too early. Similar dilemmas are the order of the day; in Darfur and Sierra Leone, in Sri Lanka and East Timor, and in many other places in the past and in the present and, we may sadly prophesy, also in the future. What may be demanded and expected of the international community?

The fall of the Berlin wall did not lead to the end of democides, but it became increasingly difficult for public opinion to accept them. In which cases, with what institutions, and using what tools must the international community intervene? How would the history of Bosnia-Herzegovina have changed if the international community had drawn upon its political and military resources to defend Srebrenica? How many Albanians would have been killed in Kosovo if NATO had not intervened? The question of whether or not it is effective to act will always accompany

1. Klaus Naumann, "Nato, Kosovo, and Military Intervention," *Global Governance* vol. 8, no. 1 (2002): 13–17, on p. 15.

each humanitarian intervention, but history is not counterfactual. Humanitarian intervention cannot even be assessed solely in terms of contingent efficacy: scandalous violations of human rights must be prevented, opposed, and even repressed in order to deprive possible perpetrators of the certainty of impunity.

Humanitarian intervention is not a concern specific to cosmopolitan thinking alone. Quite the contrary. Nationalists and communitarians, realists and idealists have on a number of occasions raised the problem of how to oppose genocides and mass murder.[2] However, cosmopolitanism adopts a specific approach to humanitarian intervention that is different from all the others as regards both the principles on which the intervention is based and the ways and means used. Cosmopolitanism undertakes to guarantee individuals a whole range of fundamental rights, even when their own state is violating them or is incapable of defending them. Without guaranteeing these fundamental rights, hopes that the citizens can participate in the management of world affairs become empty and void. Having established that it is necessary to intervene, it nevertheless also becomes necessary to determine who the actors are who are *duty bound* to intervene and above all which institutions and ways and means can most effectively be used to discharge this responsibility. As far as these aspects are concerned, the response offered by cosmopolitanism is substantially different from that of other schools of thought. It is not difficult to side with a cosmopolitanism of good intentions; very few are willing to actually put their opposition to saving a people from genocide down in writing. But when it comes to combining the ends with the means and the institutions, choices become more controversial.

7.2 Present and Future of Humanitarian Intervention

The demand for humanitarian intervention, like much else, changed radically with the end of the Cold War.[3] The very term *humanitarian intervention* rather than *war* is a linguistic indication of the fact that it

2. For a list of different kinds of reason for intervening, see Kaldor, "Decade of Humanitarian Intervention," p. 130.
3. For a precise history of humanitarian interventions after World War II, see Nicholas J. Wheeler, *Saving Strangers: Humanitarian Intervention in International Society* (Oxford: Oxford University Press, 2000). For a more comprehensive analysis of how the use of force has changed, cf. Martha Finnemore, *The Purpose of Intervention: Changing Beliefs about the Use of Force* (Ithaca, NY: Cornell University Press, 2004).

is an action carried out by an external agent—another state, a group of states, or an IO—for altruistic rather than selfish reasons. In recent times, this has been pushed as far as to say there is not just a "right" but a "duty" to intervene.[4]

The conventional arguments in favor of humanitarian intervention are appealing. The idea that secular powers can use their military force to save the inhabitants of other communities or indeed to punish those responsible for committing atrocities has always exerted a strong intellectual appeal. When, in internationalist culture, the dual principles of state sovereignty and noninterference were gradually established, the first exceptions also came to the fore. Today, however, we feel uncomfortable when we read the reasons for military action deemed valid by sixteenth- and seventeenth-century authors.[5] Theologians and jurists have justified armed intervention in other countries to convert infidels, to prevent cannibalism, and to punish incest, sodomy, and bestiality. A king's ill-treatment of his parents could be used to justify humanitarian intervention.

At the same time, two quite different and contradictory reasons for a community to intervene elsewhere emerged: on the one hand, the desire to *save* certain populations from the abuses to which they were exposed by their own secular power; on the other, the intention to *punish* behaviors so different from their own. *Punish*, indeed, and in many cases the punishment could be extended to take in both the perpetrator and the victim, as both shared the practices carried on in those remote communities and considered deviant. Instances of double standards were also quite frequent: the ritual of human sacrifice, for instance, shocked those traveling to the newly discovered Americas without any of the "Conquistadores" realizing that the witches burned at the stake in Spanish squares belonged to the same category.[6]

There was no lack of jurists who strove to rationalize the rules governing intervention in other countries, which led to the emergence of a discipline such as the *ius gentium*, although historical investigation has shown how sensitive they were to the arguments of their employers, thus

4. See, for instance, Gareth Evans and Mohamed Sahnoun, eds., *The Responsibility to Protect: A Report Presented to the UN by an Independent Commission*, 2001, Web site www.iciss.ca and United Nations, *A More Secure World*.
5. Richard Tuck, *The Rights of War and Peace: Political Thought and International Order from Grotius to Kant* (Oxford: Oxford University Press, 1999) provides a penetrating account of these motivations.
6. For an enlightening account of the encounter with "the other" in the Americas, cf. Tzvetan Todorov, *The Conquest of America: The Question of the Other*, trans. Richard Howard (New York: Harper & Row, 1984).

justifying the epithet of "sorry comforters" that Kant addressed to them.[7] It is therefore an excellent mental exercise, whenever a secular authority seems ready to use the means at its disposal to the benefit of some other people, to ask whether there is any underlying vested interest. At the same time, it should be asked whether means other than war exist that could prove to be equally effective.

The atrocities crying out for humanitarian intervention were not infrequent in the past and are still present in today's world. However, the cases in which interventions presented as humanitarian actually mitigated suffering are rare: the failures seem vastly to outnumber the successes. In many cases, the victims one proposes to save suffer to a greater extent the fallout from the intervention than the perpetrators, as the means used are too clumsy to strike at the criminals without harming their potential victims.

Can a historical account of humanitarian intervention provide significant lessons that can be generalized? From the fascinating account given by Wheeler, three cases of success emerge: that of India in East Pakistan (which later became Bangladesh) in 1971, that of Vietnam in Cambodia in 1978, and that of Tanzania in Uganda in 1979.[8] All three took place at the height of the Cold War; all three were carried out by nonwestern states and, at least in two cases out of three, by nondemocratic states. None of them were justified by appealing to humanitarian reasons, but all three were carried out to safeguard the national borders from the exodus of refugees or because of border clashes. All three were viewed by western states with suspicion and were not condemned by the SC, in two cases thanks to the veto imposed by an emblematically authoritarian state, the Soviet Union. Recent historical experience should at the very least be an embarrassment for western partisans of democracy: the best humanitarian interventions in no way comply with the stereotype of a well-intentioned white man rushing to the aid of black and brown peoples.

In the present political scenario, the situation has changed drastically. It is highly unlikely that humanitarian interventions can take place without the approval of western countries. Indeed, in recent years, the western states have done all they can to boost the legitimacy of their own interventions under the humanitarian heading, widening the difference between legality and legitimacy.[9] The stage has been reached in

7. Kant, "Towards Perpetual Peace," p. 103; Tuck, *Rights of War and Peace*.
8. Wheeler, *Saving Strangers*, p. 286.
9. The Independent International Commission on Kosovo distinguished between legality and legitimacy in the use of force for humanitarian purposes in the *Kosovo Report: Conflict, International Response, Lessons Learned* (Oxford: Oxford University Press, 2001). The usefulness of such a distinction is

which every war fought by the West has "humanitarian" motives.[10] This was observed in the case of the interventions in Afghanistan (2002) and Iraq (2003), when the specific reasons of self-defense—to dismantle the infrastructures of terrorism and defuse the alleged weapons of mass destruction—were coupled with humanitarian reasons, that is, "to free" the Afghan and Iraqi peoples from totalitarian regimes (cf. chapter 8).

Let us define humanitarian intervention as *a military intervention by an institution in an external territory without the authorization of the ruling government in that area for the purpose of saving persons from democide or from other serious human rights violations.*

The lack of authorization of the government "in power" may be dependent on the fact that there is no government or that the existing government is deemed illegitimate, as in the case of civil war, revolution, and secession. This definition also makes it clear that, at least in principle, the intervention is being carried out mainly or exclusively for the purpose of helping a population exposed to intolerable abuse. This does not necessarily mean that the intervention must be totally altruistic. As Michael Walzer pointed out, the fact that an actor has implicit or explicit vested interests could be received as good news by people exposed to a massacre, as it would make the external agent more inclined to accept the risks involved in the rescue intervention.[11] But as soon as it becomes a matter of setting up the institutions necessary for humanitarian intervention, the presence of selectivity and discrimination diminishes the moral authority of the action and makes it less effective.

Two different possibilities are available for assessing humanitarian intervention: either on the basis of the agents' *intentions* or their *effects* on the populations to be saved. In the first case, the assessment is ex-ante; in the second case it is ex-post. An agent might have the best possible intentions at the time in which it is decided to intervene, but the situation could develop in such a way as to make it impossible to prevent harm to the population that has to be saved. Likewise, an agent can decide for purely selfish reasons to help a population at risk and nevertheless carry out a very successful operation. The fact that the ex-ante and ex-post

---

discussed in Richard Falk, ed., *Legality and Legitimacy in International Order* (Tokyo: UN University, 2008).

10. See the criticism by Noam Chomsky, *The New Military Humanism: Lessons from Kosovo* (Monroe, ME: Common Courage Press, 1999); Danilo Zolo, *Invoking Humanity: War, Law and Global Order* (London: Continuum, 2002); David Chandler, "International Justice," pp. 27–39 in *Debating Cosmopolitics*, ed. Archibugi.

11. Michael Walzer, "The Argument about Humanitarian Intervention," *Dissent* vol. 48, no. 2 (2002): 29–37.

appreciations can differ considerably shows how difficult it is to pass judgment on a humanitarian intervention that stops short at addressing contingencies. The public opinion is not in a position to see behind the agents' motives and, even if it were, would find them complex and contradictory, like all human behavior. An ex-post appreciation, however useful it may be as a lesson for the future, is irrelevant to the present. For as long as a situation in which each case must be judged on its own merits persists, there will be uncertainty over the actual advantage produced by the intervention. Accepting the idea of humanitarian intervention means implicitly limiting the sovereignty of states.[12] Also in the existing judicial system, we are faced with a typical case of conflict between the principles of sovereignty and noninterference. Some blame the principle of sovereignty as being the main cause of the lack of timely humanitarian interventions.[13] However, this is a badly distorted view: it would almost seem that the world is swarming with powerful, benevolent nations willing to invest resources and even spill their own soldiers' blood to rescue foreigners in peril and that they abstain from doing so only because they are reluctant to violate the principle of sovereignty. In fact, states possessing the means to do so violate the sovereignty of other states without worrying too much about it when it is in their interest.

7.3 For a Humanitarian Intervention Based on Cosmopolitan Principles

Cosmopolitan logic is wary of those who demand an emergency military intervention without being willing at the same time to put the appropriate institutional instruments in place. The most common practice of humanitarian intervention is actually dictated by the logic of emergency. It often happens that public opinion is suddenly bombarded with news and information concerning ongoing or looming catastrophes which must be rapidly warded off by means of an ad hoc intervention.[14]

---

12. See Brown, *Sovereignty, Rights and Justice*, chapter 8.
13. Michael Ignatieff, *Human Rights as Politics and Idolatry* (Princeton: Princeton University Press, 2001). For an opposite perspective, see Costas Douzinas, *Human Rights and Empire: The Political Philosophy of Cosmopolitanism* (London: Routledge, 2007).
14. Typical cases of media campaigns leading up to humanitarian interventions are the Somalia crisis (1993), where TV crews preceded the spectacular landing of U.S. troops on the beaches, and the already mentioned case of Kosovo (1999). In neither case were the mass media persevering enough to document the conditions of these areas at the end of the intervention, just as today there is an abso-

The slogan is "something must be done" and the metaphor most frequently bandied about is that of a fire: when faced with an unexpected event, do the neighbors have the right and duty to intervene? While one is instinctively responding, in the grip of urgency, equally important questions remain in the background, such as: How come this situation of crisis emerged? Are we sure that the consequences of humanitarian intervention will produce benefits that outweigh the disadvantages? Is there any link between the declared emergency and the interests of those intending to intervene?

The regulatory debate has only too often dodged these questions. Some authors indeed argue as though the existing system, dominated as it is by sovereign states that, on a voluntary basis, can decide how and if to intervene, is unchangeable,[15] to the extent that any humanitarian intervention lies in their hands. It is not surprising that the regulatory precepts that derive from them are largely based on the five pillars of the just war doctrine:

1. Just cause for intervening;
2. Legitimate authority to intervene;
3. Impossibility of resolving the crisis without the use of military means;
4. Proportionality of the intervention;
5. Consequentiality, that is, reasonable expectation that the intervention will be successful.[16]

Today any intervention pretends to be "cosmopolitan" any time a state, in the grips of an uncontrollable fit of generosity, is willing to intervene to save from peril the individuals of another state.[17] However,

---

lute lack of information on the Darfur tragedy, probably because no state is seriously willing to commit resources to it. On the selectivity of media coverage, see Mariano Aguirre, "The Media and Humanitarian Spectacle," pp. 157–76 in Humanitarian Studies Unit (ed.), *Reflections on Humanitarian Action: Principles, Ethics and Contradictions* (London: Pluto Press, 2001).

15. Walzer, "Argument about Humanitarian Intervention"; Tom Farer, "Cosmopolitan Humanitarian Intervention: A Five-Part Test," *International Relations* vol. 19, no. 2 (2005): 211–20.

16. The revival of the just war doctrine in the modern political discourse is largely due to Michael Walzer, *Just and Unjust Wars: A Moral Argument with Historical Illustrations* (New York: Basic Books, 1977). For an application to humanitarian intervention, see Mona Fixdal and Dan Smith, "Humanitarian Intervention and Just War," *Mershon International Studies Review* vol. 42, no. 2 (1998): 283–312.

17. Farer, "Cosmopolitan Humanitarian Intervention," p. 212.

this is only cosmopolitanism by halves, as it continues to leave to state institutions the task of attending to a problem that is not of individual states. If it were, all those who intervene in other people's territory would find their justification in cosmopolitan ethics. A full cosmopolitan spirit would, on the contrary, not only accept responsibility for the intervention but also ensure that it took place through institutions legitimized to obtain such objectives. Arguing from the above-mentioned premises, a cosmopolitan logic would impose severe limitations on the criteria cited. In particular, as far as point (2) is concerned, it is denied that a state has the legitimate authority to decide on an intervention, while legitimacy is invested in multilateral institutions to which the states have previously delegated authority in the matter. Likewise, multilateral institutions would have to be in a position to assess the other points on the agenda. We know only too well that these institutions do not yet exist, but this does not exonerate us from the responsibility of establishing them.

Walzer observed that multilateral institutions can have interests of their own just like states.[18] All institutions have interests of their own, and the task of political theory is to identify institutions that perform their task properly precisely because it is in their interest to do so. State institutions were created to serve the purposes of the state, not for humanitarian intervention. To come back to the fire metaphor: it is certainly a good thing to be able to rely on the neighbors' good will, but if fires are frequent it would be wise public policy to see that a fire brigade was set up. Both neighbors and firemen can have their own interests, with the important distinction that firefighters are publicly accountable for their actions.

The rest of this chapter discusses what genuine cosmopolitan logic can be used to underpin humanitarian intervention. It has been attempted to put some order into several fundamental questions so as to see which institutions can respond more adequately. In a word, we have retained the logic underlying cosmopolitan institution building. The questions to which it will be attempted to find answers are:

a. In which cases is it necessary to intervene?
b. Who is authorized to decide when a humanitarian intervention is needed?
c. How is it necessary to intervene?
d. Who is going to intervene?

18. Walzer, "Argument about Humanitarian Intervention," p. 32.

A. IN WHICH CASES IS IT NECESSARY TO INTERVENE?

When discussing humanitarian intervention, it is not a question of re-tracing the fascinating saga of the universality of human rights that, ever since the diatribe between Antigone and Creon, has continued to rage for more than twenty-five centuries. Even if it were to be deter-mined that certain human rights have been violated, this would not jus-tify military intervention, for the simple reason that war in any case en-trains a violation of other human rights. For example, it may be discussed whether such practices as infibulation or stoning to death are to be con-sidered violations of fundamental human rights or tolerated on the strength of some kind of cultural relativism. But there is no doubt that no one will go so far as to demand *military* intervention to ban them. Humanitarian intervention is merely a last resort to prevent serious vio-lations of fundamental rights at a collective level.

It may be useful, however, to lay down a code of conduct to define which cases require military intervention. A need was perceived right from the end of the Cold War to make a prior assessment of when hu-manitarian intervention is required, even if subsequently too little was done in this direction.[19] It would be alarming if each state were to come up with different codes of conduct, as this would imply a return to the state of nature in which each government attributes to itself the right to use force as it itself determines. To bring humanitarian intervention into the sphere of multilateralism and of the UN in particular, it would be useful if the International Law Commission or equally authoritative in-stitution could draw up guidelines for those cases requiring military in-tervention that would be submitted to the GA for approval. A code of conduct would have the beneficial effect of providing transparent ex-ante boundaries for cases justifying humanitarian intervention.

Such a code of conduct could also provide a more solid basis for UN action and law. It is a known fact that the UN Charter does not envisage the use of force for humanitarian reasons unless there is a threat to peace and security.[20] Democides like the one that occurred in Cambodia between 1976 and 1979 or in Argentina between 1977 and 1983 are unlikely to be considered a threat to international security. Internation-alist jurists have discussed whether humanitarian intervention can have a legitimacy based on consuetudinary law, or whether it is preferable to overhaul the charter. The codification of actual practice into specific

19. With the exception of Evans and Sahnoun, *The Responsibility to Protect.*
20. For a legal overview, see Simon Chesterman, *Just War or Just Peace? Hu-manitarian Intervention and International Law* (Oxford: Oxford University Press, 2001).

guidelines seems to be the most effective away of updating the legal framework of the UN without being caught up in the controversy that could derive from an amendment of the charter.

As this is an ex-ante task, and therefore not limited to a specific situation, the commission itself should lay down the rules of intervention, taking into account what is regulated by wartime law but applying it to the case in which the intervention is carried out to protect civilians. Indeed, humanitarian intervention is justified by the need to protect the populations of certain countries, and this calls for a code of conduct that is even more restrictive than normal wartime law. It should establish an important cosmopolitan principle, namely, that the populations to be protected must receive the same degree of protection as the forces carrying out the rescue. In other words, the rules of engagement would have to be more like those of the police than of the army.

B. WHO IS AUTHORIZED TO DECIDE WHEN A HUMANITARIAN INTERVENTION IS NEEDED?

While it is an important step to reach the stage of setting out guidelines, they need to be interpreted. What specific situation needs to be defined as a humanitarian emergency? This represents one further step. If the guidelines are the result of a multilateral process, there is no reason why their interpretation should not also be. Clearly, both citizens and institutions can make a different assessment of individual situations. Over the past few years, there have been interventions in Somalia but not in Rwanda, in Iraq but not in East Timor, in Sierra Leone but not in Darfur, because different assessments were made concerning the intensity of the crisis.

It is often pointed out that there are not enough resources to intervene in all humanitarian emergencies. Walzer claimed that "we do only what we can," and Smith that "the fact not everything can be done everywhere does not mean that nothing must be done in any circumstances."[21] However, these considerations refer to the capacity and the determination to carry out a relatively successful military intervention. It may be difficult or even impossible to carry out humanitarian intervention with any degree of success against a superpower. Not even the most fervid interventionists proposed taking military action against China after the Tienanmen massacre or against Russia in order to protect the Chechen

21. Walzer, "Argument about Humanitarian Intervention," p. 30; Michael J. Smith, "Humanitarian Intervention: An Overview of the Ethical Issues," *Ethics and International Affairs* vol. 12, no. 1 (1988): 63–79, on p. 78.

people, simply because the intervention would have been unsuccessful because of the strengths of the players involved.

But even if it is not possible to intervene, it is necessary to have a legitimate authority that can declare such situations to be emergencies. Politics must indicate when humanitarian interventions may be undertaken, but ethics must at least be able to denounce organized violence when it causes a humanitarian emergency. To lay down a procedure whereby a state of emergency may legitimately be declared would be an important achievement: that is, to place all crises, and consequently all the political authorities directly or indirectly responsible for the crisis, on an equal footing before the international community and the public opinion. Impartiality and nonselectivity cannot be attained in the moment in which it is necessary to intervene militarily, but at least each situation can be assessed and denounced using the same yardstick. This would at least lead to the political discrediting of states committing the violations as well as to economic or political sanctions.

So far the opposite has been true: states have decided whether to intervene not by assessing the nature and degree of the human rights violations but by agreeing to provide the military and financial resources for intervention. Some have defined conflicts as "genocide" simply when they decided to set their soldiers on the march. However, this is an ambiguous situation for two reasons. First, crises may be defined as humanitarian catastrophes because no one is willing to shoulder responsibility for them. The paradox is reached that not even the western mass media bother to inform public opinion, perhaps because they realize there is no point. Second, as soon as there is a state willing to send troops, the situation immediately becomes a humanitarian emergency. In this way, all wars are liable to become humanitarian.

There have been cases in which the SC declared a state of emergency and no one took any steps to protect the population. The most significant case is that of the crisis in Rwanda in 1994. Viewed through the eyes of a citizen of Rwanda, there must have been small consolation in the fact that the SC, in its Resolution 912 of April 21, 1994, declared that it was "appalled at the ensuing large-scale violence in Rwanda which has resulted in the death of thousands of innocent civilians, including women and children."[22] But at least it was clear that the problem was not a question of principle (throughout this tragic genocide, no one declared themselves to be noninterventionist) but one of political will. For this reason a distinction must be made between the *declaration* of the situation of emergency and the *implementation* of humanitarian military intervention.

22. UN, *The United Nations and Rwanda, 1993–1996* (New York: UN, 1996), p. 268.

Which multilateral institutions should assess the crisis? A problem of this kind was raised during the Kosovo crisis in 1999: Russian hostility to the intervention meant that the western countries carried out the intervention without a UN mandate. The states wishing to intervene felt the need to obtain legitimization from other multilateral institutions such as NATO and the EU. NATO was originally set up as a military institution and does not really lend itself to the defense of populations of non–member states. Regional organizations are a different kettle of fish. Owing to their proximity to a region in crisis, they might have a better perception of the problems than that available elsewhere. However, it does not appear that regional unions such as the African Union or the Organization of American States are always more sensitive to local crises than the SC. The SC has often come out in favor of humanitarian interventions; however, if the aim is merely to declare which crises must be defined as "emergencies," the SC does not seem to be the most appropriate body. Under the present conditions, each of the five permanent members can paralyze the decision by using its own veto, and authoritarian regimes could prevail in conserving the principle of noninterference. For example, this is the recurrent attitude of China, which is generally inclined not to weaken the principle of sovereignty (unless it is that of Tibet or Taiwan).

The body with the greatest legitimacy could be a world parliamentary assembly (§ 6.5). Until the advent of such a body it would be reasonable to attribute these responsibilities to the ICJ. If a judicial institution had the power to determine when an emergency existed such as to legitimize the use of force against a sovereign state, it would increase the force of the idea that the operations carried out have the nature of international policing. How many divisions has the ICJ?[23] None, of course, but if its powers proposed here do not refer to the intervention but merely the assessment of the degree of emergency, it is appropriate, as William Penn said, that *cedant arma togae* (arms should give way to law).[24]

C. HOW IS IT NECESSARY TO INTERVENE?

Having defined the need, we now come to the specific features of the intervention. During the war in Kosovo, several hopeful commentators actually claimed that NATO was becoming the secular arm of Amnesty

23. Stalin is reported to have once asked his military high command: "The Pope? How many divisions has he got?"
24. William Penn, *An Essay towards the Present and Future Peace of Europe, by the Establishment of an European Diet, Parliament, or Estates* (London: Friends House, [1693] 1993), p. 5.

International. In the same way, the wars in Afghanistan and Iraq were justified by the need to free peoples from the yoke of totalitarian regimes. In fact, these wars may have had humanitarian intentions but were certainly not humanitarian in practice. The Italian prime minister Giulio Andreotti, in 1991, defined the Gulf War as an "international police intervention." Observing how this war and other humanitarian interventions were carried out, however, there was not one case in which the same methods were used as those involved in a police operation in a democratic country. Most of the victims were civilians, so that the occupying forces did not even bother to collect data and information concerning the civilian and military deaths caused by their humanitarian intervention.[25] As far as the "humanitarian" component is concerned, the operations often had a counterproductive effect. The argument proposed here is that a genuine military intervention should apply the same methods as those accepted within the borders of a state. It is inadmissible that, as a result of escalating violence in an area inside a liberal state, such as the Basque region, Northern Ireland, or quarters having a high density of mafia in Sicily, aerial bombing should be carried out rather than police operations. Each political community desirous of performing a genuine humanitarian intervention must be prepared to risk the lives of its own soldiers in order to save those of the community in peril. Policemen, firefighters, and doctors already do this daily in their own country.

The experience of the past decade shows that it is not enough to want to intervene; it is also necessary to use appropriate ways and means that have not even been tried out in the last ten years or so. It is surprising that in an era of sensational technological breakthroughs, which have led to the development of increasingly sophisticated military technology, the tools of intervention are still very similar to those used in World War II. We should not be complacent about the fact that nowadays, in the so-called asymmetric wars, one of the warring parties can intervene without putting even one of its soldiers in harm's way, as

25. In the case of the wars in Afghanistan and in Iraq, the number of civilian casualties has been estimated by NGOs opposed to the wars. For civilian victims in Afghanistan, 2001–2003, see the database put together by Marc W. Herold on the Web site http://pubpages.unh.edu/~mwherold/AfghanDailyCount .pdf. For Iraqi civilian victims, only on December 14, 2005 did President Bush present a U.S. estimate of the number of victims, which according to him amounted to about thirty thousand. Figures estimated by medical sources referring to the increase in mortality rate since the beginning of the war were actually twenty-one times greater. Cf. Gilbert Burnham, Riyadh Lafta, Shannon Doocy, and Les Roberts, "Mortality after the 2003 Invasion of Iraq: A Cross-Sectional Cluster Sample Survey," *The Lancet* vol. 368, no. 9545 (2006): 1421–28.

happened, for example, during the war in Kosovo. It is, however, true that if there is no risk of incurring casualties, it is easier for a state to decide to intervene in defense of a foreign population. But if the intervention is not costly, it is also more likely that the foreign state will pursue its own interests. The measure of the success of a humanitarian intervention is therefore its capacity to minimize the number of casualties on both sides.[26]

The UN is once again the most suitable institution for developing new methods to use in the case of humanitarian interventions. Even today, however, the UN leaves it to the governments that have decided to carry out the intervention to decide which military tools to use. The governments then leave this principally to their own military experts. One alternative to this disappointing practice could be to give the job to a UN commission composed of military and civilians that decides on a case-by- case basis the most suitable methods to use in each emergency. The commission would make a prior assessment of whether an intervention—after it had been deemed necessary on the basis of the procedures set out in subsection (b)—is, in the first instance, actually feasible.

A humanitarian catastrophe might not, for instance, be amenable to military intervention for various reasons attributable to the lack of consequentiality:

1. The government responsible for the democide might be too strong to be overthrown by outside intervention. Other instruments, such as international isolation, might prove more effective.
2. The crisis area might be too remote and the violations already committed in conditions in which they are unlikely to be repeated. In this case, judicial prosecution of those responsible by means of criminal tribunals might be the best approach.
3. The estimated losses in the case of intervention might be greater than the number of victims saved. Other channels for the protection of the victims could be sought, such as "smart sanctions" aimed at those responsible.

D. WHO IS GOING TO INTERVENE?

The application of the above proposals would lead to interventions decided by organs lacking the power of coercion, and that would be more hazardous for those carrying them out and less harmful for the popula-

26. Kaldor, "Decade of Humanitarian Intervention," p. 130.

tions expected to benefit from them. This means that it would become more difficult to find secular powers willing to make their own troops available to rescue foreigners. The more remote the peoples to be rescued—geographically and culturally—the less willing a given community will be to put its soldiers in harm's way. Placing too many restrictions on how the interventions are decided and carried out may mean scuttling them. Paradoxically, a growing number of crises may be declared humanitarian emergencies by the international community (precisely because it is not costly to carry them out) without finding any state willing to put its own forces at risk to intervene.

The only way to resolve this problem is to have the political will to set up organizations that have an institutional mandate to carry out humanitarian interventions. Already in 1992, French President François Mitterrand suggested that about fifty of the largest and most powerful states should each make available about one thousand soldiers to the UN secretary-general. In this way, about fifty thousand troops would be on standby for peacekeeping purposes. Since then, other authoritative voices have urged making peacekeeping soldiers available on standby.[27] Others have suggested creating a permanent volunteer force of blue helmets.[28] Its multinational nature would avert a single country's (on most occasions, the United States) having to take the risks and responsibility, suffering the losses, and in many cases being subjected to criticism. UN peacekeepers total more than one hundred thousand (May 2008). Quantitatively, Mitterrand's proposal has already been overtaken by events without the troops currently deployed even being sufficient to fully satisfy all the needs. Moreover, a peacekeeping intervention is much less demanding than peace enforcement.

It is not just a quantitative problem but also a qualitative one, as the effectiveness of peace keeping is linked to the way the intervention is implemented.[29] First, it would be necessary to give these specialist troops a different status from those of the other armed forces. Second, the

27. Both the commissions chaired by Gareth Evans and Mohamed Sahnoun, *The Responsibility to Protect* and by Panyarachun, *A More Secure World* stressed that the stability of the international system also relied on the availability of consistent armed forces for peacekeeping and peace-enforcing operations.
28. Carl Kaysen and George Rathjens, "The Case for a Volunteer UN Military Force," *Daedalus* vol. 132, no. 4 (2003): 91–103.
29. For a historical assessment of peacekeeping, see Roland Paris, *At War's End: Building Peace after Civil Conflict* (Cambridge: Cambridge University Press, 2004) and Michael Doyle and Nicholas Sambanis, *Making War and Building Peace: United Nations Peace Operations* (Princeton: Princeton University Press, 2006).

countries providing these troops would also have to be those that respected human rights inside their own borders. Third, it is very important that the troops receive appropriate professional training for the functions they are to perform to ensure they are suitable for international police tasks rather than for war. Fourth, it would be a good idea to back up these blue helmets with at least the same number of "white helmets," that is, functionaries such as doctors, social workers, teachers, and engineers who have experience in civilian operations. These functionaries would also have the task of explaining to the civilian population that the intervention does not have only military objectives but also that of assistance. The experience of the former Yugoslavia shows that an external military operation can be successful only if it has close ties with the civilian populations.[30] Within a decade, this permanent rescue army could become the most sophisticated and best trained of the national armed forces. These forces would be the only ones authorized to carry out humanitarian interventions and would be supported at different levels by the conventional armed forces. Only the armed forces currently have the capacity to rapidly transport troops and to provide them with air cover. In many cases, national armies geographically close to the crisis areas are able to intervene more rapidly. However, the existence of an institution whose main objective is to intervene in emergency areas would demonstrate a budding global responsibility in defense of survival.

7.4 One Step Forward and Two Backward

In recent years, the debate on humanitarian intervention has focused mainly on the conditions that justify it and much less on the ways and means of implementing it. In this chapter a different approach has been followed: states willing to intervene should be asked to do so in a cosmopolitan institutional framework. If it is believed that the states can act as ethical agents, why should they not be asked to act accordingly and to not only supply their troops but also set up the necessary multilateral institutions? This approach is alternative to that of unilateral interventionist practice or even to that carried out through military alliances such as NATO. If the states are so altruistic as to cherish the destiny of humanity outside their own frontiers, they should not be reluctant to accept this type of proposal. This type of proposal requires drastic changes in the theory and practice of military intervention. The

30. Mary Kaldor, *New and Old Wars*; Giulio Marcon, *Dopo il Kosovo. Le guerre nei Balcani e la costruzione della pace* (Trieste: Asterios, 2000).

proposals presented here are aimed at linking the grassroots demand for safeguarding human rights in all corners of the Earth to institutions that can protect them. Table 7.1 summarizes the proposals suggested herein. It might be objected that, even when implemented, these proposals would not lead to a more effective and timely military intervention and that, as the procedures required to obtain authorization have become too complex, no one would be willing to carry out dangerous, which could even be politically and legally criticized interventions in the field. Some believe, however, that in a world dominated by a select club of democratic states, the creation of these institutions could be interpreted as an unequivocal message that the dominant countries refuse to tolerate massive violations of human rights. It would be a step toward collective security, a fundamental ingredient to achieve a genuine global commonwealth of citizens.

One could easily object that such reforms might prove useful but any interest in implementing them would be highly unlikely. In the current international climate, these proposals must certainly be considered unrealistic. The obstacle obviously comes from the states, which are reluctant to agree to multilateral codes of conduct that curtail their autonomy. By accepting the proposed framework, the states would commit themselves on the one hand to participation in a permanent rescue army and on the other not to carry out unilateral interventions.

It has already been asserted that the motive is not the best way to assess humanitarian intervention and that priority should instead be given to the outcome. However, the procedures are not independent of the outcome. A more coherent institutional framework is necessary not only for moral coherence reasons but also to increase the effectiveness of the intervention. Hitherto, the governments and factions to which the humanitarian intervention is addressed have had an easy task in highlighting the contradictions encountered by the interventionists. In Somalia, Bosnia, Kosovo, Afghanistan, and Iraq, those opposing the intervention claimed easily that the UN, NATO, and the unilateral occupation troops were not impartial judges but that the interventions were selective and self-interested. This reduced the support these interventions might otherwise have received from local civil society. Some believe, on the basis of the recent experiences, that any idea of humanitarian intervention is dangerous, as it legitimizes the action of the stronger against the weaker. It is not difficult to make a devastating criticism of the harm caused by the new humanitarian activism,[31] although this does not justify a return to isolationism. The solution therefore does not lie in hiding behind a shabby sovereignty that is juridically shaky and not always effectively

31. See, for instance, Zolo, *Invoking Humanity*.

Table 7.1

Procedures for a Military Intervention for Humanitarian Purposes: Some Institutional Cosmopolitan Proposals

Stage	Issue	Proposal
A	In which cases is it necessary to intervene?	Assign to the International Law Commission the task of drafting guidelines on the crises that deserve to be labeled "humanitarian emergencies" and that would require a military intervention without the consent of a legitimate government. The guidelines should be approved by the UN General Assembly.
B	Who is authorized to decide when a humanitarian intervention is needed?	When a situation that seems to be a humanitarian emergency arises, the Security Council should ask the World Court if a military intervention is justified.
C	How is it necessary to intervene?	A joint committee of military and civilian humanitarian organizations would develop guidelines on acceptable methods to be used when humanitarian intervention is needed. The same committee would assess whether the intervention is feasible.
D	Who is going to intervene?	Create a permanent rescue army composed of soldiers, police, and civilians from a large group of countries. Each of these countries would supply at least 1,000 soldiers and 1,000 civilians. These corps would be deployed in real time at the request of the UN Secretary-General.

restorable rather than seeking suitable ways and means to prevent, halt, and repress massive human rights abuses.

The question, however, is whether military interventions are the best way to bring solace to suffering humankind.[32] In the developing coun-

32. For a critical analysis, see David Kennedy, *The Dark Sides of Virtue: Reassessing International Humanitarianism* (Princeton: Princeton University Press, 2004); Douzinas, *Human Rights and Empire*.

tries, the persons who die of hunger, curable diseases, and natural disasters unfortunately still outnumber those who die from political violence. Yet, since the fall of the Berlin wall, the very states that zealously flexed their muscles in humanitarian interventions have subsequently reduced aid for economic and social development. Some liberal thinkers might claim that the responsibility of a state outside its own borders is limited to affirming civil and political rights, as these represent a prerequisite for the endogenous attainment of development and thus also of economic and social rights. However, this argument does not apply in the case of natural disasters that cause humanitarian catastrophes. And it does not at all seem that western countries have been more generous in these cases. What should be done, if anything, is to understand how come that liberal countries have this peculiar propensity to intervene more willingly and zealously when a single person is killed by another person than when ten or even one hundred persons die of hunger.

It would therefore not be absurd to put the altruism of the liberal states to the test in natural catastrophes, when there is no need to oppose other political communities and even less to violate the principle of sovereignty. Such testing could provide a good opportunity to try out the combined effect of armed forces and civilian humanitarian organizations to save the population from poverty or catastrophes without the need to fight against other human beings. Once a permanent rescue army has proved its worth, thereby gaining respect and authoritativeness in the world, it would be possible to take the next step, namely, military intervention in defense of threatened human rights.

Chapter 8
Can Democracy Be Exported?

8.1 The Image of the Past

The idea that freedom and democracy can be exported all over the world is an ancient dream. Athenian democrats, French revolutionaries, and Russian Bolsheviks, to mention only the better-known cases, were convinced that their own political system was good enough to be donated to all peoples. But not even the path to freedom is carpeted with rose petals: enthusiasm is often mingled with fanaticism; idealism must come to terms with the harsh laws of realpolitik.[1]

At the end of the last world war, democracy was a gift made by the Americans to the Europeans. An Italian cannot be unmindful of the glorious days of the Summer of 1944 and the Spring of 1945, when the main Italian cities were being liberated by Allied troops. I use the term *liberated* because this was the feeling of the vast majority of Italians, who considered that the Allies' arrival marked the end of Nazi and fascist brutality, of civil war, and of the air raids. However, we often overlook that at the time the Allies referred to Italy as an "occupied" country, and rightly so, since until only a few months before, it had been an active ally of Hitler's Germany.[2]

1. For a skeptic's view, cf. Luciano Canfora, *Esportare la libertà* (Milano: Mondadori, 2007).
2. This perception seems reversed in Afghanistan and in Iraq: the civilian population tends to regard the United States as an occupying power, while Washington sees itself as a liberator.

But even if Italy had been the enemy until the day before, not a single shot was fired in anger against the Allies. As soon as the Allies arrived on the ground, hostilities ceased. The heavy Allied bombing of the Italian cities, which had caused numerous deaths among the civilian population comparable to the number of deaths caused by the ruthless Nazi reprisals, was immediately forgotten. On the ground, the Allies, and the Americans in particular, did not arouse feelings of fear but were immediately regarded as friends and brothers, who handed out cigarettes and joined in the dancing and singing. Above all, they spoke of freedom and democracy.

If the Italians welcomed the Americans so warmly, it was partly because Italian immigrants on the other side of the Atlantic had explained what the United States was like, but it was above all because the Resistance, fighting against the Nazis and fascists, had spread the idea among the population that the Allies were not enemies of the people but rather, as they had been promptly rechristened, *Allies*, not just because the troops came from an alliance of countries but because they could be considered *our* allies against dictatorship.

In Germany and Japan there was no civil war as in Italy, and the Resistance was much weaker in those countries. Indeed, the Allies were not greeted there by a flurry of flags as they were in Italy, France, Belgium, and the Netherlands, even though they were not actually attacked by anyone. In all three defeated countries, the winds of change were felt promptly because there was awareness that the occupation troops would be staying for only a brief period and that before leaving the country they would plant the seeds of a political system—democracy—that would benefit the whole population. The idea that it was a matter of setting up not trusted regimes but rather democratic governments was much more deeply rooted in the Americans than in the British. Great Britain headed a world empire and was more interested in having faithful regimes than democratic ones. Despite the looming rivalry with the Soviet Union and its recent satellite states, the United States believed in the value of democracy for the purpose of consolidating the bonds among free peoples. Political parties, trade unions, information agencies, judicial apparatuses—all received substantial support from the American administration. Ever since, U.S. foreign policy has repeatedly declared that its objective is to spread democracy, often by means of armed intervention.

To export democracy has actually always been one of the declared priorities of US foreign policy.[3] The successes achieved at the end of

3. See Tony Smith, *America's Mission: The United States and the Worldwide Struggle for Democracy in the Twentieth Century* (Princeton: Princeton University

World War II gave rise to the idea that any military action could produce the same outcome. Not even years and years of supporting dictatorships, for instance, all over the Latin American continent at the time of Henry Kissinger, not even the CIA plots against elected governments could erase from the mind of the American public opinion that its country was not only the freest in the world but also better able than any other to liberate the others. Neither the isolationists nor the interventionists have ever denied the good intentions of the exporter and the advantages accruing to the importer: the American debate focused on whether it is in the country's interest to carry out these interventions.[4] Yet, the sentiments expressed by the vast majority of the world public opinion no longer supports the United States' concept of its mission. Since the end of World War II, skepticism has continued to grow concerning the legitimacy and efficacy of external action. American intervention outside its frontiers is increasingly perceived as an imperial projection. As a result of the uncertain outcome of the mission in Afghanistan and the Iraq disaster, this skepticism has spread also to the American population.

The present chapter reexamines the question of the exportability of democracy in the light of the cosmopolitan project. Unlike the humanitarian intervention discussed in the preceding chapter, exporting democracy involves not only preventing acts of genocide but also imposing a specific regime, democracy. It is *proactive* and not just *interdictive*. The question raises much greater conceptual problems: while it is only to be expected that all individuals wish to survive, it cannot be taken for granted that they wish to participate in the management of public affairs. A humanitarian intervention by definition refers to political communities in which peaceful coexistence has ceased, while an intervention to export democracy can also be directed toward communities that, although authoritarian, guarantee their citizens' security. Anyone wishing to export democracy must therefore be sure that their intervention will be appreciated and not perceived by the population as merely replacing one internal authoritarian regime with another imposed from the outside.

Press, 1994); Michael Cox, G. John Ikenberry, and Takashi Inoguchi, eds., *American Democracy Promotion: Impulses, Strategies, and Impacts* (Oxford: Oxford University Press, 2000).
4. Ole R. Holsti, "Promotion of Democracy as Popular Demand?" pp. 151–80 in *American Democracy Promotion*, ed. Cox et al., demonstrated that the American public opinion is often less inclined than its government to support interventions aimed at modifying the internal regime of other countries, above all because of the costs that the country incurs.

CAN DEMOCRACY BE EXPORTED?

    This chapter examines whether it is legitimate, and what means may be used, to bring about a regime in autocratic countries in order to convert them to democracy. The cosmopolitan project holds that all political communities can embrace the values and rules of democracy, but who can legitimately and effectively extend the values of democracy geographically, and how can they do so? Consideration is given in the following section to the theoretical implications of exporting democracy. Section 8.3 addresses the available ways and means and their efficacy in this perhaps decisive issue. Section 8.4 assesses the role played by IOs in fostering democracy.

8.2 Can Democracy Be Legitimately Exported?

REGIME CHANGE AS AN ACT OF POWER

Why should democracies be concerned with exporting their own system instead of enjoying its fruits in their own home? Imposing a regime from the outside is above all an act of power, and democratic countries are certainly not the only ones to be led into temptation. The most frequent reasons that convince a political community to invest its own resources to change a regime elsewhere are its own interests and the hope to acquire resources from other societies. In some cases, this offensive inclination involves annexation and the subjugated peoples will claim self-determination, as will be discussed in the following chapter. In other cases, a state may attempt to achieve its objectives by imposing from the outside a given internal regime by setting up "puppet" governments.

    A wide-ranging historical review covering the past five centuries has taken into consideration nearly two hundred cases of countries imposing internal institutions on other countries from the outside.[5] A report on such heterogeneous cases that covers a long period of time helps to frame the problem in a perspective that is less dominated by contemporary ideology. It is not surprising to find that the countries imposing the change are usually the great powers, while the countries whose regime is changed through external imposition are the less powerful ones: you cannot impose if you do not have the power to do so. The cases reviewed show that whenever a country set about imposing regimes from the outside, it tends to do so repeatedly. The regimes imposed from abroad vary widely, ranging from absolute monarchies to republics, from constitutional

5. John M. Owen, "The Foreign Imposition of Domestic Institutions," *International Organization* vol. 52, no. 2 (2002): 375–409.

monarchies to democracies, from nationalist dictatorships to communist systems. As might be expected, the regime promoted tends to correspond to that of the promoting power, although there is no general rule. In many cases, a political community imposes a different regime, sometimes one of an opposite political nature, as is demonstrated by the colonial domination of the European powers.

The external imposition of internal regimes tends to be concentrated into given historical periods characterized by massive ideological confrontations, such as the European wars of religion of the early seventeenth century, the disorders following the French Revolution, and the period after World War II. Those favorable to the stability of the international system understandably are concerned over these upheavals, and it is not surprising that after a period of furious conflicts arising out of the desire to dominate from the exterior there are attempts to dampen enthusiasm by boosting the principles of national sovereignty, noninterference, and self-determination. The Treaty of Münster, the Congress of Vienna, and the San Francisco Charter may all be viewed as attempts to set up counterbalancing forces by treaties, rules, and institutions designed to safeguard each player's autonomy.

Is there any substantial difference in imposing a democratic regime rather than a Catholic, Protestant, Islamic, communist, or fascist regime? Today the democratic countries are politically dominant and could, like any other regime, feel tempted to expand their own geographic area of influence out of self-interest. A democratic country could, for example, consider that states having a similar regime are more reliable trade partners and less inclined to start a war or to threaten their security, as well as being probable allies in the case of conflict. In other words, a democratic state might have a vested interest in living in a condominium of democratic states simply in view of the benefits involved. If these are the reasons, there would be no greater legitimacy underlying the intention of exporting democracy than there would be in imposing any other regime. The attempt to export democracy would represent a new version of undue interference of one state in the internal affairs of another.

For these reasons, it is necessary to assess the intentions of not only those offering to carry out an intervention but also those living in the political community where the intervention is intended. It seems logical to attach greater weight to the wishes of those who intend to "import" democracy than to those who wish to "export" it. The exporter should ask himself whether signals exist on the interior that indicate a widespread desire for regime change.

EXTERNAL INTERFERENCE IN THE CASE OF INTERNAL INSURRECTION

Interference may be justified in support of peoples seeking to free themselves from an authoritarian system, but why would a people need an external intervention instead of taking its destiny into its own hands? If a people is under the yoke of an authoritarian government, it can revolt against it and set up a government that complies more closely with its desires. When the social contract between a government and its people is broken, until an open contrast becomes apparent between the government in power and the rebels, one would expect that external forces may take sides with one of the factions without foreigners being accused of upsetting the state of peace or of interfering in another country's internal affairs. But in the absence of any overt or at least latent rebellion, external intervention will verge on undue interference. Above all, it is difficult to ask the citizens of the democratic countries to put their lives at risk and to put their hands in their pockets to provide a more satisfactory government to citizens who are unwilling to do the same for themselves.

An overt rebellion does not necessarily signify a commitment to democracy by the rebels. History is filled with revolts that have replaced an authoritarian regime with one that is even more authoritarian. In the many cases in which a people is split into several factions, the main aim of external intervention must therefore not be to support one of the warring factions but to find an agreement among them all. For pacification to be effective, the conflicting parties must also agree on how to manage public affairs, and democratization becomes the principal instrument for doing this. Rather than as an ally of one of the factions, external intervention is required to act as a mediator or arbitrator.[6] However, in these cases, the external intervention takes place when a civil war is already under way and those who intervene from the outside cannot be blamed for breaking the state of peace.

One would expect the democratic countries to unconditionally support those struggling for democracy. Historical experience shows, however, that this is not a general rule. Just as the very Catholic France supported the Dutch Protestants against the very Catholic Habsburgs and the French monarchy supported the Republican rebels against the British monarchy, the United States supported General Pinochet rather than

---

6. For an analysis of pacification interventions undertaken by the UN, including those carried out by democratization, cf. Doyle and Sambanis, *Making War and Building Peace*. Paris, *At War's End*, on the grounds of the peacekeeping interventions of the 1990s, rightly warns against the use of a fast democratization as a method for ending a civil war.

the elected government of Salvador Allende. During the Spanish civil war, Germany and Italy consistently supported Francisco Franco, while Great Britain and France were much more ambivalent in their actions. No unequivocal solidarity seems to emerge between democratic governments and movements fighting for democracy.

REGIME CHANGE AFTER AN AGGRESSION

Regime change often occurs as the result of a compulsory transition after a war. A government that starts a war of aggression and loses it also loses its legitimacy as a member of the international community and in the eyes of its own subjects. In such circumstances it is not surprising that internal and external pressures combined can lead to a radical change of regime. One typical case occurred in the aftermath of World War II. The Allies deemed it necessary to remove all traces of national-socialism from Germany and its allies. This policy was legitimized not only by the crimes against humanity carried out by Nazism but also by the obvious argument of self-defense, that is, to prevent the same regime from committing new acts of aggression. However, the action taken by the Soviet Union was opposite to that of the Allies: while in East Germany a government was set up under direct Soviet control, the Allies expressed complete confidence in West Germany's capacity for self-government, provided that West Germany carried out a radical and irreversible regime change. The Allies decided implicitly not to blame German citizens for the crimes committed by their government and concentrated instead on the individual prosecution of those who were directly involved with the crimes of the old regime. Recognition of individual responsibility for the crime of aggression or for crimes against humanity was used to provide legitimacy for a new leadership based on completely different values.

The approach taken by the victors of World War II was quite the opposite to that followed after World War I. At the 1919 Paris Peace Conference, the victorious powers imposed sanctions and reparations on Germany, implicitly considering the German people fully responsible for their government's actions. The victorious powers also implemented a number of "containment" actions aimed at preventing Germany from ever again representing a threat to its neighbors. The democratic institutions of the Weimar Republic failed to mitigate the victors' claims. The disastrous outcome of the Treaty of Versailles induced the Allies to radically change tack after World War II. Unfortunately, these long-standing lessons were ignored at the end of the Gulf War in 1991: after winning the war, the allied countries left power firmly in the hands of the existing ruling class, further isolating Iraq from the international community and weakening it by implementing "containment," thus making the country's oppressed citizens pay a higher price than the regime's ruling class.[7]

The lesson that may be learned from World War II is that if a country suffers an aggression, it acquires the right and the duty to set up a different regime in the defeated country, if for no other reason than for self-protection. However, this does not represent a specific justification for exporting democracy; otherwise a state having suffered an aggression for religious reasons could, if it won the war, claim the right to remove the religious institutions underlying the aggression.

THREE INTENTIONS

Must we conclude thus that exporting democracy has no greater legitimacy than exporting any other regime? Some claim that it is not possible to achieve democratization if there is no internal pressure, that democracy can be imported but not exported.[8] This does not alter the fact, however, that the international framework plays a decisive role, although no general rule can be established.[9] Exporting democracy can gain legitimacy provided that it is based on three intentions.

The first intention is related to the willingness to sound out *the intentions of the peoples* of third states with regard to a democratic regime. It must be assumed not only that it is in the interest of these peoples to have a democratic government but also that peoples may not succeed in attaining their objective because they are repressed by the ruling government. A

---

7. Unlike Michael Walzer, "Regime Change and Just War," *Dissent* vol. 52, no. 3 (Summer 2006) at www.dissentmagazine.org, I therefore believe that "containment" is the policy least likely to encourage regime change.

8. Philippe C. Schmitter, "The Influence of the International Context upon the Choice of National Institutions and Policies in Non-Democracies," pp. 26–54 in *The International Dimensions of Democratization: Europe and the Americas*, ed. Laurence Whitehead (Oxford: Oxford University Press, 2001, exp. ed.); Sunil Bastian and Robin Luckham, eds., *Can Democracy be Designed? The Politics of Institutional Choice in Conflict-Torn Societies* (London: Zed Books, 2003). See also Nadia Urbinati, *I confini della democrazia* (Roma: Donzelli editore, 2007), chapter 2.

9. This is the lesson to be learned from the experiences described in Laurence Whitehead, ed., *The International Dimensions of Democratization*. See also Kristian S. Gleditsch and Michael D. Ward, "Diffusion and the International Context of Democratization," *International Organization* vol. 60, no. 3 (2006): 911–33.

democracy-exporting agent acting in good faith should, in other words, give priority to the importer's reasons over the exporter's own reasons. Otherwise, one of those typical cases arises that, in Robespierre's words, reflects the mania to make peoples happy against their will. In some cases, the intentions of a people may be explicit, for instance, when a government in power refuses to step down after losing free and fair elections, as happened in the Philippines in 1986 and Myanmar in 1990. In these cases, international law has begun to be used to safeguard internal norms.[10]

The second intention is related to giving the population *freedom of choice* regarding its own form of government. It is clearly antidemocratic to want to export democracy without allowing the people to decide which constitutional form they prefer. Exporting democracy means giving people the chance to decide which constitutional form to apply. What can be exported from the outside is the power of self-government, while the specific democratic form must be decided on the inside.

The third intention refers to the *way of assessing* the political regimes involved. Since exporting democracy requires the existence of at least two agents, the importer and the exporter, it would be necessary to perform an independent assessment to establish whether the importer actually needs a change of regime and whether the exporter is in a position to develop an alternative regime. It has already been seen how controversial it is to assess democratic regimes and how reluctant also consolidated democracies are to accept external assessments (§ 2.5). Ideally, only global legislative and judiciary institutions can legitimately define such criteria and apply them. In the absence of such power, the would-be exporter of democracy would have to rely on the opinion expressed by existing institutions or third-party organizations.

8.3 The Means for Exporting Democracy

The discussion presented in the preceding section may seem abstract. Indeed, much of the controversy arising over the idea of exporting de-

10. Cf., for instance, Thomas M. Franck, "The Emerging Right to Democratic Governance," *American Journal of International Law* vol. 86, no. 1 (1992): 46–91; James Crawford, "Democracy and International Law," *British Year Book of International Law* (1993): 113–33; Susan Marks, *The Riddle of All Constitutions: International Law, Democracy and the Critique of Ideology* (Oxford: Oxford University Press, 2000). Contrasting opinions are collected in Gregory H. Fox and Brad R. Roth, eds., *Democratic Governance and International Law* (Cambridge: Cambridge University Press, 2000).

mocracy is not related to its theoretical legitimacy but to the means used. While few would deny the utility of exporting democracy through persuasion, the matter becomes much more controversial when it is intended to use coercive means. What are the consequences of using coercion (the stick) instead of persuasion and incentives (the carrot)?

THE STICK

The means of coercion par excellence for exporting democracy is war, as in Afghanistan and in Iraq. In this case, the means (war) is clearly in conflict with the end (democracy). The violent means represented by war does not involve despots alone but inevitably ends up affecting also the individuals who are expected to benefit from the regime change. The use of such means is the least suitable for effectively promoting a regime based on nonviolence and for protecting the citizens' interests. Rather than establishing a ruling class alternative to the one in power, a war of aggression creates a vacuum and only aggravates local conflicts. In the case in which an explicit will is expressed by the public to have a democratic government, this does not mean that the same public will accept a military invasion. Let us take the case of Panama in May 1989, when, after losing the elections, Manuel Noriega and his regime refused to hand over power. Although the Panamanian citizens had expressed their desire to have a different government, they feared an armed intervention by the United States to overthrow Noriega.[11] This was a classic case in which the population would have preferred external help of the nonviolent kind, for instance, a naval blockade.

But as well as representing a clear-cut contradiction between means and ends, historical experience shows that only in rare cases can a democratic regime be set up using external military means. What happened in Germany, Japan, and Italy in 1945 represents a unique experience that is unlikely to be repeated. A survey by the Carnegie Endowment for International Peace dedicated to U.S. involvement in military operations abroad in the twentieth century indicates that only rarely was democratization the result. In the first half of the twentieth century, the failed military operations involved countries that were neighbors of the United States and apparently easy to control, such as Panama (1903–1936), Nicaragua (1909–1933), Haiti (1915–1934), the Dominican

11. Cf. Eytan Gilboa, "The Panama Invasion Revisited: Lessons for the Use of Force in the Post Cold War Era," *Political Science Quarterly* vol. 110, no. 4 (1995): 539–62. It is estimated that the U.S. intervention cost the lives of 500 to 5,000 Panamanians and 23 U.S. soldiers.

Republic (1916–1924), and a good three times Cuba (1898–1902, 1906–1909, and 1917–1922).

Other military occupations, such as in Korea in the 1950s and South Vietnam and Cambodia in the 1960s and 1970s, were dictated mainly by the intention to block communist expansion, and democratization was not even attempted. Since the end of the Cold War, the U.S. administration has not achieved any lasting success even in Haiti. After World War II, the only clear-cut successes have been Panama (1989) and Grenada (1983), two small states closely linked to the U.S. economy and society. In the case of Panama, a heavy price was paid.[12]

Even more discouraging is the record of the two old European colonial powers, France and Great Britain. France and Great Britain almost never explicitly intended their military interventions abroad to favor democratic forces but rather to follow the the traditional logic of maintaining political influence. According to Pickering and Peceny,[13] French and British interventions after World War II almost always led to reduced political liberalization and to support of the existing regimes, even when those regimes were oppressive. The current failures in Afghanistan and in Iraq actually have numerous precedents. How can such disappointing results be accounted for?

One of the first ingredients that seems to be missing in the attempt to export democracy is the determination of the exporters, who are more often inclined to promote reliable and faithful regimes than to allow the self-determination of peoples. In a situation in which the intentions are controversial and the successes achieved questionable to say the least, it is understandable that the developing countries should view with some distrust the good intentions of western countries, especially when they propose using coercive means, and that this distrust should be cultivated even by the greatest champions of the democratic cause.

12. Cf. Minxin Pei and Sara Kasper, *Lessons from the Past: The American Record on Nation Building* (Washington, DC: Carnegie Endowment for International Peace, 2003). The studies by James Meernik, "United States Military Intervention and the Promotion of Democracy," *Journal of Peace Research* vol. 33, no. 4 (1996): 391–402; Margaret G. Hermann and Charles Kegley, "The U.S. Use of Military Intervention to Promote Democracy: Evaluating the Record," *International Interactions* vol. 24, no. 2 (1998): 91–114; and Karin Von Hippel, *Democracy by Force: U.S. Military Intervention in the Post-Cold War World* (Cambridge: Cambridge University Press, 2000) confirm the negative outcome regarding democratization of the majority of U.S. military interventions.

13. Jeffrey Pickering and Mark Peceny, "Forging Democracy at Gunpoint," *International Studies Quarterly* vol. 50, no. 3 (2006): 539–60.

When the intention is to export democracy using coercive means, one other decisive aspect is overlooked, namely, the consequences that involvement in a war has for the exporter. In war each state is compelled to forgo some of its own freedom. The citizens are sent to war, civil freedoms are reduced, the relative weight of the strong powers (army, secret service, and security apparatus) increases at the expense of transparency and control. Democracies that are perpetually at war develop chronic diseases. The United States and Great Britain, which have been involved in a never-ending series of high- and low-intensity conflicts since the end of World War II, have so far resisted incredibly well in preserving their own democratic system at home. But not even these two states have been able to avoid sacrificing part of their own democratic institutions on the altar of national interest. In the state of necessity produced by war, torture and the killing of unarmed prisoners have been committed and justified, and they would have never been tolerated by public opinion in peacetime. Exporting democracy by military means also signifies reducing democracy on the home front.

At the height of the enthusiasm for the exportation of freedom at bayonet point, at the beginning of the French revolutionary wars, a few wise voices were raised to warn against the looming dangers:

> Invincible within, and by your administration and your laws a model to every race, there will not be a single government which will not strive to imitate you, not one which will not be honored by your alliance; but if, for the vainglory of establishing your principles outside your country, you neglect to care for your own felicity at home, despotism, which is no more than asleep, will awake, you will be rent by intestine disorder, you will have exhausted your monies and your soldiers, and all that, all that to return to kiss the manacles the tyrants, who will have subjugated you during your absence, will impose upon you; all you desire may be wrought without leaving your home: let other people observe you happy, and they will rush to happiness by the same road you have traced for them.

These words were taken from the *Philosophy in the Bedroom* by the Marquis de Sade.[14] Perhaps because they were contained in a book whose raving author had been put away in a madhouse, they had little effect at the time. But it is never too late to meditate upon them.

---

14. Donatien-Alphonse-François de Sade, *Philosophy in the Bedroom* (New York, Grove Press, [1793] 1965), p. 339.

THE CARROT

Must it therefore be concluded that nothing can be done to export democracy outside one's borders and, as the Divine Marquis suggests, the only useful thing that democratic countries can do is to perfect their own political system so much that other peoples will want to imitate them? There is no reason to be so skeptical. If democratic states support the self-determination of other peoples, they will soon discover other peoples want to participate in the way power is managed in their own society. The error implicit in the mania to export democracy refers solely to the means, not to the end. If the end is legitimate, what instruments are therefore available to the democratic states?

The first and most obvious instrument is linked to economic, social, political, and cultural incentives. The present-day domination of the West is so widespread that, if their priority is truly to expand democracy, they ought to commit more resources to it. But we are far from moving in this direction: in 2005, the U.S. defense appropriation amounted to more than 4 percent of its gross domestic product, and that of the EU countries to more than 2 percent. In view of this military expenditure which, considering the present international scenario, it is quite euphemistic to call "defense" expenditure, only the small change is dedicated to development aid currently only 0.1 percent of the U.S. GDP and 0.3 percent of that of the EU GDP.[15] Only a small proportion of these funds are explicitly earmarked for encouraging democracy.

But the carrot does not consist solely of economic aid. Economic aid can be effective but may also be perceived as a form imposition by a rich and powerful state on a small and weak one. The logically most convincing way to export democracy is to have it transmitted by the citizens of the democratic countries opening up direct channels between themselves and the citizens of the authoritarian countries. Professional and cultural associations and other transnational organizations play an important role in connecting citizens. During the Cold War, these channels proved fundamental in supporting the opposition in the eastern bloc countries and in forming an alternative ruling class.[16] These channels

15. World Bank, *World Development Indicators*.
16. See, for instance, Mary Kaldor, ed., *Europe from Below: An East-West Dialogue* (London: Verso, 1991). The existence of nongovernmental channels may itself be considered an excellent indicator of the feasibility of exporting democracy: the civil society in the democratic countries had numerous contacts with the eastern European countries during the years of the Iron Curtain despite control and repression. Nothing comparable exists today between Afghan and Iraqi citizens and those of the occupying countries.

are often politically weak pressures that are easy to counter: the leaders of the opposition that maintain personal contacts are often placed under surveillance and are the first to be repressed. The governments in power are capable of brushing off for decades all requests for political liberalization, as we learn from the case of Burma and the persecution suffered by the opposition leader Aung San Suu Kyi, in the face of a pressing international solidarity campaign. Yet, one must not discount the political importance of these channels. At least they demonstrate to the oppressed inhabitants of authoritarian regimes that political societies that express solidarity for their aspirations exist. Without this solidarity, Vaclav Havel, Nelson Mandela, and Lech Wałęsa would never have been transformed from political prisoners to heads of state.

Using persuasive means also reinforces instead of weakening democracy in the exporting countries. Involving civil society in the foreign policy choices, for example by directing trade, tourism, and economic aid flows toward countries that respect human rights and where self-government prevails, helps the populations of democratic countries to pursue the values underlying their own social contract. If the citizens themselves become ambassadors for their own political system and plead its cause abroad, the citizens themselves become defenders of the democratic values.

It is equally important to offer countries that might choose democracy the chance to join the club of democratic states on equal terms, rather than establish a clear-cut hierarchy in which a state deems it can export its own system instead of allowing different states to participate in a political union in which the various systems are compared and reinforced. If democracy can be defined as a journey, some peoples could benefit from traveling together. It is therefore not surprising that IOs continue to play an extremely useful role in spreading democracy.

8.4 The Role of International Organizations in Spreading Democracy

IOs act on behalf of democratization by exerting pressure on authoritarian governments, both when the IOs accept the membership of heterogeneous regimes (as in the case of the UN) and when they accept only democratic states (as in the case of the EU). The UN exerted weak pressure in the direction of democratization in the 1960s and 1970s. This pressure has increased considerably since the 1990s also because the number of the UN's democratic members has gradually increased. A virtuous circle has been set up in which the greater the number of democratic states, the tougher it has become for the others not to be democratic.

The capacity of regional organizations may become extremely strong,[17] even though they depend on the nature of their membership and the available incentives. The EU has a greater force of persuasion than the Arab League because the EU may reach a greater degree of consensus on democratic values and because the EU has more instruments and resources to commit. IOs can act on internal democratization through at least three channels: stable center of gravity, crafting of rules, and economic integration.

The IOs often represent a point of reference and stability during the transition process. The elites in power often fear that regime change will be accompanied by a violent change in the economic and social base, will wipe out their acquired privileges, and will expose them to reprisals.[18] In many cases they fear that the regime they control may be replaced by one that is equally authoritarian. These fears can make the ruling classes extremely reluctant to liberalize the political system and can induce them to defend the existing regime even at the cost of unleashing a civil war. IO membership may instead prove useful in defining the future rules of coexistence a priori, allowing the ruling faction to become one of the political parties represented in the new regime. The other member states can act as models on which to base the future regime. Likewise, once political liberalization has been achieved, the IOs can contribute to stabilizing the existing political regime and sheltering it from attempted coups d'état. Not surprisingly, countries increase their propensity to participate in IOs after democratization.[19] Several IOs have undertaken in the past to suspend countries whose governments seized power in a coup. Article 30 of the statute of the African Union, for example, states, "Governments which shall come to power through unconstitutional means shall not be allowed to participate in the activities of the Union."

One typical case in which the effectiveness of IOs can be appreciated is the design of constitutional systems and electoral assistance.[20] In the

17. See the important line of research opened by Jon C. Pevehouse, "Democracy from the Outside-In?" and *Democracy from Above? Regional Organizations and Democratization* (New York: Cambridge University Press, 2005).
18. Pevehouse, "Democracy from the Outside-In?" p. 524.
19. See Edward D. Mansfield and Jon C. Pevehouse, "Democratization and International Organizations," *International Organization* vol. 60, no. 1 (2006): 137–67.
20. For a conceptualization of international electoral assistance procedures, see Mathias Koenig-Archibugi, "International Electoral Assistance," *Peace Review* vol. 9, no. 3 (1997): 357–64; for a case history, cf. Peter Burnell, *Democracy Assistance: International Co-operation for Democratization* (London: Frank Cass, 2000).

transition from an authoritarian regime to a democratic one, the parties and factions involved distrust each other. A supranational institution can not only certify the outcome of the electoral process but also contribute to planning the constitutional system. Precisely because IOs are multilateral, they are less likely to dominate one state or to be perceived as an instrument of domination. It is therefore not surprising that the UN electoral assistance office has become increasingly active and that numerous IOs, including the Organization of American States and OSCE, receive a growing number of requests for collaboration in organizing or certifying elections. Among NGOs, the action of the IDEA of Stockholm is particularly dynamic and effective.[21]

The IOs open up channels of communication among states involving not only governments but also enterprises. IOs whose principal aim is free trade boost the dialogue between players operating in different countries, making it more difficult for authoritarian regimes to control economic agents.[22] Furthermore, a growing number of IOs tie free trade agreements to the existence of democratic regimes. If a democratic regime were overthrown, the enterprises could have their access to foreign markets revoked, which for purely economic reasons would induce them to defend the democratic institutions. After the 1967 coup, Greece was suspended from the Treaty of Association with the European Community, which set up considerable internal pressure to restore democracy, which Greece achieved in 1974.[23] Likewise, the attempted 1981 coup in Spain was resisted by enterprises owing to the consequences the coup would have had on Spain's proposed membership in the European Community.[24] Other regional organizations such as Mercosur, which are open solely to democratic countries, are also helping in consolidating democracy.[25]

---

21. For a practical guide accompanied by numerous national case histories, see IDEA, *Electoral Management Design: The International Handbook* (Stockholm: IDEA, 2006).

22. Russett and Oneal, *Triangulating Peace*; Youngs, *International Democracy and the West*.

23. Basilios Tsingos, "Underwriting Democracy: The European Community and Greece," pp. 315–55 in *International Dimensions of Democratization*, ed. Whitehead.

24. Charles Powell, "International Aspects of Democratization: The Case of Spain," pp. 285–314 in *International Dimensions of Democratization,* ed. Whitehead.

25. Francisco Domínguez and Marcos Guedes de Oliveira, eds., *Mercosur: Between Integration and Democracy* (Pieterlen: Peter Lang AG, 2004); Patomaki and Teivainen, "Critical Responses to Neoliberal Globalization in the Mercosur Region."

The EU represents the most successful case of an IO setting up and consolidating democratization. The EU has some of the toughest membership criteria of any organization: countries must attain a given level of democracy and maintain it over time. In two distinct historical periods, and in completely opposite international climates, the EU has played an extremely useful role in launching democratization. In the 1970s and 1980s, the EU played a central role in allowing southern European countries (Greece, Spain, and Portugal) to emerge from fascist regimes.[26] In more recent times it played the same role for European countries in the Soviet bloc. The EU has also very effectively promoted democracy outside its own continent.[27] The fact that the EU is a "civil power"[28] composed of numerous countries often in disagreement among themselves has meant that the EU's interventions were perceived not as imposition but as collaboration.

While much attention has been focused on economic incentives, as represented by access to the largest market in the world, the political incentives have often been underestimated. As soon as new members are admitted to the club, they enjoy the same status as founder members. Romania, admitted only in 2007, has a larger number of deputies in the European Parliament than the Netherlands, which is one of the six founder members. Even though each country has a different amount of economic muscle, each country has the same clout in defining institutional politics and foreign policy. Exclusion from the EU is in itself already a severe penalty. The EU does not simply give lessons in democracy, but once new members have been admitted, those new members define common policies jointly and democratically.

Europe must reproach itself for not having played the membership card when the former Yugoslavia broke up. Perhaps it would have been possible to avoid the savage civil war in Yugoslavia if the EU had demanded that each ethnic community should break off hostilities and be rewarded by being given a fast-tracked admission to the EU. It would thus have been possible to reduce the importance of the fight to delimit the frontiers, as EU membership would have guaranteed free circulation of persons, goods, and capital and the protection of human rights for each ethnic group. In that case, the EU failed either to offer a carrot or to use the stick. It was a failure, but the only one.

26. Whitehead, *International Dimensions of Democratization.*
27. Richard Youngs, *The European Union and the Promotion of Democracy* (Oxford: Oxford University Press, 2002).
28. Mario Telò, *Europe, a Civilian Power? European Union, Global Governance, World Order* (Houndmills: Palgrave Macmillan, 2006).

It may justly be objected that so far the EU has accepted new members from among countries that, owing to their economic level, infrastructures, and social capital, were considered likely to democratize, those deemed by the literature on the transition to be closest to success.[29] In the next years we will see if the EU will be able to take in countries that are culturally different (such as Turkey) and have substantially lower income levels (such as the southern Mediterranean countries). The lesson to be learned from the EU, however, is that as soon as a state takes seriously the political destiny of another community, that state should be coherent enough to bound with the other to form an institutional union. And since no one offered Afghanistan and Iraq the opportunity to become the twenty-eighth and twenty-ninth members of the EU, not to speak of the fifty-first and fifty-second states of the United States, the skepticism of those who believe that these wars do not encourage self-government is further reinforced.

8.5 Is It Still Possible to Export Democracy after the Invasion of Iraq?

The war in Iraq has reaped an unquantified but growing number of victims on the ground, made international relations stormier, and caused the West to forgo the role of leader among the developing countries that it had acquired thanks to its material and cultural resources. The war in Iraq has had another detrimental effect: it has shown the world's peoples that the West has not shaken off the habits of old colonialism and new imperialism, aggravated by its use today of the noble values of freedom and democracy as a rhetorical screen behind which to conceal the interests of restricted elites in power. Inside the West, this has produced a dramatic rupture between democratic governments and, at the same time, between governments and their own public opinion. Since the West possesses the resources and the will to export democracy, the Iraqi adventure is destined to decisively impact a future agenda.

A long list of factors explains why democratizing Iraq and Afghanistan proved so much more difficult than democratizing Germany, Italy, and Japan. It has been claimed that the former countries did not satisfy the minimum conditions regarding income level and political and religious culture. It has been claimed that a complete defeat of the previous regime is necessary to allow the transition. It has also been claimed that numerous errors were made in the way the transition administration

29. Cf. Linz and Stepan, *Problems of Democratic Consolidation*; Przeworski, *Sustainable Democracy*.

was handled.[30] All these arguments are valid, but none seem decisive. I claim that a war of aggression is a means that contradicts its end and this, more than any other factor, explains why the Iraqi people, instead of accepting a regime imposed by occupation forces, launched into a ferocious civil war and a stubborn resistance.

The damage was done not only in Iraq; just as the Vietnam War discredited the leadership of western countries and for more than a decade pushed many developing countries and national liberation movements toward political systems that were antagonistic toward those of liberal democracies, today an opposition has developed to the foreign policy of the western countries that will have unpredictable consequences. The wave of democratizations that started in 1989 has come to a sharp halt, and there are even dangers of regression: after 2003, and for the first time since 1990, the number of democracies has decreased rather than increased. It will take a long time and a lot of patience before the democratic countries regain the authority on the international scene that has been dissipated by Bush and Blair. Yet it would be mistaken to believe that the dramatic civil wars occurring in Iraq and Afghanistan are signs that there are people who are not "mature" enough for democracy or that the international context cannot contribute to its spread and consolidation.

The analysis in this chapter has revealed that the opportunity for self-determination may be exported, while the specific form of democratic government can only be imported; that is, the democratic government needs to be formed starting from a suitable endogenous political fabric. This rules out the possibility that democracy can be exported militarily, unless this exportation takes place after democratic countries have been attacked. The historical experience considered confirms that the cases of successful exportation of democracy were carried out by means of persuasion, incentives, and international collaboration. In this case there is no dilemma regarding the choice of means and ends: the aim of democracy is achieved much more easily when coherent means are adopted. This lesson is fully compliant with the cosmopolitan project outlined herein: the external conflict reinforces the authoritarian regimes, while an international system based on peace and collaboration

30. See the wide-ranging debate in Kuper, *Multilateral Strategies to Promote Democracy*, with interventions by Thomas Carothers, John Cavanagh, Sakiko Fukuda-Parr, Adam Przeworski, Mary Robinson, and Joseph Stiglitz. Larry Diamond, *Squandered Victory: The American Occupation and the Bungled Effort to Bring Democracy to Iraq* (New York: Times Books, 2005) blames the failure to democratize Iraq on a series of errors committed by the occupation troops rather than on the aggression itself.

makes life difficult for despots and encourages the internal oppositions required for an effective political liberalization.

The policy of persuasion, incentives, and sanctions is not always effective and is rarely timely. In South Africa, the apartheid regime, in spite of its extensive international isolation, remained in place for several decades before being removed, and also the despotic regimes in Myanmar and many other countries are still under the yoke of dictatorships. However, the carrot has a huge advantage over the stick: it does not cause any damage or harm for which the democracies have to take responsibility. No collateral damage is caused by the attempt to convince other countries to become democratic. At a time in which there is no certainty that evil means allow desirable goals to be achieved, it is wise to refrain from carrying out actions that compromise the democratic cause.

Chapter 9

A Cosmopolitan Perspective on the Self-Determination of Peoples

9.1 Self-Determination in the Globalization Era

The self-determination of peoples is one of the most frequent causes of conflict. Within consolidated states no less than in states that are breaking up, relatively dominant groups make use of the notion of self-determination to support their own project. The statistical data set out in table 9.1 show that the number of these claims is decreasing only slightly and that in the early years of the third millennium the demands for self-determination still underlie as many as twenty-five armed conflicts. Numerous other conflicts exist that have not exploded into war: in twenty-three areas of the world, a hybrid mixture of political and military means is implemented, and in fifty-four areas, traditional political methods are being used.[1] These conflicts vary widely: they range from demands for greater tolerance of the religious practices and the uses and customs of minorities to the desire to redraw the frontiers or create new states. Self-determination is an umbrella for many different, often mutually conflicting aspirations. One stark fact is obvious: the persistence of self-determination conflicts, which last much longer than conflicts due to other reasons, a persistence that perhaps indicates the difficulties involved in finding solutions and of the often irrational roots of the conflicts.

---

1. Marshall and Gurr, *Peace and Conflict 2005*, pp. 21 and 25.

Table 9.1

Armed Conflicts for Self-Determination and Their Outcome, 1956–2006

Period	New Armed Conflicts	In Progress at the End of the Period	Conflicts Contained	Conflicts Won or Resolved
Before 1956		4	—	—
1956–1960	4	8	0	0
1961–1965	5	12	0	1
1966–1970	5	15	2	0
1971–1975	11	23	0	3
1976–1980	10	31	2	0
1981–1985	7	37	0	1
1986–1990	11	43	2	3
1991–1995	20	45	9	9
1996–2000	6	38	7	7
2001–2006	8	26	15	6
Total	87	—	37	30

Source: J. Joseph Hewitt, Jonathan Wilkenfeld, and Ted Robert Gurr, eds., *Peace and Conflict 2008* (College Park, MD: Center for International Development & Conflict Management, 2007), p. 34.

A more attentive reading of these claims to self-determination reveals that underlying the "right to self-determination" are three quite different categories. The first category is the self-determination of colonized peoples. This is the meaning expressed in the UN Charter and in many other sources of international law. The international community widely accepts the legitimacy of this claim nowadays, with only a few lamentable exceptions. The second interpretation refers to the claims of minorities desirous of seceding from the state to which they belong. This was the meaning most in vogue at the end of the Cold War and the one most directly associated with the armed conflicts and civil wars of the last decade. The third interpretation is related to certain ethnic or cultural groups that, although willing to continue to be part of their state of origin, want to obtain specific collective rights. The third interpretation is the most innovative and has given rise to an intense debate, particularly in the democratic states. All three interpretations have a theoretical and practical validity, although accompanied also by powerful political and intellectual obstacles. In all three cases, self-determination appears as a claim, a subjective right, that has still to find a precise correspondence with an objective right. This chapter explores the relationship between the self-determination of peoples and cosmopolitan democracy. Self-determination is, as illustrated in the preceding chapter, the first of a democratic system. But this points to a still unresolved issue: how can a "people" be defined, identifying thus the political community that has the right to self-determination? A people is not an element that can be traced back to a state of nature but rather a historical and social construct.[2]

The term *self-determination* can refer to different situations. It may refer to the *internal* forms of government of the community, whereby citizens can nominate and instruct their rulers. But the association of the term *self-determination* with that of *people* presupposes that the people is free from *external* pressures. We are thus dealing with *two* forms of self-determination: internal and external. How does the internal component interact with the external one? The concept of self-determination therefore immediately suggests another: sovereignty. As soon as a given political community is identified with a people, it indeed demands that sovereign power set its own norms. Even though this identification conforms with democratic rules, it may clash with cosmopolitan thinking, which instead assumes that each community's norms must be compatible with the norms of other communities. This causes tension between the principle of the self-determination of peoples and the cosmopolitan view. It is not surprising that it has been attempted to distinguish between the principle of nondomination and that of noninterference, between autonomy and self-determination.[3] Outside a cosmopolitan system, the self-determination principle is liable to stir up particularistic and chauvinistic claims that may clash with certain fundamental rights. I do not intend to address the never-ending controversy between relativism and universalism but rather the more specific issue of how to define the boundaries of a political community. To what extent can a cosmopolitan democracy help minimize the use of violence?

The next section concisely indicates of a few steps in the evolution of meta-state law, in order to show how peoples have on several occasions appeared on the scene in the history of juridical thinking. The following

2. See Rainer Bauböck, "Paradoxes of Self-Determination and the Right to Self-Governance," pp. 101–28 in *Bulwarks of Localism: Human Rights in Context*, ed. Christopher L. Eisgruber and Andras Sajo (Leiden: Martinus Nijhoff Publishers, 2005).
3. Bauböck, "Paradoxes of Self-Determination"; Iris Marion Young, "Self-Determination and Global Democracy: A Critique of Liberal Nationalism," pp. 147–83 in *Designing Democratic Institutions*, ed. Ian Shapiro and Stephen Macedo (New York: New York University Press, 2000).

section examines what a people consists of from the point of view of political and institutional organization and concludes that "a people" is a fleeting and ambiguous concept. For this reason, seeking to equate state and people is as unfeasible as it is harmful. The concluding section presents and analyzes three meanings of self-determination, showing that a cosmopolitan juridical system must support each meaning. The final section indicates ways and means of recovering what is essential in each of the three interpretations of the self-determination of peoples.

9.2 Patterns in the Rights of Peoples Over Time

The concept of the self-determination of peoples is based on the assumption that the people themselves hold certain rights. This means establishing rights that are different from those recognized as belonging to states and individuals. The problem is certainly not a new one; on numerous occasions in the course of the evolution of law, lawyers, diplomats, and politicians have perceived the need of juridical categories of a different nature from those of state and interstate public law. The Romans at the height of the imperial period, the Spanish at the time of their encounter with the new world, and the European states before and after the French Revolution, albeit for different reasons, felt the need to support and sometimes even to guarantee the rights of "peoples" even when those peoples did not form a "state."

The problem of the self-determination of peoples again came to the fore during World War I. Similar terminology was used by the Bolsheviks and President Wilson: both preached the self-determination of peoples, albeit attributing different significance to the term. The Bolsheviks referred above all to self-determination on the inside, in the belief that the main factor of division on among peoples is representated by the dominance of autocratic governments and by a social minority that oppresses the majority of the population. President Wilson, on the other hand, promised to achieve the self-determination of peoples from the outside, if necessary by redrawing the frontiers in such a way as to create state communities that were homogeneous from the cultural, ethnic, geographic, and linguistic points of view. The collapse of a great multilingual organization such as the Austro-Hungarian Empire—which was cosmopolitan, but not democratic!—marked the transition from one era to another.

At the Paris Peace Conference, Wilson was obliged to mediate between the European governments and the U.S. Congress itself. The Bolsheviks, who might have been his most precious allies in the matter, were kept at arm's length. Aside from personal interests, however, which were destined to prevail, Wilson's rationalist principles had to come to terms with history and geography. It emerged at the conference that the self-determination of peoples could not technically lead to the creation of a state for each people. In a Europe based on the existence of nation-states, new states were established with very large ethnic minorities: Czechoslovakia, Yugoslavia, Poland, and the Baltic Republics all became new countries in which the various peoples were forced to cohabit.[4]

Not wishing to appear as dupes, the great powers at the Paris Peace Conference demanded and obtained that the governments of the new states should undertake to recognize and guarantee certain rights for their minorities. The new states would also be obliged to accept restrictions on the exercise of their own internal sovereignty by allowing the international institution being set up at the time, the League of Nations, to act as guarantor on behalf of the minorities. As pointed out by Arendt, the fact that minorities needed their rights guaranted by international institution signified in truth declaring a state of political minority of the minorities.[5] An equally significant case is that of Germany; the Treaty of Versailles imposed many international obligations on Germany (starting with reparations), but paradoxically no obligation to safeguard ethnic minorities. The birth of the Weimar Republic, which was proud to be based on the guarantee of individual rights, seemed to suggest that, at least in this regard, the Paris Peace Conference had been far-sighted and that in Germany being citizens of the state was enough to have one's individual rights respected. However, it was in Germany that the fundamental violation of the rights of a people, the Jews, occurred, that is, of a people that up to only a few years earlier could consider themselves fully integrated into the German society.

It was perhaps because of the still-fresh memory of the mistaken judgments made at the Paris Peace Conference that, after the tragedy of World War II, the UN Charter was much more cautious in accepting the dichotomy between states and peoples. In the charter, the reference to peoples is interpreted as being to the colonized peoples who, in a relatively distant future, would become states.[6] No provision was made to solve the problem of the ethnic or linguistic minorities inside states that had already been established; if the UN meant to protect certain rights of the peoples, they did so by protecting individual rights.

4. Cf. the vivid account given by Arendt, *Origins of Totalitarianism*, in particular chapter 9, § I.
5. Arendt, *Origins of Totalitarianism*, p. 276.
6. See, for instance, art. 73.

9.3 What Is a People?

The concept of the self-determination of peoples instinctively arouses strong feelings of sympathy among the champions of democracy. Suffice it to imagine the opposite—*hetero*-determination—which takes place in external occupation or under authoritarian governments. But in order to give the concept of the self-determination of peoples a complete meaning, it is also necessary to define what is meant by a people. This concept, a people, is one of the vaguest imaginable. When we refer to a state, there is no ambiguity; we know where the state's frontiers are, what the prevailing law is inside each state, and what international norms the state has agreed to respect. But a people has no unequivocal definition. Language, religion, race, and a shared history can all contribute to the definition of a people without, however, any one of these aspects unequivocally determining who is to be included and who excluded. The U.S. Constitution opens with the emblematic words "We the People of the United States" and is a rare case in which *people* coincides with *citizens*. Basques, Irish, Padanians, Palestinians, Kurds, Armenians, Georgians, Quebecers, Serbs, Croats, Chechens, Luxemburgers, Red Indians, Sardinians, Ladins, Val d'Aostans, Walloons, the Flemish, Scots, and the Welsh are all groups that may be identified on a territorial basis and can be defined as a people, although without this implying any corresponding citizenship. But *people* may be defined also with reference to categories of persons that have no territorial contiguity. Catholics and Protestants, Arabs and Jews, Arsenal and Tottenham fans may also be defined as peoples. No limits may be imposed on a group that wishes to construct an "imaginary identity."[7] The confused list of groups wishing to be classified as a "people" clearly shows how the definition can be applied to a wide range of situations, and it is not surprising that this can easily become the cause of armed conflicts. My current interest is focused on a specific interpretation, namely, the interpretation in which a people is identified with a political community and that consequently opens up the way to certain rights and duties.

David Miller proposed a few criteria that can be used to identify a nation, such as: (1) an internally shared set of convictions, (2) an identity inclusive of a historical continuity and the commitment to preserve and develop it, (3) a geographic space, and (4) several distinctive elements such as a national character arising out of a shared public culture.[8] Although these criteria may be widely accepted academically, the real problem is to get the parties in conflict to agree to them. If the par-

7. Benedict Anderson, *Imagined Communities* (London: Verso, 1991).
8. David Miller, *On Nationality* (Oxford: Clarendon Press, 1995).

ties do not agree, political conflict often turns into military conflict. The definition of *people* has always been arbitrary, although this arbitrariness has more direct implications today when the inhabitants of the planet are subdivided into states that impose a criterion of disjunctive membership. When the state becomes the agent that gives specific form to a people, the state inevitably ends up not only by including but also by excluding. And exclusion is more frequently at the root of conflict than inclusion.

Each state on the planet is an imperfect representation of a people in two different senses. In one sense, a state may represent more than one people; the United States is made up of dozens of peoples, and this has actually become a reason for national pride. In the other sense, a state may not necessarily represent an entire people; its members can be citizens of several states. Irish, for example, may refer to the citizens of Ireland, the United Kingdom, or the United States. That peoples can voice their opinion and are represented in world political life just as when they are subjects or citizens of a specific state is therefore a source of richness; that they must form states in order to have their voice heard is instead anachronistic.

From the cultural and sociological point of view, nothing prevents any community of persons that recognizes itself as having a given identity from being defined as a people. Here there is no discussion about the fact that the Irish hold St. Patrick's Day celebrations, the Rome football club supporters identify with the yellow and red jersey, and the Scots wear kilts. The freedom to engage in this behavior actually belongs to the sphere of individual liberties. In order to obtain a collective identity, a group of persons does not necessarily have to set up its own state or indeed claim its own sovereignty. Separating the two aspects, Ferrajoli has suggested giving any collective group that asks for it the power to call itself a people.[9] This kind of generosity, however, could remain an empty gesture unless it associates some specific right with the definition of a people. If, instead, this approach involves the recognition of specific rights, it may clash with the rights recognized for individuals. For example, does a people also have the right to exclude other subjects? Could the majority of German citizens of Aryan race decide that the German citizens of Jewish race should not belong to the German people and should even be deprived of their German citizenship? These are only rhetorical questions, and agreement is easily reached regarding extreme

9. Luigi Ferrajoli, "Il diritto all'autodeterminazione nell'età della globalizzazione," in Fondazione Basso, *Il diritto all'autodeterminazione dei popoli alle soglie del 2000* (Roma: Fondazione Basso, 1999).

cases. In numerous cases, however, substantial disagreement exists on the collective rights accorded to some citizens and not to others.

If every people in the world corresponded to a state and if each of these peoples lived solely and exclusively inside the borders of their own state, we would certainly not need to turn to the notion of people's rights. The conventional notions of public law and interstate law would be necessary and sufficient, and the concept of self-determination would be valid exclusively within and not outside states. History and geography oblige us to acknowledge, however, that state and people do not coincide. The member states of the UN total 192, while the ethnic communities are in the hundreds and active languages total nearly 7,000.

The idea of establishing a correspondence between political community and a people is a very old one: in the early fifteenth century, this was Joan of Arc's political program. During and after the Napoleonic Wars, at a time in which the formation and abolition of states had become a military academic exercise, many thinkers believed that they could put an end to European political disorder by creating states that represented homogeneous ethnic and linguistic communities. But even during the Napoleonic era, it was found difficult to associate ethnic, linguistic, cultural, and religious identity with a given territory. Increasing globalization, the great migrations, and the subdivision of the planet into territorial states have meant that nowadays it is impossible for state and people to coincide. Can we imagine how to go about setting up 7,000 linguistically homogeneous states? The international community could easily cope with such a transformation; the diplomatic system, the IOs, including the UN, could continue to function even with 700 or even 7,000 member states instead of 192—the solution would not be unfeasible from the international point of view. The problem would arise above all inside the states, as the fragmentation of states would mean redrawing the frontiers, thus flouting both history and geography. It would be necessary to deploy such means as war, ethnic cleansing, forced deportation, or even genocide on a hitherto unprecedented scale.[10]

10. It is quite disturbing to note that a brilliant liberal like David Miller, merely in order to have political communities correspond to his principle of nationality, could suggest resorting to a kind of preventive ethnic cleansing. Cf. "Secession and the Principle of Nationality," pp. 110–24 in David Miller, *Citizenship and National Identity* (Cambridge: Polity Press, 2000), on p. 121. The solution suggested herein is exactly the opposite, namely, the formation of state political communities capable of accommodating several cultures and several nationalities.

9.4 The Three Interpretations of the Self-Determination of Peoples

In order to take a closer look at the notion of the self-determination of peoples, we should assess at least three interpretations from the point of view of the subjective law claimed by political agents:

i.   the right of colonized peoples to form a state of their own;
ii. the right of the minorities of a state or states to form an autonomous state;
iii. the right of ethnic minorities to enjoy certain collective rights inside the state

This taxonomy is slightly different to that suggested by Ronen and Cassese in that it groups together similar categories and underlines the internal/external relationship.[11] Of course, the three categories are interconnected; the same people can further their case by using one of the three interpretations depending on the circumstances. A people can, for example, demand that certain collective rights be recognized by their own state (third meaning) and, should these demands be ignored or indeed repressed then demand their own political independence in order to pursue their own rights (second meaning). This is the case of the Kurdish people, whose pressure to set up a sovereign state of their own is directly proportional to the repression exerted by the other states (whether Turkey, Iraq, Iran, or Syria) on their cultural, religious, and linguistic identity. Depending on its policy toward minorities, a state may thus find it has to cope with claims of the second or third type.

Demands of the first and third type can be alternative. Some peoples who were colonized by European powers have not asked to set up autonomous states because they were satisfied with their degree of internal self-determination. Greenland, for example, continues to be an autonomous territory under the Danish crown, as the autonomy it has obtained on the basis of point (iii) above did not trigger the desire to set up an independent state.

It is also difficult, more in theory than in practice, to trace out a clear dividing line between the first and the second interpretation. Many nationalist political movements aspiring to become independent (for example, several Basque factions) claim their people has been colonized. A difference may be detected, however, between the ethnic minority of a

11. Dov Ronen, *The Quest for Self-Determination* (New Haven: Yale University Press, 1979), pp. 9–12; Antonio Cassese, *Self-Determination of Peoples: A Legal Reappraisal* (Cambridge: Cambridge University Press, 1996), pp. 316–17.

state and a colonized people: in the first case, the state recognizes both the "minority" and the "majority" as having the same rights and duties, while in the second case the state envisages different rights and duties for the "colonized" people than for the "colonizers." On the basis of this distinction it may be claimed that, at the time of apartheid, the black population of South Africa was included in the first category and that of the Basques in the second.[12] The following sections examine the three different meanings.

9.5 The Right of Colonized Peoples to Form a State

It is certainly not a coincidence that the principle of self-determination was resuscitated after World War II as a reaction to colonial domination by the western states. In the 1950s, 1960s, and 1970s, self-determination was interpreted mainly as the right of peoples to set up their own state, adopting the same conceptual and juridical categories as were used to reorganize European society after World War I.[13] "Nearly 100 territories designed as colonial under Chapters XI and XII of the UN Charter have become independent and have been admitted to the United Nations," recalls the jurist James Crawford.[14] The largest group of UN members is represented by peoples that have gained the right to self-determination.

In cases such as that of India or Algeria, self-determination meant allowing these peoples to set up sovereign states in opposition to those who had conquered them. England and India, France and Algeria had no shared cultural, geographic, ethnic, or religious affinity. In addition, the rights accorded to Indian or Algerian citizens were quite different from those recognized for British or French citizens. In these cases, the notion of people's right takes on a *transitory* configuration: as soon as

12. Not even this qualification can get the opposing parties to agree, however. The separatist movements, although formally enjoying the same civil and political rights, probably suffer from economic and social discriminations or do not enjoy adequate guarantees, for instance, in terms of security.
13. See the overview by Cassese, *Self-Determination of Peoples*. The crowning point of this phase was represented by the Charter of Algiers, a document agreed upon by a set of NGOs. Cf. François Rigaux, *La Carta d'Algeri* (S. Domenico di Fiesole: Edizioni cultura della pace, 1988).
14. James Crawford, "State Practice and International Law in Relation to Secession," *British Yearbook of International Law*, vol. 69 (1998): 85–117, on p. 90.

the people in question obtains its own sovereignty, peoples' law is replaced by state and interstate law.

We can now reexamine the events related to the self-determination of colonized peoples with a pinch of critical sense. The liberation movements that aimed at setting up their own states intended to achieve self-determination from the outside. The mode of exercising self-determination on the interior was instead set aside during the national liberation struggles. World public opinion, which actively demonstrated in favor of the independence of India and Algeria, and of the respect of the sovereignty of states such as Vietnam and Cambodia, demanded self-determination from the outside, relying implicitly on the assumption that the liberation movements in question would allow also self-determination from the inside. Too much insistence on the mode of self-determination on the inside for as long as these peoples were under the colonial yoke at best was paternalistic and at worst would lead to the conservation of colonial domination and imperialist occupation. The Indians and Algerians had certainly much to learn from the democratic system in force in Great Britain and France, but this issue was of secondary and subordinated importance vis-à-vis the sacred request by these countries to attain their own self-determination from the outside. As long as the noble western liberal democracies were tarnishing their reputation with colonial crimes, those democracies could not be taken seriously as models of democracy by the peoples in the developing countries.

The decolonization experience showed that self-determination from the outside and the inside do not necessarily coincide. This divergence has often caused serious political difficulties: the world public opinion which for years had supported certain liberation movements in order to uphold the right of peoples to self-determination from the outside, suddenly found itself having to oppose the same liberation movements as soon as those movements conquered power because they denied self-determination on the inside. Cambodia in the 1970s is a case in point. It is not hard to see why the successes of self-determination on the inside, that is, of democracy, were so few and far between. An authority that could decide on the form of internal government to adopt has always been absent. With what possible legitimacy could the British, French, or Americans, who until the day before had often been brutal overlords, credibly recommend that the Indians, Algerians, Vietnamese, or Cambodians adopt the institutions characterizing modern representative democracy? Giving full power to the right of peoples to self-determination would have required juridical norms and institutions that would interfere in the internal affairs of the states. The international institutions themselves, starting with the UN, which had nevertheless played a very important role in the decolonization process, proved incapable of helping the peoples that were laboriously setting up their own states to achieve their internal self-determination.

This further aspect must be emphasized: the national liberation movements, although opposed to the colonizing western powers, accepted the frontiers inherited even when they had been drawn quite arbitrarily. What, indeed, made India a homogenous political community? Why should India set up a single state instead of three or twenty-five different states? And what about a case in which the various local communities might have disagreed? Who would ultimately resolve the disagreement? The cement binding together the many national liberation movements was often simply having been oppressed by the same country. These liberation movements did not represent homogeneous communities in terms of language, race, or religion. Once freed from the colonial yoke, these liberation movements had to invent a national identity they did not possess.[15] Also in the widely accepted case of the self-determination of the colonized populations, it thus emerges that the notion of the right of peoples is insufficient to resolve two essential problems: self-determination on the inside and redrawing existing frontiers. This notion leads to the need to incorporate self-determination in a broader juridical framework, that of the cosmopolitan system championed herein.

9.6 The Right of Minorities to Form a State

The 1980s also saw the beginning of a substantial increase in another kind of claim, that of ethnic, linguistic, or religious minorities wishing to form a state.[16] Croats, Ukrainians, Chechens, Basques, Quebecers, Scots, and even Padanians have appealed to the right of peoples to justify secession from their state of origin and set up an autonomous state. Other peoples, such as the Kurds, have put forward the same claim versus the various states over which their people is scattered.

In a small number of fortunate cases, secession has taken place without conflict.[17] In many other cases, the dreams of independence of some peoples clashed with other aspirations. In the contested cases, which sadly became more numerous after the end of the Cold War, the demand

15. Anderson, *Imagined Communities.*
16. See the well-thought-out review by Allen Buchanan, "Theories of Secession," *Philosophy and Public Affairs* vol. 26, no. 1 (1997): 31–61.
17. For an analysis of peaceful secessions, cf. Robert A. Young, "How Do Peaceful Secessions Happen?" *Canadian Journal of Political Science* vol. 27, no. 4 (1994): 773–92.

to secede led to civil wars and bloody conflicts. This is not surprising, as the configuration of modern states means that each secession leads to the birth of a new ethnic minority. As Habermas pointed out, the redrawing of borders only causes new minorities; as in Chinese boxes, whenever a minority community is discerned, a minority appears within the minority.[18] The few cases of bloodless secession (Slovakia from the Czech Republic and Slovenia from the Yugoslav Federation) were those that did not have any significant ethnic minorities on the inside of the newly forming state.[19]

The former Yugoslavia was the tragic test laboratory for this process. A spiral was set up in which (a) the Yugoslav state discriminated against several ethnic minorities; (b) these ethnic minorities aimed to protect themselves from discrimination by affirming their own identity and demanded to set up a sovereign state of their own; (c) at the same time, also in reprisal against the established state powers, these minorities denied the rights of the ethnic minorities living inside them; and (d) this caused the Yugoslav state to defend the minorities of the minorities. The result was a vicious circle in which weapons and violence became the only right.[20] The multiplication of states was unable to resolve the problem; not even creating a separate state for each family would have established homogeneous states.

All the groups involved in the conflict in the former Yugoslavia appealed to the right to self-determination of their *own* people. Those who wanted the separation of Croatia or Kosovo appealed to the right of the Croatians or Kosovars to form a sovereign state, while those who wanted to retain the Yugoslav federal state appealed to the rights of the newly established Serb minorities in Croatia and Kosovo; those who wanted an independent Bosnian state appealed to the right of the Bosnian people, who wanted the union of Serbs and appealed to the right of the Bosnian Serb people, and so on. Unfortunately, appealing to the right of peoples and the principle of self-determination was not enough to avert the spread of violence.

The various conflicting demands for self-determination were settled in the most brutal and traditional of ways: by military force to win sov-

18. Jürgen Habermas, "Struggles for Recognition in Constitutional States," *European Journal of Philosophy* vol. 1, no. 2 (1993): 128–55.
19. Crawford, "State Practice and International Law," p. 86, points out the juridical difference between secession, which is unilateral, and devolution or grant of independence, which follows an agreement between the parties involved.
20. See the passionate accounts by Kaldor, *New and Old Wars* and Marcon, *Dopo il Kosovo.*

ereignty. Each ethnic community, whether real or imagined, fought with all its might to obtain sovereignty over a given territory. The international community proved incapable of proposing solutions in which the frontiers of the states and the rights of the ethnic minorities and individuals to be guaranteed were jointly defined.[21] The international community proved even less capable of imposing peace and the enforcement of human rights within each political community. The lesson to be learned from the former Yugoslavia and the wave of ethno-nationalism that we have witnessed over the past decade is that a people's demand to form an independent state does not always solve the problem of obtaining the respect of individual rights; the new state is often compelled to accommodate minorities to the same extent as the original state. The peoples involved often felt the lack of a power of arbitration at a higher level than the parties involved that could offer a peaceful solution and guarantee each community. The legitimacy and functionality of the claims by the various ethnic groups should be assessed on the basis of three criteria:

1. *Actual verification of the will of the people to form an autonomous state of their own.* The demand for secession has no political value in the absence of a deliberate claim by the majority of citizens involved. The cases of the Basque countries, Padania, and Croatia actually show how relatively unrepresentative political groups can claim to speak in the name of a people. If they deliberately pursue a strategy of increasing conflict, they obtain the result of compelling a large part of the population to take sides, however reluctant the population may be to do so initially. Fomenting strife is the simplest way to increase consent. Whenever it has been ascertained that the majority of the population wants to set up an autonomous state, the claim must be pursued on the basis of existing constitutional norms. The constitutionalization of the right to secession is the best way of rendering separatist demands harmless.[22] If such a right is not envisaged in the states' constitutional system, as in the case of Italy, it is necessary to activate the channels already available in the international system.

2. *Protection of the rights of individuals and minorities.* Before setting up a new state, it is necessary to guarantee the rights of

---

21. The various plans for dividing up Bosnia presented by the EU and the UN (Carrington–Cutileiro, September 1991; Vance–Owen, January 1993; Owen–Stoltenberg, August 1993) focused more on the territorial boundaries than on the safeguarding of human rights.

22. Daniel Weinstock, "Constitutionalising the Right to Secede," *Journal of Political Philosophy* vol. 9, no. 2 (2001): 182–203.

groups that are about to become new ethnic minorities. The problem of a minority that deems itself to be oppressed cannot be solved by turning it into an oppressive majority. The experience of the republics that arose after the dissolution of the Soviet Union has shown that the resident Russian populations suddenly changed from oppressive majorities to oppressed minorities. A right should not be safeguarded by sacrificing one people rather than another. The fight for land could be made much less bitter if the contending parties, before discussing the possible formation of new states or redrawing the frontiers, were to agree on how to guarantee the protection of both individual and collective rights.

3. *Monitoring and control by supranational institutions.* The secession of one region of a state cannot be considered a purely internal problem. In the presence of massive conflicts between the state and the ethnic groups seeking autonomy, the principal element for a peaceful composition of the conflict is disregarded—namely, mutual confidence. Problems such as the drawing new frontiers and assigning rights to minorities are unlikely to be solved without the action of a third, superior, political authority above the parties.

Two questions remain to be solved: (a) what rules of conduct must this third party obey, and (b) which institutions of the international community are supposed to carry out these interventions. So far, the international community has been rather reluctant to play a more active role in cases involving the demand for secession. Crawford's review suggests that the international community prefers not to "accept unilateral secession outside the colonial context. This practice has not changed since 1989, despite the emergence during that period of 22 new states. On the contrary, the practice has been powerfully reinforced."[23] It is not surprising that the international community, the main actors of which are represented by the states, are so unwilling to recognize new states without the prior consent of the existing state. For the states, sovereignty must be respected and interference avoided. However, such a passive role is not necessarily a good thing and often leaves the parties in conflict (namely, the existing state on the one hand and the separatist movements on the other) with the sole alternative of using force. The international community could play a more useful role in preventing conflicts by acting as an ex-ante arbitrator in cases requiring the redrawing of the frontiers, and as a guarantor of individual and collective rights, rather than merely recognizing ex-post what has in the meantime become a de facto reality owing to the use of violence.

23. Crawford, "State Practice and International Law," p. 114.

9.7 Right of the Minorities to Certain Collective Rights inside the State

A third interpretation of the self-determination of peoples is used by peoples that do not demand the establishment of a state but simply the recognition and safeguarding of certain collective rights. These peoples do not question their membership in their own state of origin, nor do they claim to have any valid reason for obtaining special protection insofar as they are minorities. In this interpretation, the peoples claim their rights versus the territorial state of origin. This is the case of some indigenous peoples, for instance, the native Indians in Canada and the United States and the Australian aborigines.[24] Very similar situations have occurred after recent settlements by ethnic communities in foreign countries, for instance, the Turkish community in Germany and the Arab community in France. Migrations in the contemporary era and the increasingly large ethnic communities in foreign countries (suffice it to consider that Berlin has become one of the largest Turkish city in the world) will result in this type of claim becoming ever more frequent. Self-determination is not associated with the demand to set up a state but is addressed to the state of origin for the purpose of obtaining, for example, autonomy in certain fields, such as education and the language in which this is imparted, or else waivers to allow certain religious practices to be performed. In such a context, the right to self-determination is no longer totalizing but identified with the collective rights of minorities with regard to education, welfare and other specific aspects.

In the global society, if the states do not intend to pursue ethnic cleansing, isolationism, or the compulsory integration of minorities, the states are obliged to become multicultural and multiethnic.[25] This interpretation of the right of peoples thus represents an important juridical instru-

24. For these cases, cf. James Crawford, ed., *The Rights of Peoples* (Oxford: Oxford University Press, 1988). On the specific condition of indigenous peoples, see Benedict Kingsbury, " 'Indigenous Peoples' in International Law," *American Journal of International Law* vol. 92, no. 3 (1998): 414–57; Nieves Zúñiga, *Los pueblos indígenas y el sistema internacional* (Barcelona: Obra Social Fundación la Caixa, 2005).

25. In the increasingly vast literature dedicated to multiculturalism, see Kymlicka, *Multicultural Citizenship*; James Tully, *Strange Multiplicity: Constitutionalism in an Age of Diversity* (Cambridge: Cambridge University Press, 1996). Alain-G. Gagnon and James Tully, eds., *Multinational Democracies* (Cambridge: Cambridge University Press, 2001); and Michael Keating, *Plurinational Democracies; Stateless Nations in a Post-Sovereignty, Era* (Oxford: Oxford University Press, 2004) address the more specific case of states that must accommodate several nations.

ment for helping the states to manage communities having highly different traditions and cultural values. Here self-determination is not so much a matter of international law as of internal public law. Not even this interpretation rules out the external component entirely. Some ethnic minorities inside states may demand that their voice be heard separately in IOs, as is the case of the Roma people in Europe (this is what a reformed UN should endeavor to do; cf. § 6.5). As soon as the minorities are no longer adequately guaranteed by the existing laws of the state, the minorities can also attempt to obtain protection via international law and institutions.[26]

In some states, specific citizens are allowed to benefit from additional rights, as they belong to particular peoples. This is a quite frequent case: in Alto Adige, German-speaking Italians receive certain benefits from the state that are not extended to Italian-speaking citizens. In Canada and Australia, the aborigines have rights that are not granted to the other citizens. In Great Britain itself, multiculturalism has led to the introduction of different norms for various groups.[27] The Sikhs, for instance, are allowed to ride motorcycles without having to wear crash helmets. In the case in which the minorities enjoy rights, waivers, and limited concessions, the latter run the risk of coming into conflict with the notion of the universality of law and de facto oppose individual rights to collective rights.[28]

Guaranteeing some collective rights may also lead to conflict with the community in which these ethnic minorities live. The use of the *chador* and *burqa* by the Muslim minority in Europe has led to a passionate debate, and the member states of the EU have often reacted differently, with the United Kingdom being more permissive and France more restrictive. How far can the principle of liberal tolerance be pushed? Infibulation, for example, is treated as a criminal offence in most western countries,[29] while tattooing and piercing carry no criminal penalty. While agreement exists on the extreme cases (no one is prepared to allow an adulterous wife to be stoned to death), intermediate cases are controversial and produce different attitudes in similar countries.

26. See Benedict Kingsbury, "Reconciling Five Competing Conceptual Structures of Indigenous Peoples' Claims in International and Comparative Law," *NYU Journal of International Law and Politics* vol. 34, no. 1 (2001): 189–250; Philip Alston, ed., *Peoples' Rights* (Oxford: Oxford University Press, 2001).

27. See, for instance, the analysis made by the Commission on the Future of Multi-ethnic Britain, chaired by Lord Bhikhu Parekh, *The Future of Multi-Ethnic Britain* (London: Profile Books, 2000).

28. The most radical criticism of multiculturalism from the liberal standpoint was made by Brian Barry, *Culture and Equality* (Cambridge: Polity Press, 2001).

29. The issue is reviewed by the UN Population Fund at www.unfpa.org.

In a world characterized by mounting migratory flows, conflicts between state norms and the claims made by particular ethnic and cultural communities inside the state will tend to increase further. A truly multi-ethnic and multicultural state should therefore provide in its own system for ways and means of dealing with these conflicts. At the same time it is difficult to think that minorities will acknowledge the state institutions as sufficiently legitimate. A French law court called upon to make a decision regarding the chador will be considered by the Muslim minorities as disrespectful of Muslim cultural traditions. This interpretation of self-determination, in order to be considered fully valid, needs a cosmopolitan law and institutions that can as needed decide on which norms may be accorded to the minorities and which not.

9.8 The Inconsistency of the Self-Evaluation of Self-Determination

The problem of the self-determination of peoples causes numerous and often bloody conflicts. What prospects can cosmopolitan democracy offer to reduce the number and the violence of these conflicts and at the same time to enforce democratic norms and human rights? In this chapter, three meanings of the self-determination of peoples have been identified. Table 9.2 summarizes the reasoning followed. All three cases show that the principle of self-determination has a specific validity if it is incorporated in a cosmopolitan juridical system that represents the point of view of the citizens of the world as much as it does that of states and individual peoples.

Let us summarize the three meanings. The first meaning, that of the right of peoples to establish their own state, has been appealed to by national liberation movements and their supporters. As a political project, this meaning encountered success with decolonization. This meaning has a transitory value, as it works toward its own replacement: as soon as the peoples achieve self-determination from the outside, they set up a state of their own and therefore replace the right of a people with the right of a state. Historical experience shows, however, that liberation movements, having achieved self-determination from the outside, are often ill-inclined to allow self-determination on the inside or to guarantee the rights of the newly formed minorities. The UN's reluctance to interfere in the internal affairs of the new states and the lack of a wide recognition for the values of democracy at the end of decolonization certainly did not help. If ways and means had been found to link self-determination from the outside to that on the inside, many civil wars and genocides would probably have been avoided.

Table 9.2
Different Meanings of the Self-Determination of Peoples

Subjective Right Claimed	Paradigmatic Historical Cases	Objective Law Inside States	Suprastate Objective Law
Right of colonial peoples to become states	India, Algeria, Angola, etc. Nearly 100 UN member countries.	Existing: lacking. The independence of colonial peoples has generally been the result of a conflict.	Existing: United Nations Charter, pacts on civil and political rights, pacts on economic, social, and cultural rights, and subsequent developments.
Right of peoples to secede from state	Achieved: Republics of the former Soviet Union, Slovakia, Slovenia, Croatia, Macedonia, etc. 22 new states since 1989.	Existing: generally not envisaged save as outcome of conflict. In some cases, envisaged in the constitutional system (e.g., Canada).	Existing: absent. The international community recognizes peoples only if they have rebelled or following the conquest of a given territory.
	Claimed: Kosovo, Basque Countries, Quebec, Scotland, Kurdistan, Padania, etc.	To be claimed: creation of procedures to evaluate the legitimacy of the secession, consulation of majorities and minorities, protection of human rights, sharing of resources.	To be claimed: arbitral activity of international institution in redefining controversial frontiers and guaranteeing protection of human rights in new states.

Right of peoples as minorities inside the state		
Native populations: Australian aborigines, Indigenous peoples in the United States and Canada, etc.	Existing: in some states collective rights are envisaged to protect minorities.	Existing: the right of minorities is mainly considered an internal affair of sovereign stages.
Ethnic minorities: Basques, Quebecers, South Tyroleans, etc	To be claimed: creation of institutions and procedures designed to periodically match the rights of minorities with those of majorities.	To be claimed: monitoring and evaluation of minorities' claims for protection of their cultural and political identify.
Immigrants: Turks in Germany, Arabs in France, Mexicans in the United States, Albanians in Italy, etc.		

On the strength of the second meaning, the right of peoples refers instead to cases in which a few ethnic or cultural groups demand to secede from their state of origin and form a state of their own. In this case we are also dealing with a transitory meaning: if secession is achieved, you leave the right of peoples and return to the dichotomy between internal and international law. It is really difficult to decide when such a request is legitimate, as redrawing state borders necessarily entails creating new minorities.[30] In the first instance, the process demands that the world community should enforce the rights of individuals and minorities, and secondly, that institutions should be set up with an arbitral and jurisdictional function to settle conflicting claims from ethnic groups. It would certainly be an advantage if the constitutions of the states included "a suitably restrictive right to secession,"[31] but only a few constitutions envisage norms to regulate secession, just as only a few persons getting married sign a contract to regulate a possible divorce. External mediators could help defuse the vicious circle leading from the discrimination of minorities to their radicalization and so on.

The third meaning refers to the collective rights that certain ethnic groups claim from the state to which they belong (and from which they have no intention of seceding). This is a problem more of public law than of interstate law, and the supporters of multiculturalism have dwelt at length on the topic. In this meaning, several collective rights and individual rights may clash. The right of peoples takes on a permanent and no longer merely transitory dimension. In this case, the cosmopolitan institutions could play an important role in striking a correct balance between the collective claims of the minorities and the principle of equality among citizens.

If we wish to avoid the noble and necessary principle of the self-determination of peoples being used to form a new kind of tribalism,[32] by encouraging several of the more retrograde tendencies of contemporary society, we must be clear on the fact that the claims contained in self-determination must envisage the inclusion in a juridical system that does not belong exclusively to the community claiming self-determination. The norms of the individual states, but also that specific to the interstate system, are insufficient. Likewise, the self- evaluation of self-

30. For a review, see Allen Buchanan, *Secession: The Morality of Political Divorce from Fort Sumter to Lithuania and Quebec* (Boulder: Westview, 1991).
31. Weinstock, "Constitutionalising the Right to Secede," p. 202.
32. As warned by Thomas Franck, "Postmodern Tribalism and the Right to Secession," pp. 3–27 in *Peoples and Minorities in International Law*, ed. Catherine M. Brolman, Ren Lefeber, and Marjoleine Zieck (Dordrecht: Martinus Nijoff, 1993).

determination is not able to solve the matter and can only reduce it to a state of nature in which force prevails over reason.

The ambitious project of a cosmopolitan democracy would solve the problem of the individual claims, as it would entrain the creation of a level of governance to which both the states and the individual groups could refer. When Claude-Henri de Saint-Simon, at the end of the Napoleonic Wars, boldly proposed to emerge from the chaos that reigned on the old continent by setting up a European Parliament, he already imagined that the new institution would also have to be capable of settling disputes:

> If a particular part of the European Population, under a particular government, wishes to form a separate nation, or to come under another government, it is for the European parliament to decide the issue. It will decide, not in the interest of the governments, but of the peoples, bearing in mind always the best possible organization of the European Confederation.[33]

The stakeholders appealing to self-determination do not necessarily have to wait for a cosmopolitan system to be set up, however. It is sufficient for the stakeholders to accept that impartial institutions should vet their claims. This would mean simply accepting the principle that no one can be a judge of his own cause and consequently that the self-evaluation of self-determination is a contradiction in terms. It would certainly be useful for the parties involved (be they the Russian state or the Chechen secessionists, the Spanish state or the Basque separatists, the aboriginal populations of North America or Australia or their respective states) to be willing to accept the independent opinion of third organizations and to respect their decisions.

Northern Ireland is a significant case in which arbitration—through the 1998 Good Friday agreement—proved effective in settling the conflicts associated with self-determination. For many years, the British government had considered the issue a purely internal matter and had failed to quell the reciprocal violence committed in the region or to prevent Irish Republican Army terrorist attacks in Great Britain. In 1985, the British government decided to involve the Irish government in the talks, thus implicitly acknowledging that the question was not exclusively under British jurisdiction. Over the years the British and Irish govern-

33. Claude-Henri de Saint-Simon, "The Reorganization of the European Community," pp. 28–68 in *Social Organization, the Science of Man and Other Writings*, ed. and trans. Felix Markham (New York, Harper and Row, [1814] 1964), on p. 38.

ments co-opted a growing number of external mediators, in particular the U.S. government. In 1996, former U.S. senator George Mitchell chaired the peace talks. Other figures participating in the various stages of the talks included the Canadian general John de Chastelain, who monitored the decommissioning of the paramilitary force's weapons. This led up to the Good Friday accords, which represented a milestone in the peace process and were ratified by the referendum voted in Northern Ireland and the Irish Republic in May 1998. All sides were a party to the agreements and the text thereof was distributed to each household in Northern Ireland. The result was the disarmament of the paramilitary groups, the end of terrorist attacks, and a substantial reduction of violence in the region.[34]

This is one of the many cases in which the "absent third party," to quote Norberto Bobbio, appeared on the scene and helped reduce the conflicts.[35] The persistence of conflicts to obtain self-determination, often extending beyond even the ruthless logic encountered in the case of wars, shows that the parties in conflict are not pursuing a rational plan in which the benefits that the parties hope to obtain exceed the disadvantages. The existing judicial institutions, such as the ICJ, could more actively mediate, for example, by offering consultative opinions at the request of the IOs, which are, however, still the expression of an interstate logic. So far IOs are depositaries of the principle of sovereignty, which is precisely what the peoples' claims to self-determination aim to undermine. In the absence of truly cosmopolitan institutions, the parties involved could entrust arbitration to NGOs in which they have confidence.[36] If the parties involved were willing to listen to an impartial opinion, we would already be moving in the right direction to solve the conflicts peacefully.

34. For an assessment of the Good Friday agreement, see Stefan Wolff and Jörg Neuheiser, eds., *Peace at Last? The Impact of the Good Friday Agreement on Northern Ireland* (New York: Berghahn Books, 2002).
35. Norberto Bobbio, *Il terzo assente* (Torino: Edizioni Sonda, 1988). On the figure of the third party, cf. Pier Paolo Portinaro, *Il terzo. Una figura del politico* (Milano: Franco Angeli, 1986).
36. One potential candidate organization for performing this role could be the Permanent Peoples' Tribunal, an independent international opinion tribunal that since 1979 has used the judicial approach to assess conflicts and people's claims. See Gianni Tognoni, ed., *Tribunale permanente dei popoli. Le sentenze: 1979–1998* (Verona: Bertani editore, 1998).

Chapter 10
Is a Multilingual Democracy Possible?

10.1 In Search of a European Lingua Franca

A chronicler of exception, Gustave Flaubert, tells how during the European riots of 1848, there were people in Paris, the city that had triggered the revolutionary rumble, who posed the problem of finding a language capable of becoming a means of communication for the new Europe: "Michel-Evariste-Népomucène Vincent, a former professor, votes that European democracy adopt a single language: a dead language, for example an updated form of Latin, might come in handy."[1]

Suggesting Latin as a new language for the continent was a way of putting all populations on the same plane and scaling down the aspirations of French as a *lingua franca*. A French-language-dominated Europe would not have displeased the old European aristocracy (the French of Frederick II and Catherine II was no worse than Louis XVI's) and had been explicitly demanded during the Great French Revolution. Anacharsis Cloots, for example, preached the universal republic, claiming that

---

1. Gustave Flaubert, *L'éducation sentimentale* (Paris: Bordas, [1869] 1974). With detached irony, Flaubert also fills us in on the debate that followed:
   "No, no Latin!" said the architect.
   "Why not?" asked a teacher.
   And these two gentlemen started up a discussion, in which others joined in, each trying to dazzle the others with the points he made; it soon became so annoying that many moved away.

Paris was the capital of the world and French the planetary language.[2] These wild imaginings had been hoisted on the muskets of Napoleon's troops, tardy and incoherent offspring of the Jacobins, who had imposed universal units of measure, codes, and even festivities across the whole of Europe but always in French. If, in short, there were Parisians in 1848 who felt Latin ought to replace French as a lingua franca, that should be viewed as an act of humility intended to place all nations on the same plane—including the youngest ones that were crowding onto the European stage.

Yet the equality among nations that was to be assured by reviving a dead language did not entail rendering *individuals* equal too. Latin was widespread throughout Europe but was always known by the same social classes: aristocrats, intellectuals, and priests. More than French, and certainly more than English or German, Latin brought together the members of the communities of letters, religion, science, civil matters, and politics but at the cost of excluding the vast majority of the population. Language, as much as the sword, brought different cities, peoples, and nations into contact, but those who held the reins of this contact were not the majority of the population—the demos—but the elites—the *oligo*. Hereditary dynasties supported by diplomats and learned men held a firmer grip on foreign policy than on domestic policy partly because they enjoyed a monopoly over linguistic communication. Democracy obviously seeks to break this monopoly, and to do so requires a suitable linguistic means. The question is therefore whether the absence of a common language limits the scope of a democratic process among different linguistic communities.

The idea that a common language is needed recurs periodically in European and world history whenever there are revolutionary upheavals: the issue pops up in peace conferences, the various Workers' Internationals, and today in the World Social Forums. Even the *Osservatore romano*, the official newspaper of the Catholic Church, refloated the idea of disseminating Latin to curb the expansion of the new hegemonic language—English.[3] These movements did not necessarily intend to proceed from a common language to a single political community, however. In the present chapter, I look at the circumstances in which a political community can operate in a multilingual context. Since the aim of the cosmopolitan democracy project is to set up a world political community, the question is whether cosmopolitan democracy is compatible

2. Anacharsis Cloots, *La république universelle: ou, adresse aux tyrannicides* (Paris: Chez les marchands de nouveautés, 1792), p. 9.
3. Mario Gabriele Romano, "La questione del latino," *L'Osservatore Romano*, August 12, 2006, p. 3.

with a planet peopled by a population that speaks a myriad of different languages. Already John Stuart Mill argued that "free institutions are next to impossible in a country made up of different nationalities. Among a people without fellow-feeling, especially if they read and speak different languages, the united public opinion, necessary to the working of representative government, cannot exist," and the adversaries of European integration repeated this harsh judgment again and again.[4] If democracy were possible solely in linguistically homogeneous communities, the project supported here would be unfeasible until the world inhabitants all spoke the same language.

The preceding chapter illustrated what the cosmopolitan project offers in the challenging task of delimiting the various communities so that each community may enjoy maximum autonomy and self-determination. In the present chapter we step through the reasoning underlying one of the more distinctive aspects of a human community even before that community becomes political: the linguistic medium used for communication. The definition of linguistic community is less controversial than the definition of political community: the individuals concerned either understand each other or do not. However, political communities do not coincide either in theory or in practice with linguistic communities, which raises theoretical and practical problems. While the problem of self-determination often gives rise to conflict, the problem of linguistic variety opens up a wider range of problems, including acceptance, assimilation, discrimination, or even expulsion.

10.2 Linguistic Rights and Political Communities

The language problem has become impelling over the past twenty years. Where the languages of minorities were repressed for a long time, as in Spain or the former Soviet republics, the importance of diversity has reemerged, leading to multilingualism or even to secession. But new conflicts and demands have also emerged in consolidated states such as Belgium and Switzerland.[5] In other contexts, linguistic diversity emerged

4. John Stuart Mill, "Considerations on Representative Government," pp. 205–447 in *On Liberty and Other Essays* (Oxford: Oxford University Press [1861] 1991) on p. 428.
5. See Gagnon and Tully, *Multinational Democracies;* Keating, *Plurinational Democracy.* The trilogy by Kenneth D. McRae dedicated to Switzerland, Belgium, and Finland is also very instructive. See Kenneth D. McRae, *Conflict and Compromise in Multilingual Societies* (Waterloo, Ontario: Wilfrid Laurier University Press, 1983, 1986, and 1997).

as a consequence of changes in demographic structure: more than thirty-five million Hispanics continue to preserve their language and customs in the United States; if the present demographic trends are confirmed, the United States could become one of the countries with the largest Spanish-speaking populations of the world.

This is not a total novelty. The Roman Empire was made up of myriad tribes, each with its own language. Prior to "liberal neutrality,"[6] the Romans allowed each tribe ample religious and linguistic autonomy, provided the tribe paid its tributes and supplied soldiers. To preserve their empire, the Romans were also wont to take some of the more promising sons of aristocratic families hostage and provide them with an education in Latin, without asking them to pay the tuition fees demanded by Harvard or Oxford. The young men thus often became a vehicle for collaboration and dominion. After the Romans, many other linguistic communities had to come to terms with differences among languages, but it seems that these differences were tolerated, as the individuals were subjects and not citizens. Subjects, the vast majority of whom were engaged in farming, were not expected to give voice to their thoughts, but only to work the land and pay taxes. Armies were composed mainly of mercenaries who were given both training in weapons skills and taught the minimum linguistic skills needed to carry out orders. The people were neither required nor desired to be polyglot.

The resurgence of the language problem in our era resulted from two fundamental, contemporary historical processes. First, the language problem is one of the several outcomes of the increased interdependence among different communities. Globalization has a stronger effect on communication than on any other social aspect, and state political communities have become increasingly permeable to trade flows, migrations, mixed marriages, and tourism. Second, individual rights have increased in importance. This has been expressed as an extension of rights in democratic states and in an increase in the number of states in which democracy is in force. The first process is essentially guided by civil society, while the second process is driven by political institutions. If we take the state as a reference point of political organization, we may sub-

---

6. Namely, the idea that a liberal state should not take sides regarding the various aspects of its citizens' private lives, such as the religion they practice and the language they speak (cf. Alan Patten, "Liberal Neutrality and Language Policy," *Philosophy and Public Affairs* vol. 31, no. 4 (2003): 356–86). If, as Kymlicka argues, the liberal state has ever promised neutrality with regard to language, this is denied by Clare Chambers, "Nation-Building, Neutrality and Ethnocultural Justice: Kymlicka's 'Liberal Pluralism,'" *Ethnicities* vol. 3, no. 3, (2003): 295–319, on p. 301.

Table 10.1

Causes and Applications of Linguistic Rights

Applications Causes	Inside the State	Outside the State
Globalization (driven by economic and social phenomena)	Increase in number of languages used inside a state as a result of immigration, trade and cultural exchanges, tourism, etc.	Growing number of communities whose destinies are transversal to the state with common problems and different languages
Democratization (driven by political-institutional factors)	Demand for rights by original and newly formed linguistic minorities	Demand to make the international system and its organizations more transparent and accountable

divide the problem of linguistic rights into two major categories. The first category concerns the existence of different languages *inside* a state community. This is the problem the multiculturalist theorists are most concerned with. The second category concerns multilingualism in political communities *outside* the state or *through* the state. In general, this is the issue with which cosmopolitan theorists are concerned. Table 10.1 above summarizes the causes and applications of linguistic rights.

INSIDE THE STATE

Multilingual communities may be found in (a) multilingual states (such as Switzerland, Belgium, and India), (b) states with groups of immigrants who have preserved their own language (like the Hispanics in the United States), or (c) states that have incorporated indigenous populations who have maintained their own languages (such as the aborigines in the United States, Canada, Australia, and New Zealand). In all three cases, linguistic minorities address the demand for linguistic rights to an existing institution that already possesses the authority, resources, and explicit competences to assist its citizens. This has led some states to adopt more than one official language (as in Switzerland and Belgium), to promote bilingualism (as in Canada), or to allow certain regional minorities to use their own language (as in Catalonia and Alto Adige). Traditionally, autocratic regimes have banned the public use of the languages of minorities (suffice it to think of Italy and Spain during fascism and francoism, respectively), and in some extreme cases even prohibiting their use in private. But as Kymlicka and Patten have pointed out, not even liberal states have been neutral toward language, nor is such neutrality achievable.[7] Quite the contrary. Part of the process of nation building has entailed promoting the official language and repressing the other languages. In recent years, multilingualism has been a direct consequence of democratization. For instance, since Paraguay has held free elections, the country has finally raised Guarnì (the language spoken by the majority of the population) to the status of an official language alongside Spanish. Many problems remain on the agenda.[8] In which cases is it proper for the state to provide education in languages other than the dominant one? To what extent must the restrictions applied to education also apply to other public services such as health care and social security? Ought not the right to the best available defense accorded to anyone accused of committing a crime include the right to be tried in his or her own mother tongue?

OUTSIDE THE STATE

The linguistic dimension has acquired increasing importance as spheres of influence outside the state have increased. At the same time there is a growing awarness of the importance of participation of, and accountability to, the public in the life of existing IOs. As long as IGOs remained the exclusive prerogative of governments, the linguistic problem was kept within bounds. The task of the IOs was to facilitate communication among small groups of government officials by placing at their disposal mediators such as the diplomatic corps, bureaucrats, interpreters, and translators (who may be defined as *linguistic intermediaries*). Each government then transmitted significant information to their national public. However, the demands for democratization to which the IGOs have been subjected and the increased number of services they provide to citizens has aggravated the linguistic problem. The transparency of and the control over the action of the IOs and the provision of services are necessarily entrusted to linguistic intermediaries; the greater the differences among languages, the more significant the filter in the relationship

---

7. Kymlicka, *Multicultural Citizenship;* Patten, "Liberal Neutrality and Language Policy."

8. For a review of the issues from different perspectives, see Will Kymlicka and Alan Patten, eds., *Language Rights and Political Theory* (Oxford: Oxford University Press, 2003); and Dario Castiglione and Chris Longman, eds., *The Language Question in Europe and Diverse Societies: Political, Legal and Social Perspectives* (Oxford: Hart Publishing, 2007).

between citizen and political process. However, it is necessary to mention a fundamental difference between demands for linguistic rights inside and above the state. As in the case of human rights, no institutions or consolidated procedures exist above the state, which can enforce linguistic rights. Only in very rare cases can the individual demand rights from existing international organizations. A citizen cannot demand that certain services provided by the IOs be made available in his or her own language, as the official languages are decided by governments and not by their citizens.

Outside the state, the growing role of NGOs must also be taken into account. Within these organizations a lingua franca has often been found for communication, but whenever the NGOs have to deal with specific local situations, they too encounter linguistic problems. As they are NGOs, these bodies autonomously lay down the channels of communication, but whichever ones they choose, they carry on political activities in a multilingual context. The problem is by no means a new one: Karl Marx drew up his inaugural address to the International Working-men's Association in English and German.[9] The dominant language of the Socialist International was German, and this caused some discontent among the French-speaking members. The first four congresses of the Communist International relied on myriad willing interpreters, who were obliged to make long chains of translations from one language to another, which often completely altered the delegates' bellicose positions. The majority of speeches at nineteenth-century peace congresses were in French, but many orators resorted to consecutive translation. In present-day Social Forums, simultaneous translation is quite frequently offered in many languages (over a dozen in the last few WSFs), which is available also in the case of dozens of workshops held simultaneously, often thanks to volunteer interpreters.[10]

10.3 The Language of Democracy: Multiculturalist and Cosmopolitan Views

Charles V, a man proud over reigning over a truly world empire, claimed to speak Spanish to God, Italian to women, French to men, and German to his horse. Charles V belonged to that narrow circle of aristocrats who, benefiting from lessons received from a very early age from a host

---

9. Karl Marx, *Inaugural Address of the International Working Men's Association*, 1864, www.marxists.org/archive/marx/works/1864/10/27.htm.
10. A group of voluntary interpreters known as Babels was set up to facilitate the work of the Social Forums. Cf. www.babels.org.

of tutors, was able to speak many tongues with ease. A modern-day psychologist would perhaps claim that teaching children, even those destined to be leaders, half a dozen languages is a refined torture. An erudite might argue, on the contrary, that such young scions were doubly privileged, as a person has as many souls as he or she knows languages. But the phrase attributed to Charles V contains another interesting idea, namely, that each aspect of human life has its own privileged language. Even though he was no champion of democracy, it would have been interesting to ask Charles V what the language of democracy is. Although we will never hear *his* answer, Will Kymlicka's has reached us loud and clear:

> Democratic politics is politics in the vernacular. The average citizen feels at ease only when he discusses political questions in his own language. As a general rule, only elites are fluent in more than one language, and have the chance to maintain and develop their linguistic skills continuously, and feel at ease discussing political questions in different languages and in a multilingual atmosphere. Moreover, political communication has a large ritual component and these ritual forms of communication are characteristic of a language. Even if a person understands a foreign language in the technical sense, he may be incapable of understanding political debates if he or she has no knowledge of these ritual elements. For these and other reasons, we can believe, as a general rule, that the more the political debate takes place in the vernacular, the greater the participation.[11]

If these affirmations are meant as a description of how democratic politics has evolved in the course of twenty-five centuries, it is hard to disagree: democracy developed in substantially restricted communities that manage to understand one another, not only through the same language but also through a set of tacit codes their members share among themselves. The first democracies were composed of communities whose members knew each other personally. From the descriptive point of view, no one denies that a monolingual community has considerable advantages as regards democratic practice: all its citizens (except for deaf-mutes alone) can take part in political life, and any institution (from parliament to a local residents' committee) can discuss issues and make resolutions without intermediaries, while the public could follow

---

11. Will Kymlicka, *Politics in the Vernacular: Nationalism, Multicultralism and Citizenship* (Oxford: Oxford University Press, 2001), p. 214.

the acts of the government and the institutions without any need for interpreters.

The same is perhaps true for other kinds of homogeneous communities. It is conceivable, for instance, that a monoreligious or monoracial community or a community in which all the individuals have the same educational or income level facilitates political participation. Let us assume that the institutions of a liberal political community are capable of acting in a neutral fashion vis-à-vis the various characteristics of the individuals who compose the community and that those institutions therefore manage to prevent religious, racial, cultural, or economic differences from translating into political discrimination. Nevertheless, multiculturist theorists have convincingly demonstrated that a state may be neutral as regards the religion or race of its own citizens but is much more unlikely to be neutral as far as the language is concerned.[12]

Monolingual communities are becoming quite rare in the contemporary world. The diversity of languages and cultures is a fact and is likely to increase inside each political community as a result of immigration, tourism, and economic, social, and cultural integration. We need not speak of the United States, with its famous melting pot and its several hundred ethnic and linguistic minorities. Even countries such as Sweden and Hungary have to cope with new problems arising out of recent immigration. At the same time, problems that transcend the competences of single nationwide political communities are also bound to increase; for example, decisions concerning the agricultural and immigration policies of Sweden and Hungary are increasingly being made in Brussels instead of in Stockholm or Budapest.

Democratic systems have often managed to solve problems of linguistic communication. The United States granted voting rights to immigrants from all over the world and, even though the president, Congress, and the Supreme Court express themselves exclusively in English, the political parties know that in order to win the elections the votes of millions of Hispanics are also necessary. India too has become a state, despite a diversity of languages and a level of prosperity that is far below that of the United States. In order to introduce democratic institutions, India had to adopt the English of its former colonizers as lingua franca instead of the local languages. This proved much less controversial politically than the adoption of Hindi, which non-Hindi native speakers perceived as a language of some but not all Indians.[13] The same has

---

12. Kymlicka, *Multicultural Citizenship*; Patten, "Liberal Neutrality and Language Policy."
13. Neera Chandhoke, "Negotiating Linguistic Diversity: A Comparative Study of India and the United States," pp. 107–43 in *Democracy and Diversity: India*

happened in many other colonies where the language of the colonizers has become the public language while vernaculars (which often differed considerably from one another) has prevailed in private use. Even Italian became the national language only some considerable time after the foundation of the Kingdom of Italy, suggesting that the language does not develop independently of the political communities. However, there is no doubt that the current era raises new problems overshadowing those of the past. Neither the multiculturalist nor the cosmopolitan has any intention of giving up the principles and values of democracy and tolerance. Despite the controversial gusto characterizing recent debate,[14] multiculturalism and cosmopolitanism have much more in common than is generally credited. Both multiculturalists and cosmopolitans assert the following:

1. The building of nation-states was an artificial process involving the creation of "imaginary identities."[15]
2. All states practice a cultural leveling, which leads to the destruction of local cultures and languages. Even liberal states have supported this practice, directly or indirectly.
3. The diversity of the planet's languages is a value worth preserving. If we acknowledge the speed with which old languages disappear in the contemporary world, it should be the task of government and intergovernmental institutions to preserve the linguistic variety of the planet by means of specific cultural policies.[16]
4. Involving the largest possible number of citizens in the decision-making process is a constitutive value of democracy, and institutions have the job of fostering such participation.

On the strength of these assumptions, how is it possible to modify democratic practice to cater to the existence of multilingual political communities? Democratic practice must be modified and extended in such a way as to allow it to live and prosper even in environmental conditions—such as those due to multilingualism—unlike those condi-

---

and the American Experience, ed. K. Shankar Bajpai (New Dehli: Oxford University Press, 2007).

14. See, for instance, Barry, Culture and Equality.

15. Anderson, Imagined Communities.

16. For paradigmatic references to the disappearance of old languages, see Daniel Nettle and Suzanne Romaine, Vanishing Voices: The Extinction of the World's Languages (Oxford: Oxford University Press, 2000) and David Crystal, Language Death (Cambridge: Cambridge University Press, 2000).

tions experienced to date. The fundamental difference between the multiculturalist and the cosmopolitan perspectives may perhaps be said to lie in the different answers they provide to the following question: How should political communities deal with problems that cut across different linguistic communities at the same time safeguarding individual liberties, maximizing participation, and applying democratic procedures?

As far as public policies are concerned, multiculturalists tend to shift the barycenter of the decision-making process toward the local level, while the cosmopolitans are more inclined to push it toward higher-level institutions. Cosmopolitans would prefer taking away competences from the local governments and giving them to the central sites of authority, and taking competences away from the state governments and giving them to IOs. Multiculturalists set out to address common problems by preserving the linguistic identity of each community and thus implementing public policies that split the communities along linguistic lines. This approach is supposed to allow each community to retain its own democratic procedure in the vernacular and to minimize exclusion *within* each community. Multiculturalists give priority to cohesion—including linguistic cohesion—of the community in question. Cosmopolitans move in the opposite direction. Cosmopolitans do not attempt to modify the composition of the political community even when, as a result of random historical events, this political community is made up of persons who speak quite different languages. In the face of common problems, cosmopolitans seek to apply democratic procedures, implementing public policies designed to remove linguistic barriers.

From a normative point of view, the thesis that democratic politics has to be carried on in the vernacular is dangerous and even reactionary. Such a thing could, for example, instigate an attempt to use violence to force linguistically homogeneous communities, providing theoretical support to the dark side of democracy that harbors a tendency to purge those that are different, perhaps for the purpose of maintaining a high internal level of self-determination.[17] Some political forces might, in good faith, believe that the inclusion of minorities unable to speak their language properly could restrict the democratic life of their own community and that, in order to preserve it, it is necessary to assimilate, isolate, or expel those with a lesser mastery of the language or even prohibit the use of languages different from the dominant one.[18] Kymlicka's

17. Mann, *Dark Side of Democracy.*
18. As in the case of the "English Only" movement in the United States. For an account, see James M. Crawford, *At War with Diversity: U.S. Language Policy in an Age of Anxiety* (Buffalo, NY: Multilingual Matters, 2000). Assimilationist views have recently been expressed by Samuel Huntington, *Who Are We?* (London: Simon & Schuster, 2005).

approach might therefore have a completely opposite effect to the one hoped for: instead of protecting minority rights, his approach could actually lead to their violation. For these reasons, in opposition to the idea that democratic politics *is* politics in the vernacular, I propose a cosmopolitan approach: democratic politics *must* be in Esperanto. I argue against the *descriptive* thesis whereby democratic politics is carried on in the vernacular by adopting a *normative* principle: democratic politics is not necessarily in Esperanto but, wherever necessary, it *can* and *must* be in Esperanto. The Esperanto metaphor does not apply to all the linguistic rights problems addressed, but only to the problem of the language required for political communication.

Esperanto is a neolanguage not unlike the newspeak described by George Orwell in *Nineteen Eighty-Four*. Like newspeak, Esperanto is a very regular language with a limited vocabulary. It was invented by Ludwig Lejzer Zamenhof in the late nineteenth century for a practical reason, namely, to allow communication in multilingual communities.[19] Zamenhof grew up in the city of Bialystok, in present-day Poland but then part of Tsarist Russia, where the population spoke four different languages. Not surprisingly, practical misunderstandings often arose within the four communities, and Zamenhof optimistically concluded that the creation of a language that each community could easily learn as a second language could solve those misunderstandings. Zamenhof's ambition for the new language was of course greater than this: if the new language worked for a small town in eastern Europe, it might have universal value. It should be noted that Esperanto was intended not to replace existing languages but to supplement them. Since Zamenhof introduced it, Esperanto has attracted a small number of enthusiastic supporters in every country but has always been supplanted as a world lingua franca by French first and then by English. Other languages—Mandarin Chinese, Hindi, Spanish, and Russian—have become *linguae francae* in various regions of the world. Esperanto may be viewed as a positive Utopia which is perfectly symmetrical to the negative Utopia represented by Orwell's newspeak: while the ultimate aim of newspeak was actually to repress evil thoughts against the authorities, the aim of Esperanto is to facilitate communication between individuals in the remote areas of the world. Just as the introduction of a universal system of weights and measures sought to make economic and social life more transparent by breaking down the informational asymmetries among individuals and social classes, so the universal language of Esperanto was meant to make it possible for everyone to communicate with everyone else. The

19. Ludwig Lejzer Zamenhof, *An Attempt Towards an International Language* (New York: H. Holt, 1889).

universal language would become the key to cosmopolitan citizenship. The metaphor of Esperanto is used to support the argument that the language of political life should be viewed as an instrument not of identity but of communication. When a linguistic medium is lacking, it becomes a prerequisite for institutions and individuals participating in democratic life to create one—if need be artificially.[20]

10.4 Listening as a School of Democracy

The linguistic problem reveals many aspects of democracy and its conceptions. Espousing the "aggregative" model—the conception of democracy that favors the aggregation of preferences (as opposed to their formation)—considerably reduces the problem of language. The individual members of the political community (voters) have a fixed menu of choices to select from. If the political community is composed of individuals who speak different languages, it is sufficient and technically possible to make the various options available in the various languages. Today it is not unusual to find instructions on how to use a household appliance in ten languages, and even the information for the consumer printed on a tube of toothpaste appears in at least four languages. The electoral programs of political parties, from which the voters ideally choose the candidate to vote for, are usually more detailed than the information found on a tube of toothpaste but not more detailed than the instructions for a household appliance.

In an aggregative model of democracy, a political community would be able to run elections easily by providing information in all the necessary languages. It would be the duty and in the interest of each political party to make its program accessible to voters in the most appropriate linguistic medium. In this model, voters are asked to formulate their preferences and to check that the political party that has won the election carries out its program, while their direct participation in political life is reduced to a minimum. If citizens were granted access to the administration and public services, language problems would obviously arise. However, it is not impossible, as required by the advocates of multiculturalism, to provide public services such as education and health care in the main languages spoken by the citizens. In many regions where two linguistic communities live side by side, public functionaries are already bilingual.

20. This is part of what Ulrich Beck labels *The Cosmopolitan Vision* (Cambridge: Polity Press, 2006).

However, the aggregative model does not accurately describe of how democracies effectively operate, still less how democracies should operate. In particular, the political project of cosmopolitan democracy, as that of multiculturalism, gives priority to a different model, which Habermas defines as deliberative, Dryzek as discursive, and Young as communicative.[21] In this model, one finds the essence of democracy in communication, that is, in the capacity to understand the reasons of others and to be able to expound one's own. In many respects, the two models of aggregative democracy are not opposed (as they are too often believed to be), but rather two phases of the same democratic process. The first phase is that of the formation of parties and political programs, in which dialogue and persuasion prevail. The second phase is that of choosing and aggregating preferences at election time, during which the competitive arguments of the political parties prevail. Two phases also mark parliamentary life: in the first there is a clash between political parties, and in the second the vote is cast. Even the government's activity takes into consideration public opinion and the debate taking place in it.

If we abandon the merely aggregative conception of democracy, the linguistic problem emerges as a significant practical hurdle. It is not possible to generate democratic culture unless the single components, be they constituencies, neighborhoods, schools, grassroots associations, political parties, trade unions, or local government, are prepared to accept the inclusion of participants, irrespective of their linguistic ability. Wherever obstacles to participation exist, it is up to democratic politics to remove them. The Esperanto metaphor thus bears witness to the willingness to resolve linguistic variety constructively (that is, without forced assimilation, segregation, or deportation).

To ask citizens to make an effort to understand one another is not a neutral act with respect to the preferred conception of democracy. Understanding others requires patience and an investment of time and resources in education. To ask citizens to make this effort means, in Benjamin Constant's words (and to argue against him), opting for the freedom of the ancients as opposed to that of the moderns, in that it means asking the members of the community to devote time and energy to overcoming existing barriers to communication, albeit for the sole purpose of democratic practice. A cosmopolitan would probably be inclined to view the opportunity to learn an extra language as an intrinsic and not exclusively instrumental value: learning languages is an oppor-

21. Habermas, *The Inclusion of the Other*; Dryzek, *Deliberative Democracy and Beyond* (Oxford: Oxford University Press, 2002); Young, *Inclusion and Democracy*.

tunity to understand human nature and not just a professional or touristic facility.[22] However, even if we stop short at the instrumental aspect, it is surprising that multiculturalists should attribute such great importance to several aspects typical of the freedom of the ancients (solidarity within the community and, more generally, the value of participation in community life) while attaching so little significance to the first aspect that characterizes a community—the will to understand those who are different.

10.5 Political Options: A Comparison between Multiculturalists and Cosmopolitans

Perhaps the best way to understand the difference between the multiculturalist and the cosmopolitan positions is to address some specific cases. In this section, four paradigmatic cases are discussed: a local school, a multilingual city, a great multiethnic country, and a supranational parliament. Of course one may find significant differences among the multiculturalist theorists[23] and among the cosmopolitans (in particular, between liberal cosmopolitans and democratic cosmopolitans). Without attempting to provide a faithful representation of all the positions, let us seek to identify the differences between the two approaches, even at the cost of forcing them somewhat.

A STATE SCHOOL IN CALIFORNIA

In a state school in a district of Pasadena, California, where English-speaking pupils are traditionally dominant, demographic trends and successive waves of immigration are producing a sizeable increase in the number of Hispanic pupils. Since a degree of demographic decline has been observed among the Anglos, the school has been able to assimilate the new Hispanic students quite easily, and indeed their presence has saved the school from being closed for lack of students. The problem is that the two communities differ in terms of income level, culture, religion, and language. The Hispanic students do not speak English well and their parents speak it even worse. School parent-student

22. Take, for example, the (small number of) Berliners who learned the rudiments of Turkish to communicate with an essential component of the city's population.
23. In particular, between Kymlicka, *Multicultural Citizenship* and Bhikhu Parekh, *Rethinking Multiculturalism: Cultural Diversity and Political Theory* (Cambridge, MA: Harvard University Press, 2002).

meetings end in pandemonium, with the Anglos complaining that their children are starting to make frequent spelling mistakes and the Hispanics that meals are served cold. At the end of one stormy meeting, a Hispanic father ended up by slapping an Anglo father in the face as the result of a trivial linguistic misunderstanding. The headmaster, a man with a fine sense of intuition, perceives that the Anglos are worried that the identity of the neighborhood is going to be lost. In the corridor he heard an Anglo mother say that "not only do they come and live here but they breed like rabbits." The Hispanics have identity problems of their own and are worried about the lower marks their children receive. In sports, too, the Hispanics are not as good as the Anglos, perhaps because the most popular game is American football. Although a number of the Hispanic parents were born and bred in the United States, they still do not have a good command of English. Because many of them are cleaners in the homes of the Anglos, they hope to enable their children to live in conditions that will prevent the class distinctions based on ethnic factors from being perpetuated.

The headmaster calls in a multiculturalist researcher and asks him to study the problem and come up with a solution. After a few weeks, the researcher submits a plan in which the pupils are divided into two different sections—A and H. By means of an ingenious restructuring program, the multiculturalist shows that it is possible to teach in English in section A and in Spanish in section H. The parents are free to choose the section they want for their children, although Anglos might be expected to enroll in A and Hispanics in H. Above all, the project makes it quite clear that, once the section has been chosen, no leniency will be shown for linguistic shortcomings. Without any extra costs, the project also allows for teaching the other language in both sections, enabling the Anglos to pick up some Spanish and Hispanics to study English as a second language. The multiculturalist also notes that sports are a central element of group identity and that it would be wrong to prevent Hispanics from playing the game they prefer and perform best at. Hence different sports are provided for in the project: while American football is played in section A, soccer will be introduced in H.

But the headmaster is puzzled. He wonders whether the project complies with the American Constitution, and although California benefits from constitutional waivers, the headmaster decides to call in a cosmopolitan researcher. A few days later, the cosmopolitan submits his project. On the frontispiece is a quotation from Thomas Pogge: "The best education for children is the education which is best for each child."[24]

24. Thomas Pogge, "Accommodation Rights for Hispanics in the United States," pp. 103–22 in *Language Rights and Political Theory*, on p. 118.

The plan envisages that all pupils receive the same education in English, because English is the dominant language in the country in which the pupils live and the dominant lingua franca worldwide. The plan is accompanied by tables showing that American citizens with a good knowledge of English have (a) higher incomes, (b) less risk of being unemployed, (c) less risk of being imprisoned, and (d) greater life expectancy. Another table shows how English is spreading rapidly over all continents as a second language and controversially asks whether it is the state school's job—at least in terms of statistical probability—to condemn the pupil to earning less and to the risk of being unemployed, ending up in jail, or even having a shorter life merely to preserve the language of his or her linguistic community. As regards sports, the study proposes the adoption of baseball, popular in both the Caribbean and North America.

Not content with demonstrating once and for all the advantages for the well-being of young pupils of teaching in English, the cosmopolitan also suggests introducing compulsory courses of Spanish language and culture for all, proposing as core subjects for a common identity the legend of Zorro, Ernest Hemingway, and Isabel Allende. The adoption of a single section allows the school to save money that the school can use to fund evening courses in English for the parents of Hispanics. Preempting a predictable objection from the Anglos—namely, that the parents of the other group would benefit from greater resources—the cosmopolitan proposes organizing classes of salsa and other Latin American dances for the Anglo parents. He also proposes setting up a tourist association to organize holidays in the Caribbean and Central America. After a careful reading of the project, the headmaster is still perplexed. In an attempt to synthesise the differences in a nutshell, the headmaster concludes that the cosmopolitans favor teaching in the language of the majority and that the language of the minority should be taught as a second language, while the multiculturalists prefer the opposite, namely, that each community can study principally in its own language, using the other as a second language.[25]

THE BIALYSTOK PROBLEM

An emblematic case is that of Zamenhof's hometown, Bialystok. We have already seen how, in the second half of the nineteenth century, four linguistic communities lived in the town: Poles (3,000), Russians

25. Stephen May, "Misconceiving Minority Language Rights: Implications for Liberal Political Theory," pp. 123–52 in *Language Rights and Political Theory*.

(4,000), Germans (5,000), and Jews (18,000). This multiplicity of linguistic groups caused many practical problems for the commerce, education, and basic public life that the Tsarist regime permitted in a territory that it had only recently conquered. The largest linguistic community, the Jews, had no large written corpus to rely on in their own vernacular language, Yiddish, while two other linguistic communities, the Germans and the Russians, could count on the consolidation of the language and culture of the two great neighboring states.

Acknowledging the differences, a multiculturalist probably would have suggested setting up four ethnic councils and endowing each with broad autonomy in the provision of services such as education and health care. The multiculturalist also would have set up a "clearinghouse" to make it easier for the citizens to exchange homes so as to allow the town to be divided into four linguistically homogeneous districts. This would have greatly reduced the number of problems of linguistic misunderstanding in commerce and facilitated education in the languages of the four communities. As we have seen, the ingenious solution proposed by Zamenhof, a true champion of cosmopolitanism, was to invent an artificial new language, Esperanto, designed to place the various communities on the same footing and, moreover, to allow them to communicate with all the other citizens of the world. That the solution proved unworkable in practice should not overshadow its greatness: a local problem provided the thrust toward a universal language. A less ingenious solution—but arguably more likely to yield tangible results—would have been to introduce bilingualism in education and public communication in the dominant Slav language (Russian) and German (which has many similarities with Yiddish), allowing and developing the private use of other vernacular languages. Zamenhof would probably have agreed with Van Parijs's proposal, according to which the linguistic communities required to study the language of the others, in this case the Jews and the Poles, would be entitled to tangible compensation from the communities not required to study other languages.[26]

26. Phillipe Van Parijs, "Linguistic Justice," pp. 153–68 in *Language Rights and Political Theory*, on p. 167. Parijs's proposal could be implemented at least in the academic community, where English has asserted itself unequivocally as a lingua franca and where the most widely circulating, read, and cited academic journals are Anglo-American. This affords English native speakers a considerable advantage over all the others. It would not be a bad idea for academics from other countries to ask their privileged native English-speaking colleagues to correct any howlers they themselves make.

THE CASE OF INDIA

India is the second largest country in the world in population after China, accounting for about one sixth of the world's inhabitants. India is home to a vast number of different ethnic groups and languages. Yet, after independence, India managed to establish a parliamentary democracy that has been relatively successful for a developing country.[27] One reason for this success is a national parliament whose members are elected from all the federal states. The best approach to the linguistic problem proved to be pragmatism, accompanied by a healthy dose of flexibility and tolerance.[28] Unlike in Italy, for example, all attempts to establish a unitary language as a means of boosting the national identity failed. The desire to create an Indian identity based on a common language different from that of the former English colonizers, although supported by Mohandas Gandhi himself, proved to be a factor of division rather than of union. In order to settle any linguistic conflicts, the Parliament decided to allow communication between the central government and the single states in both Hindi and English. The country currently boasts as many as 18 official languages, a tiny number compared with the number languages in actual use—1,650. A system has thus been set up in which vernacular languages are used locally: one of the official languages is used in the political life of the single states, and the languages of communication in national politics have de facto become Hindi and English.[29]

A multiculturalist would immediately note that Indian democracy is limited by the fact that the members of linguistic minorities have no control over the acts of parliament and government. In the parliament itself, the variety of different languages means there is no guarantee that the members of linguistic minorities will be able to understand each other. In 1947, a multiculturalist might have preferred separating the British possessions into eighteen independent states rather than into only India and Pakistan. This separation would have afforded each community a greater degree of political participation in their vernacular languages, and although none of the eighteen independent countries would have been linguistically homogeneous, it would have been possible to safeguard linguistic minorities by adopting the policies that multiculturalists champion in countries such as Canada or Spain.

27. For an assessment, see Atul Kohli, ed., *The Success of Indian Democracy* (Cambridge: Cambridge University Press, 2001).
28. See E. Annamalai, *Managing Multilingualism in India: Political and Linguistic Manifestations* (London: Sage, 2001).
29. Chandhoke, "Negotiating Linguistic Diversity in Democracies."

A cosmopolitan, on the contrary, would see the formation of a great nation in the aftermath of British colonization as a great advantage for the populations of the geographic area in question. In all likelihood the formation of a federal state was probably the best protection for the various ethnic, religious, and linguistic minorities. If a federal state had not been formed, conflicts probably would have broken out in the Indian peninsula, as bloody as the conflicts that took place during the partitioning of the Indian Union and Pakistan in 1947. Nor can it be ruled out that interstate conflicts like those conflicts that dominated African political life over the past sixty years might occur. The fact that everyone can consider himself or herself Indian no matter what language they speak has reduced political violence, and individuals' ability to speak their own vernacular language has prevented any traumatic changes of identity. Although Indians did not choose their colonizers, the fact that they spoke English rather than Dutch or Portuguese gave India a notable advantage in so far it afforded the country direct access to the dominant contemporary language. Although this situation has so far favored elites as opposed to the majority of the population, today suitable education policies can make English a considerable competitive advantage for the development of Indian society.[30] Looking to the future, a multiculturalist would probably seek to increase the number of official languages, along with local political autonomy and the teaching of vernacular languages. This would lead not only to a greater conservation of local languages but also to a more difficult economic, social, and political integration at both national and international levels. A cosmopolitan, on the contrary, would tend to invest more in education in English alongside local languages in order to make English the lingua franca used for both *intra-* and *inter-*national purposes.

THE EUROPEAN PARLIAMENT

The European Parliament currently has twenty-two official languages. So far the number has increased with that of EU member states. The de facto official languages coincide with the member states. There are no official languages for substate linguistic communities (the most significant claim for recognition being that of Catalan). The members of the European Parliament rely on simultaneous translation, and documents are translated into the official languages. As the number of official lan-

---

30. Estimates provided by the International Corpus of English indicate that the portion of the Indian population able to speak English varies from 4 to 20 percent (cf. www.ucl.ac.uk/english-usage).

guages has increased, the translation procedure has grown more complex: there are currently $22 \times 21 = 462$ possible language combinations ("into" and "from"), and finding interpreters capable of translating, for example, from Portuguese to Lithuanian, or from Greek to Finnish, and vice versa is not always easy. Hence the recourse to "double translations" (for example, from Portuguese to French and from French to Finnish). Yet even this vast linguistic "menu" fails to accommodate all the European languages, and members of linguistic minorities sometimes speak their own mother tongues, albeit rarely.[31]

Of the nearly six thousand employees of the European Parliament, a large number are translators and interpreters. In such a situation, the problem of reducing the number of official languages in the European Parliament understandably arises, although it is a politically thorny issue.[32] The benefit would be a more effective debate; the disadvantage would be—de facto if not de jure—limiting the passive electorate to elites who speak foreign languages. MEPs may express themselves in any of the official languages (Art. 117 of the European Parliament Rules of Procedure), although they generally use the language of their own country. Willy Brandt was one of the first members to address the European Parliament in a language that was not his mother tongue, speaking in English rather than in German. His choice was justified by the fact that the number of members who understood English was far greater than those who knew German. The choice was greeted with warm applause and some booing. Multiculturalists would probably have booed him, as he would not have been understood by voters in his own constituency who nevertheless have the right to exercise control over their elected member. Brandt also compelled his German colleagues who did not understand English (possibly because they did not belong to an elite group) to listen to the speech of a fellow countryman in translation. Cosmopolitans would have applauded him heartily insofar as he was bridging the linguistic gap between members of parliament, thus promoting a common language for European politics.

It is worth mentioning the case of Mario Capanna, an extreme left-wing MEP who provocatively made a speech in Latin at the parliamentary

31. For example, during the meeting of October 30, 1987, devoted to discussing the *Resolution on the Languages and Cultures of Regional and Ethnic Minorities in the European Community* (Doc. A2–150/87), three Spanish MEPs spoke respectively in Catalan, Asturian, and Basque, providing interpreters with a written text in Spanish.

32. Virginie Mamadouh, "Dealing with Multilingualism in the European Union: Cultural Theory Rationalities and Language Policies," *Journal of Comparative Policy Analysis* vol. 4, no. 3 (2002): 327–45.

debate of November 13, 1979, causing waves of panic in the interpreters' booths. One of the few who understood Capanna's speech perfectly was his colleague Otto von Habsburg, a direct descendant of the royal family of the Austro-Hungarian Empire but also a member elected in the right-wing Catholic party CSU in the Bavaria constituency. Since his Habsburg ancestors lost Lombardy-Veneto in 1861, his Italian was a little rusty and Otto congratulated his colleague in Latin. This is perhaps one of the last few cases in which the elites of two countries, although of opposite political tendencies, used Latin.

Today proposals are being made to reduce the languages used in parliament to 2, 3, or 4, and the organs of the European Parliament are addressing the problem of limiting the extensive use of interpreters and translations. Multiculturalists are probably against these proposals because these proposals would reduce the number of candidates effectively eligible (only citizens with a good knowledge of at least one official language could perform their role as MEPs). Moreover, though all parliamentary documents would continue to be available in the twenty-two official languages, there would always be the danger that an assembly working in only a few languages would distance itself from the electorate and ultimately turn into an oligarchy. The cosmopolitans, on the contrary, believe that communication in one or only a few languages would make parliamentary debate more authentic and direct. Cosmopolitans suggest leaving just two official languages, English and French, and placing all members on the same plane, asking the English to speak in French and the French to speak in English. Cosmopolitans point out that, although elected in one country, MEPs have to answer to the population of Europe, not only to their own constituencies.[33] Besides, to be able to work effectively in a legislative assembly, one must be able to speak, albeit only informally, with one's colleagues. In order to do this, one needs a knowledge of the more common languages. To avoid having to be escorted by a squad of interpreters, MEPs would need to have at least one language in common in order to communicate among themselves. In short, cosmopolitans would prefer an impoverished but directly understandable language to a myriad of more colorful yet inaccessible languages.

A parliament in which each member speaks only his or her own vernacular knowing that the other members do not understand it would be not only ridiculous but also useless. The very etymology of the word

33. The European Parliament allows all European citizens to run as candidates in any constituency and not necessarily that corresponding to their own nationality. So far only a small number of parties have chosen candidates who are citizens of other countries.

parliament expresses the purpose of the legislative assemblies—to speak, because it is assumed that those who speak are also prepared to listen. Without the willingness to listen, no political democracy can be constructed.[34]

10.6 For a Linguistic Cosmopolitanism

The cosmopolitan position is founded on an assumption that needs to be made clear, namely, that nothing prevents human beings from mastering two or more languages. Linguistic research has clearly shown that there is no obstacle to children learning two languages,[35] and whole countries in the civilized world run compulsory education programs to enable students to learn properly not only their own mother tongue but also a lingua franca. This is not necessarily to the detriment of the vernacular language, whose cultural value may be better understood (as an expression of the diversity of humanity) precisely by individuals who speak more than one language. The choice between vernacular and national language is too often presented as something inevitable: if the cosmopolitans support a common public language it is because they believe it is possible to retain it side by side with one or more local languages.[36] Mastery of a universal language does not entail having to sacrifice the language of one's ethnic group. Aldous Huxley, in his novel *The Island*, suggested a more realistic solution than Esperanto. In this novel, a small, utopian community in the Pacific is described—the imaginary forbidden island of Pala—which, although highly advanced, is deeply rooted in its own traditions.[37] This community has preserved its own local language, but all its members speak English, which affords them access to technology, information, and culture from the most advanced regions of the world. In the real world, the countries ranking highest in the classification of human development—Norway, Sweden, and the

34. For a passionate defense of the possibility to generate a common European multiple political identity, in spite of linguistic barriers, see Patrizia Nanz, *Europolis: Constitutional Patriotism beyond the Nation State* (Manchester: Manchester University Press, 2006).
35. Colin Baker and Sylvia Prys Jones, eds., *Encyclopedia of Bilingualism and Bilingual Education* (Clevedon, PA: Multilingual Matters, 1998); in the multiculturalist camp, this argument is supported also by May, "Misconceiving Minority Language Rights."
36. See, for instance, Patten, "Liberal Neutrality and Language Policy," p. 381.
37. Aldous Huxley, *The Island* (New York: Harper Perennial, [1962] 1989).

Netherlands—are very close to Huxley's ideal and almost all their citizens are fluent in English.

On a planet on which one third of the population is still illiterate, it is undoubtedly wishful thinking to expect to institutionalize a kind of bilingualism that would provide for an international lingua franca both inside and outside the state. However, political theory is useful if it works for the future, not for the past. Linguists tell us that two thirds of the world's inhabitants are already bilingual,[38] but this does not bring the peoples of the world together, as there is still no language of communication: what is missing is a single language spoken by everyone as a second or third language. But it does not appear impossible that multilingualism will allow linguistic diversity to be preserved without having to sacrifice the possibility of human beings practicing democratic politics. In the space of two or three generations, it may be possible to find a universal linguistic medium. Rather than choosing today between vernacular and Esperanto, we should perhaps support investment in education to allow individuals to improve their language skills. In India and in Europe, multilingualism can already be seen in action.[39] The British in Europe and the Hindis in India are among the privileged who can afford to speak a single language, while many others have to be able to speak at least two (English as a lingua franca and their own vernacular language) and others already speak three (like the Catalans, who need to speak Spanish and English as the languages of national and international communication). Linguistic access is still not available to all: as Kymlicka rightly points out, elites are still at an advantage and, in a globalized world, also enjoy a linguistic privilege. It is only too easy to make a society more egalitarian by making polyglots illiterate, but an enlightened social policy must strive to make the illiterate polyglot.

Language is the acid test for the two conceptions of democracy set out in chapter 1: the inclusive conception based on de facto citizens and the organicistic conception better described as ethnocracy. Whereas the difference in race or religion does not modify the functionality of the democratic institutions, language differences create serious problems. These problems must be taken into account, not ignored. Since the project presented here aims to develop a democratic system that includes virtually all the inhabitants of the planet, the language problem becomes essential. The larger the scale, the more difficult linguistic diversity makes political communication, transparency, and control over the rul-

38. Baker and Prys Jones, *Encyclopedia of Bilingualism and Bilingual Education.*
39. David D. Laitin, "The Cultural Identities of a European State," *Politics & Society* vol. 25, no. 3 (1997): 277–302.

ers' actions. Using different examples, I have nevertheless tried to show that, in the first instance, there is a problem of attitude. Linguistic diversity is not just a problem for a future world parliament, but also for the schools and neighborhoods of a very large number of today's cities. I have examined the prospects offered by two paradigmatic approaches, multiculturalism and cosmopolitanism. In order to fully affirm democracy, multiculturalism relies on the intensification of participation, even at the cost of introducing divisions. Cosmopolitanism, on the contrary, aims at uniting, even though this may reduce participation over a relatively long transition period.

The cosmopolitan project, in this and in other cases, is based implicitly on the philosophy of history of the age of the Enlightenment, namely, that humankind is able to progress, which is also linked to the possibility of getting to know different peoples, traditions, and cultures. This may give rise to a comparison with what is different, which represents an antidote to both compulsory assimilation and exclusion. The will to communicate with those who are different, to the point of seeking the medium required for doing so, is not only an engagement that a liberal society must undertake but also a school of both democracy and cosmopolitanism.

Chapter 11

Conclusions: The Prospects for Cosmopolitan Democracy

It appears to me more appropriate to follow up the real truth of a matter than the imagination of it; for many have pictured republics and principalities that in fact have never been known or seen, because how one lives is so far distant from how one ought to live, that he who neglects what is done for what ought to be done, sooner effects his ruin than his preservation; for a man who wishes to act entirely up to his professions of virtue soon meets with what destroys him among so much that is evil.

—Niccolò Machiavelli, *The Prince*, chapter 15

In the present book, I have deliberately chosen to ignore the authoritative warning of an Italian who dominated the art of government, Niccolò Machiavelli, to base action on political reality rather than precepts applied to imaginary communities. I have thus laid myself open to facile criticism: my proposals can be accused of utopianism and, as such, rejected as an unrealistic agenda that is thereby insignificant in international politics. Indeed the utopianism with which the project of cosmopolitan democracy is tainted is even more extreme than that of which Moore, Bacon, Campanella and their courageous emulators were guilty: cosmopolitan democracy does not in fact describe a limited imaginary community that, if actually realized, can become a good example for all. Quite the contrary. Cosmopolitan democracy sets no geographic boundaries; it is indeed a planetary fantasy from which no corner of the world can escape.

But on one point at least let us acknowledge the merit of Machiavelli and of the many who have ably followed him along the path of political realism: the starting point I have chosen is not a "republic that has never been seen nor known in reality" but the real world in which we happen to live. Indeed, I have striven to face squarely the nature of the existing political systems without conceding anything to certain among them just because these systems could already boast of having a democratic regime. No less than the realists, I refused to take for granted what must instead be demonstrated, namely, that a good internal constitution translates into a virtuous foreign policy. On the face of it, one might have expected that a book dedicated to the possible extension to world level of the norms and values of democracy should contain greater praise for real democracies, and some may be surprised to discover how much bitterness and often anger seep out when discussing the foreign policy of the western countries, the cultural area that was the birthplace and even today the depositary of self-government. At least in this case, Machiavelli's lesson has been learned: one must shun modeling what exists on what should be and imagining political reality to be more benevolent that it actually is.

Dispassionate analysis shows that the democratic countries have succeeded in distributing substantial benefits within their own borders. Their citizens enjoy a better quality of life, have fewer fears of falling victim to political violence, are sure their own rights will be respected and above all have the opportunity to participate in the decisions that concern them. However, citizens of democratic countries have shared only a small fraction of the benefits obtained from self-government with the other parts of the world. Indeed they have often exploited their own privileged position to give free reign to their desire for dominion and have spread toward the exterior the poisons held in check on the interior. Unfortunately, this schizophrenia has never been investigated as deeply as it should have been. In international relations, the idealists have essentially ignored it, confusing reality with their own wishful thinking, while the realists have merely observed it, without succeeding in identifying its causes, and have had little incentive to find a remedy. Although there has been no lack of criticism of the democracies, the majority of them have taken as their controversial target the democratic system as such, failing to distinguish between the good the democracies have achieved on the inside and the still-evil features that mark their external behavior.

Is it legitimate to demand that the foreign policy of a democratic country be virtuous? It is not enough to maintain that the foreign policy of despotic governments is even more brutal and self-seeking, and to speculate that if those despotic governments could concentrate the power that today lies in the hands of the West they would have no scruple about using even more violent means to dominate. This observation may perhaps be exact, but it is irrelevant: there is no point in opposing an existing evil with a hypothetical greater evil. Rather than seek consolation

275

in the defects of others, the democracies should strive to do better. Increasing the number of democratic countries and improving the quality of democracy in countries that are already democratic also depend on the choices made in foreign policy. I have therefore proposed a radically different method of evaluation compared with that in common use: the foreign policy of the democratic countries should not be compared with foreign policy of the despotic countries but with the democratic countries' own internal policy. This should be the benchmark used to determine whether the democratic countries behave in accordance with the expectations of their partisans in order to decide whether their behavior is indeed virtuous.

Today there are fewer historical justifications for the schizophrenia of the democratic countries; democratic countries dominate the world and no longer need to struggle for survival. Compared with the threat posed by fascism in the first half of the twentieth century and by Stalinism in the second half, the existing enemies are weak and scattered. The so-called rogue states are few and far between and isolated. Even terrorism, although it can dispense fear, destruction, and death, as the inhabitants of New York, Madrid, and London well know, fortunately cannot undermine the solid political and social foundations of the developed democracies. The danger no longer exists that one "who wishes to act entirely up to his professions of virtue soon meets with what destroys him among so much that is evil." Yet it is indicative that the perils represented by these enemies—some real, others merely alleged—are constantly blown out of proportion by carefully orchestrated media campaigns so that potential enemies appear much larger than they really are. These enemies seem as necessary for the dominant groups in the West to keep hold of their power as the Spectre is to animate the adventures of Agent 007. Those who govern the democracies thus seem incapable of acknowledging reality: today they can live without enemies.

But no longer having enemies to be afraid of does not necessarily mean being loved. The democratic and capitalist western world has earned itself a very shabby reputation outside its own frontiers. Despite the huge material resources available to democratic governments, five billion inhabitants of the planet look upon the western powers with fear owing to their destructive power as well as with envy for their material prosperity and only rarely with admiration. While the stars of the western world of entertainment, sports, and culture are hosannaed by enthusiastic crowds the world over, their political leaders are greeted with protests and demonstrations. This is the drama of our times: the West has so far failed to attain that role of political leader that befits it. If the West has failed to attain the role of political leader, it is because of the wicked course of action it has pursued, aimed more at dominating than at persuading and involving.

The cosmopolitan democracy project restated here puts forward a strategy that is quite different to that followed hitherto by the western states: that of dialogue and inclusion. Cosmopolitan democracy is not a strategy that can be offered indiscriminately to all the political subjects and that often requires making choices. It is not intended, for instance, to be offered to the despotic elites who still employ brutal methods of subjugation, but rather to those oppressed peoples who have been unable to enjoy the benefits associated with self-government. However, the promotion of democratization through dialogue and inclusion can be effective only if partners are found who are willing to listen and political subjects ready to act; otherwise it can be counterproductive. During the closing decade of the twentieth century, the peoples struggling to achieve self-government, thanks to the support received from the world public opinion, managed in many parts of the world to attain tangible results. Without a shot being fired, the five continents and even entire regions—think of eastern Europe and Latin America—have embarked upon a course toward democracy.

However, in the last few years the situation has been reversed: the democracies have ceased to increase in number and in several countries despotism has again taken over. Is this a passing circumstance or a new trend? It is still too early to decide whether the wave of democratization triggered by the fall of the Berlin wall is about to be reversed or whether it is only a temporary phenomenon. Today we may merely point out that, after George W. Bush took over the White House, after the collapse of the Twin Towers, after the invasion of Afghanistan and, above all, after the start of the war in Iraq, the mirage of an entirely democratic world is again fading. Many oppressed peoples have ceased to fight for a democratic regime and have even been unable to preserve their recently conquered democratic institutions.

While Bush and the members of his administration tour the world, declaring that the United States aims to promote democracy everywhere, many peoples have stopped seeking alliances with western countries against the dictatorships that dominate them and have adopted an attitude of indifference and often of open opposition. The question to be asked is how it was possible for such a radical change to occur in such a short historical period. The answer is quite simple: the West had promised to treat all peoples with the same dignity and to promote the same rights for all individuals irrespective of the color of their skin and the

277

passport they held, but these promises were not kept and the wars of aggression have had the effect of blocking any authentic mass movement in support of democratization.

The western ideological apparatus has obsessively repeated three requests—market economy, democratization, human rights—but always only addressed to the others, placing itself in the position of judge and itself eluding judgment. Western governments have demanded that the capitalist model should be applied universally as a machine to guarantee prosperity, although they have been incapable of forgoing even the most elementary trade privileges, thus bringing the liberalization of international trade to a halt. The western governments have insistently preached the need to democratize the political system but have violated international legality and humiliated the institutions, such as the UN, that are its depositaries. While calling for the protection of human rights, the western governments have carried out aggressions. It is therefore not surprising that entire populations—for instance, the Iranian people—have reacted by showing their willingness to applaud their own leaders whenever they utter belligerent but vain proclamations of independence from the West.

These are the concerns generated by such attitudes that have caused deep fractures among the western countries themselves. These splits have been opened in governments and parliaments, political parties and public opinion. The front of the democratic regimes, united by powerful economic interests and cultural tradition, has become divided to the point of shaking the very architecture of multilateralism. A divided West has been obliged to reflect on the mistakes it has made and the strategies to be applied. In order to curb the interventionist frenzy, numerous voices have been raised within the West itself demanding greater caution, and appeals have been made to the longstanding principles of sovereignty and noninterference. In order to dampen the enthusiasm of those wanting to export democracy by bombing, some have claimed that the conditions for self-government were still not ripe in many countries.

In the present book, I have attempted to put forward a completely different view. I have argued that it is a mistake and counterproductive to oppose the warmongering strategy pursued by the Bush and Blair administrations using the old schemes. The project of imperial dominion pursued using the instrument of war must be countered by a project of cosmopolitan governance based on the values of democracy, which thus uses methods that are the opposite of those used so far.

The principles of non-interference and sovereignty have always been used as a rhetorical screen to conceal both internal oppression and external domination. Rather than rely on these outdated schemes, it is preferable to look ahead and propose a world political system in which self-determination establishes internal democracy, impartial institutions intervene to the people's advantage, and global constitutionalism replaces sovereignty.

As far as internal democratization is concerned, it does not seem that there are obstacles to render it unfeasible in the developing countries. Each community can embrace self-government and benefit from self-government provided each community is able to freely choose the forms of political participation that best suit the community's cultural and social traditions. This means simply remaining anchored to the principal teaching of democracy: democracy is a regime that must be constructed bottom-up and not top-down and that may be imported but cannot be exported. The true dispute is therefore not whether or not to pursue democratization but, on the contrary, what ways and means must be used to achieve this objective. In this case, there is no contradiction between the means and the end: the exportation of democracy by following a multilateral strategy and through the links that exist among civil societies has proved much more effective than the use of coercive means.

I have also emphazised the strong casual link which associates the democratization of the international community to the internal democratization. If the relations between political communities were based on enhanced collaboration, the communities could create the channels required to release the internal forces that will attain self-government. A fundamental step is to reinforce the international organizations. A recent line of research—which appears to be highly fruitful—investigated empirically the effect of participation in international organizations on internal democratization. This research is deemed a source of proposals much more relevant to global governance than those that have emerged so far from the now-hackneyed debate on peace among democracies.

International organizations not only serve the instrumental purpose of promoting internal democratization; they themselves can become institutions in which the norms and values of democracy are applied. In open disagreement with the skeptics, I have claimed that nothing in theory prevents this from happening provided there is the political will to reform them. In order for global governance to be subject to the values of democracy, international organizations must take on board more functions and greater legitimacy, embracing the principles of accountability, participation and equality.

The transformation of global governance is called for today in order to address many problems, old and new. The environmental question, financial stability, security, and communications can today be success-fully managed only by means of international cooperation. The eco-nomic and social sphere is marked by constant links between distant areas, while the possibility of acting politically is still mainly confined to state communities. As a result, a large and growing number of the choices having a direct effect on our life are taken outside the demo-cratic control exercised by the state communities and the international organizations themselves. A small number of economic and political power centers, which are better equipped than others to navigate the shoals of uncontrolled globalization, succeed in defending their own in-terests and imposing their priorities without any control.

If the tools available to global governance are unsatisfactory today, the blame cannot be laid on the fact that some countries are still gov-erned by despotic methods. In fact, the advanced democratic countries represent a practically autonomous economic and social bloc. It is enough to observe a map showing commercial fluxes, air traffic, tele-phone traffic, or electricity consumption to realize that the overwhelm-ing majority of links occur within the western countries. With the ex-ception of certain strategic raw materials, such as oil, the West is an almost self-sufficient fortress and the processes of globalization are ex-tending only slowly to other parts of the world. The democratization of global governance therefore mainly regulates relations among commu-nities that are already democratic.

There are widespread complaints over the democratic deficit plaguing world politics. Many who complain are the actors who contribute to the progress of global society and who nevertheless feel they are not ade-quately represented in the political sphere. I have discussed in this book some of the numerous proposals put forward to resolve the problem: intergovernmental fora and world business centers, the World Economic Forum and the World Social Forum each in their own way have ad-dressed the problem of reforming global governance, and demand for the form of democratic governance to be taken as the inspirational model is rising.

On a number of occasions in this book it was stressed the need to set up a World Parliamentary Assembly that can act as a privileged forum of expression for a motley and fragmented public opinion that roams restlessly between Davos and Porto Alegre. The aim is to allow the citizen of the world to act on the world stage not only as a worker, manager, consumer, or spectator, but also as a political animal. It would be reductive to think that such a parliamentary grandstand would have to resemble the one that already exists in the developed democracies. A significant proportion of the panoply of national political life is probably unsuitable for addressing world political problems. Citizens' participation in world politics must be redesigned with imagination and courage and different approaches will probably be developed to those known so far. Interests and choices might in the future be represented more flexibly and unstably than they are in today's state communities.

An examination has been made of the prospect of reforming the UN, an issue that has been on the agenda for all the sixty years of the organization's life without any significant change being introduced yet. However, the UN, the most ambitious and wide-ranging international organization, must be the pivot of a new multilateralism that is able more decisively to incorporate the basic principles of democracy that are encapsulated in the values of nonviolence, public control and political equality. Many actions can be undertaken to allow the UN and its specialized agencies to govern globalization in a more effective, participatory, and transparent fashion.

I am confident that it is possible to settle and increasing number of disputes by means of the rule of law, and I have reviewed the proposals aimed to bolster international judiciary powers. This presupposes greater powers being given to the existing organs, which have so far proved ineffectual, such as the International Court of Justice, as well as the development of new ones, as is taking place in the only recently established International Criminal Court. In addition to the formal institutions, the parties involved should also accustom themselves to using arbitration rather than force. Consideration has been given to a passionate specific case of conflict, namely those triggered by the demand for self-determination. It has been examined whether a cosmopolitan principle, namely that of an impartial third party as intermediary and arbitrator, can bring about a substantial reduction in violence.

Nevertheless violent conflicts have occurred in the past and will occur also in the future. To what extent can the international community contribute to their resolution? After reviewing the various military interventions carried out for humanitarian reasons over the past decade, I have suggested that the logic of emergency is a poor counselor. Rather than act on the spur of the emotions stirred up artificially by often-manipulated mass media, it would be preferable to set up *ad hoc* multilateral institutions. In this way it would perhaps be possible to avoid humanitarian interventions of dubious efficacy, like those in Somalia and Kosovo, as well as the recurrent painful outcries over the inability to cope with great catastrophes like those in Rwanda and Darfur.

Table 11.1
Recapitulation of the Main Proposals

Domain	Institutions	Proposals
Security	UN Security Council	– Procedurally and substantially limit the use of the veto of permanent members.
	Humanitarian military intervention	– Generate procedures for timely interventions through a permanent rescue army.
Participation	World Parliamentary Assembly	– Institute a world legislative assembly representing citizens independently of the state they belong to.
	UN Security Council	– Increase the number of seats to allow more equitable and representative participation of countries. – Provide access to regional organizations and to selected nonstate players.
	UN General Assembly	– Link national delegations to their citizens by making elective the appointment of at least one of the ambassadors.
	UN Thematic areas and specialized agencies	– Increase and formalize the access of non-governmental organizations.
Judiciary	International Court of Justice	– Strengthen its role by making its jurisdiction mandatory and by extending competencies also to nonstate actors such as insurgents and ethnic minorities.
	International Criminal Court	– Fully implement the court's treaty and increase the number of state parties.
	Right to self-determination	– Enhance the practice of mediation and arbitration of third and independent parties to minimize the recourse to violence.

Domain	Institutions	Proposals
Human rights	Council of Human Rights	– Strengthen the review of human rights, giving a greater role to non-governmental organizations and independent advocacy groups.
	World Parliamentary Assembly	– Periodically evaluate the human rights regimes in countries and activate smart sanctions for those governments that violate them.
Internal democratization	International organizations	– Provide greater support to democratic forces in authoritarian and transition states.
		– Use membership of international organizations as an incentive to strengthen and consolidate internal democratic institutions.
	World Parliamentary Assembly	– Perform independent democratic audits of national performance.
Global democratization	International organizations	– Apply to the various international organizations the core values of nonviolence, popular control, and political equality.
	World Parliamentary Assembly	– Assess and steer political actions in the direction of democratic values and norms.

The list of proposals discussed in this book is far from exhaustive (see table 11.1 for a summary), and many other actions could be undertaken to approach the cosmopolitan democracy defended herein. The question is why democratic governments, which ought to be more ideologically inclined toward developing democracy outside their own boundaries, have so far made so few efforts to build up and strengthen a network of global democratic institutions. International organizations—the most visible instrument of global governance—are the favorite offspring of western liberalism, and even today we must be grateful for their existence not only to enlightened thinkers such as William Penn, Jeremy Bentham, Immanuel Kant and Claude-Henri de Saint-Simon but also to bold politicians such as Woodrow Wilson and Franklin D. Roosevelt. But if we compare the resources expended by democratic governments for their own defense with those earmarked for international organizations, the extent to which foreign policy is still dominated by national interests immediately becomes apparent. Foreign policy is still driven by old conceptions as though the interests of a country are best safeguarded by striking fear into the hearts of its neighbors rather than by laying down rules for civic cooperation.

How can a world political community based on the values of democracy be boosted? Which political subjects would be interested in doing this? The arguments I have put forward may seem contradictory: how can a change be possible if the political subjects, including the democratic governments, respond to a desire for power? We cannot expect fresh changes in world political life to come solely from the top down, in the form of a sudden epiphany that enlightens the minds of the rulers. Rulers often succeed in eluding public scrutiny in the democratic countries, and to an even greater extent in foreign policy as is shown by the farce of the weapons of mass destruction. The hope that a radical transformation will occur in world politics lies in the entry onstage, in a more structured and institutionalized fashion, of a new political subject, the only political subject that possesses democratic legitimacy: the citizen. Only by creating a global commonwealth of citizens who will allow themselves to express in world politics can some changes be achieved. Empowering the citizen of the world means to build up at the global level those checks and balances that have nurtured the evolution of democracy.

To demand a role for the citizens of the world does not mean replacing what individuals already have in a growing number of countries but merely supplementing it. It is necessary to take into account the increased quantity and quality of the interactions among distant communities by means of increased participation. Individuals already have numerous channels they can use to express their opinion in world politics: public opinion is certainly far from being the queen of the world hoped for by William Ladd, although it already plays an important role and no government can ignore its wishes. Mass media, professional associations, the internet, and a thousand other channels today allow the public to express itself and compare its ideas, to disapprove of the decisions made and even to organize campaigns aimed at achieving certain ends. However, the role of the public opinion is still weak, especially when compared with the power with which the economic and social sphere projects us into the global society. When we go to work, go shopping, or watch TV, we are increasingly living in a global space, but as citizens we continue only and exclusively to belong to and participate in a narrow political community.

The huge body of information of which global society is composed and the interactions and repercussions of the events that have spread across the continents still have no channels through which to be transformed into a forum of political decision making. Only a minimal part of the energy released by globalization is converted into the mobilization of global civil society. The public opinion is capable of only sporadic, spasmodic action. Many have overemphasized the capacity of global civil society to effectively correct action by governments and, indeed, over the past decade, global movements have emerged as the most original political actor of our era. On a historic occasion, on February 15, 2003, the voice of the united peoples was raised to halt the war; the *New York Times* even claimed that the global movements had become a kind of superpower capable of standing up to the last remaining true superpower, that led by the White House. Field day, though, however great, is not enough to set up the checks and balances that we desperately need in world politics.

World public opinion and global movements are not always guided by unified intentions. Indeed, it often happens that the objectives pursued differ or are even contradictory. Nor is there any reason to expect that among such different subjects there can be a greater unity of intentions than that which exists within each separate state. World public opinion does not have the function of expressing a single totalizing view but rather represents a counterweight vis-à-vis the choices made by the governments. The function of world public opinion is not to converge on a single objective but to contribute to creating better and transparent context for policy making. This is why new channels of representation must open up through which the various opinions may be expressed in a dialogical rather than antagonistic fashion. To be effective these channels demand a greater willingness on the part of individuals to participate in the management of global public matters. The making of a global commonwealth of citizens requires that individuals are prepared to act on the ground of key shared values. What principles of political action must the citizen of the world subscribe to? The suggestions put forward in the present book may be summed up in three keywords: inclusion, responsibility, and impartiality.

The first principle is that of cosmopolitan inclusion. Cosmopolitanism does not entail merely observing habits and customs with curiosity but also being capable of including those that are different and incorporating them in a shared life project; it is a school of participation and sharing. Cosmopolitanism is coupled to the idea at the center of every conception of democracy: all individuals must participate in the decision-making process that concerns them. It is a principle that is much easier to state than to implement: the levels of interdependence involve an ever-growing number of individuals and communities, and each in a different way. To gear the participation of each individual or political community to its own specific interest is a difficult mission that is often impossible to accomplish. However, the mode of participation and the relative weight of each subject with reference to the decision-making process are technical aspects that can be resolved if the participants agree on the principles. Hitherto, the democratic systems have marked out boundaries and dividing lines and have decided who is in and who is out, often arbitrarily. It has now become a matter of coming up with new forms of participation and, even if the decisions made continue to be arbitrary, those decisions nevertheless will always be capable of opening up a new phase in the evolution of democracy.

The second principle is that of cosmopolitan responsibility. Political action has so far been grounded on responsibilities restricted to certain territories and groups of persons; the raison d'état favors duty toward the interior and mortifies duty toward the exterior. However, previous certainties are beginning to evaporate: as borders become increasingly uncertain, the consequences of political action are expanding. The responsibility of the public sphere must consequently be enlarged, to the point that political action can be taken in the interest of all those who are directly or indirectly involved. Cosmopolitan logic therefore tends to modify what is envisaged by democratic theory, which univocally binds those who govern to those whom they govern and who have elected them. Whereas so far it has been assumed that an exclusive relationship exists whereby decision makers act in the name of, on behalf of, and in defense of those who have elected them, today the decision makers must act with a sense of responsibility that has no frontiers.

The third principle is that of searching impartiality. Searching impartiality is a way to address difference without the intention of imposing one's own will. In a world inhabited by peoples with different customs and traditions who are nevertheless subject to constant interdependence, it is only inevitable that different views and differences of opinion should arise. These differences may be focused on particular and specific aspects, such as the dressing code required in schools, or problems of a more general nature, such as the type of regulations required controlling atmospheric pollution. Searching impartiality aims to address disputes on the basis of the principle that no one can be his own judge. Whenever disputes arise, the parties concerned must be willing to appeal to and accept an external opinion. This approach prevents certain values being imposed on others and offsetts a danger inherent in cosmopolitanism, the danger of considering one's own view to be universally valid.

The application of these principles entails moving on from the politics of the *polis*, founded on borders, to that of the *cosmopolis*, founded on sharing. A cosmopolitan democracy will certainly not result from a pre-conceived plan but will perhaps be the outcome of contradictory actions that take place on the stage of history. Above all, it will not be necessary to employ evil means even to achieve desirable ends: each step toward a cosmopolitan democracy is, at the same time, a means and an end. Many political subjects may be interested in and desirous of applying in everyday practice the principles and proposal discussed herein. The international organizations can strengthen their channels of participation, also opening up to subjects that are not states. The states themselves can become champions of cosmopolitanism not only by participating in and supporting the action of the international organizations but also by acting inside their own borders to include those who are different, whether they be minorities, immigrants, or refugees. Above all it is the individuals who must today move on from their fragmented condition as subjects of globalization and become and act daily to build their own commonwealth of citizens.